FROM THE FIELD

365 Missionary Stories To
Encourage Your Daily Walk

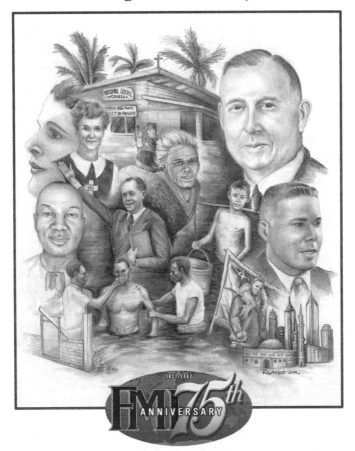

Foursquare Missions International

International Church of the Foursquare Gospel
Los Angeles, California

FROM THE FIELD

Cover Art by Robert Hunt
Cover Design by Caroline Crews and Robert Hunt

About the Cover Art: Starting from the bottom left working clockwise; 1) Construction of a church, typical of the thousands of short-term projects carried out by the Foursquare family; 2) Papua New Guinea Leaders baptizing a new convert, symbolizing the historic growth of Foursquare Missions towards indigenous church leadership; 3) The late Cote d'Ivoire National leader Severine Kouame – one of Foursquare's greatest leaders; 4) The key to the growth of Foursquare Missions, preaching the Word, Nathaniel Van Cleave in Puerto Rico 1935; 5) Sister Evelyn Thompson who received a prophetic word from Sister Aimee regarding her missionary future and who would go on to win tens of thousands to the Lord on the field (profile of Sister Aimee to her left); 6) A church in the Philippines, an older woman with child in Okinawa, a young boy with water in Cambodia; 7) The late Arthur Edwards who represents the many early Foursquare missionaries who laid the first foundation; 8) Arthur Edwards's son, Dr. Leland Edwards, who represents the many families who followed their parents' faithful footsteps and who also symbolizes the quality of FMI leadership as a former FMI Director; 9) FMI missionary in Alaska, depicting the cross-cultural missions work in the U.S; 10) A Muslim city, representing the FMI targeting of cities and focus on the Muslim world. (Posters available through FMI.)

MESSAGE FROM
THE PRESIDENT

Some of us have had the privilege of knowing our Foursquare missionaries, from the first generation of those who were sent out until the present time. As we came to know them, their families and their unique personalities, we have been awed by their daring commitment to preaching the gospel and amazed at the things that they accomplished through God's strength and supply.

How would one characterize our missionaries? The first word that comes to mind is "spiritual." These were men and women who were sensitive to the Holy Spirit and who were willing to obey the call of God to go to unfamiliar lands and cultures to bring the Gospel to people of all ages. As we witnessed their dedication, to God and our Church, our hearts were warmed. They became our heros.

Our missionaries were practical. At times, the creative ways they found to communicate the Gospel and to deal with almost impossible situations boggled the mind. Their thoughts may have been focused on heavenly truths, but their feet and hands were planted solidly on the ground. They "lived" the gospel as well as taught it, providing footsteps which national leaders and believers could follow. Their faith and faithfulness were reproducible.

They were also authentic. They were real. They were humorous. As they related stories from the field, we laughed, we cried; above all, we were encouraged. Our missionaries reminded us that God's goodness and mercy was available to us as well.

As you spend each day with these voices, "From The Field," you will feel the pulse of the very heart of our Church—Worldwide Evangelism—and enjoy the same privilege that others of us have had over the years.

Paul Risser
ICFG President

FORWARD

*A*fter reading through these amazing stories, I was awestruck by the rich history of Foursquare Missions. Our history was forged by the passion and prayers of dedicated people. When you read these snippets of their lives and mission, you will come away, as I have, with a sense of God's great purpose carried out through those who humbly serve their Lord.

This book is both a testament to our past and an insight into our future. For if Foursquare Missions continues to send the caliber of people that have marked our past (and I believe He is doing just that) then the kingdom work of the future will be in able hands.

With that being said, this book is meant for more than perusing history, it is intended to inspire. My sincere prayer is that you will be encouraged, challenged, and motivated in your daily walk with our Lord from the pages of this book. I have gained personal strength and desire for a deeper faith as I read of our missionaries exploits. Their extraordinary courage wrapped in honest humanity will make you proud to be a part of the family.

And as you read each day, please remember to pray for the ongoing work of Foursquare Missions. Your prayers are the backbone of our worldwide movement. Perhaps you yourself—through your prayers, support, or going to the field—will write the stories in our next book!

Until all have heard,

Mike Larkin
Missions Director

Foursquare Missions

ACKNOWLEDGEMENTS

Our deepest thanks to Letania Ponte who originally had the vision for this book and to Mike Larkin who made it happen. Of course we are indebted to our missionaries, both former and present, who participated; their lives and stories will inspire us daily. A special thanks to Eloise Clarno who not only submitted stories but edited hundreds of others.

To the FMI Communications staff who spent thousands of hours making this book a reality: Caroline Crews, Rev. Randy Brockett and his wife, Julie. And to Wyce Ghiacy from Foursquare Missions Press. They put their hearts into it.

Finally, without Jackie Fernandez, these great stories would have never found a home. She was the driving force and we are all very grateful.

Robert Hunt
FMI Communications/Foursquare Missions Press

OUR FOURSQUARE QUEST

*I*t has been my lifelong privilege to be exposed to many missionaries and their ministry. I have learned they are a very special breed. I have witnessed the tears in their eye at altars, praying, "I'll go where you want me to go, dear Lord." I have seen them with incredible happiness on their faces—leave their homes and earthly security behind and depart for distant lands. Fire appeared to burn in their souls—the Lord had said, "Go and I will go with you!" I have seen missionaries return on occasional furloughs when they could hardly wait for the time to return to the fields of their callings.

Several years before I was born, my mother was a missionary and my sister, Roberta, was born on the mission field a month after the death of her missionary father. As I grew up, the world became our mission call, at home and abroad. The Lord had said, "Go into all the world and preach the gospel to every creature." Though reaching hundreds of thousands of people, personally, mother soon realized the size and impossibility of the task. The Lord, speaking of the needy world, had also said, "Look on the fields for they are already ripe unto harvest but the laborers are few. Mother gave all she had and could give no more, but HER WORKS DO FOLLOW HER.

I consider myself greatly blessed to have been able to have had a part in carrying on the work the Lord started through my mother and to see the work multiply ten fold around the world. It has been thrilling to have the opportunity to visit mission fields and get to know and form lasting friendships with scores of outstanding missionaries. A great host of workers have been raised up. We have been joined by tens of thousands of nationals from all walks of life. They not only work within their own countries—they have united with us to reach the "impossible dream" of reaching the world for Christ.

Rolf K. McPherson
President Emeritus, ICFG

"Those who know your name will trust in you,
for you, Lord, have never forsaken those who seek you."

PSALM 9:10

My husband, Arthur, and I clasped our hands together and stood before the Lord saying this prayer, "Lord, we do not want to leave our home and go to other lands unless You manifest Your power though us. We do not want to go to other places and just preach. We want to see You perform miracles of all kinds. We do not want to see a few receive Christ. We want to see thousands accept the Lord. We are not young any more but we are not too old to go if You are with us in power."

The following week we were praying for the sick people in our church. A well-known doctor in the city who had suffered a stroke a few months before and had become blind came forward very slowly with a cane, and he was instantly healed of all of his infirmities.

It was the Lord saying to us, "If you trust Me, you will see what I can do." We did trust Him and the following year many families received Christ as their Savior. Many healings took place, as well as many miracles. Our church was too small to hold the people. We sold it and built a much larger church. God was building our faith, preparing us to go to faraway places.

In 1954, Arthur and I were called by the Lord to minister in the Philippine Islands. As we trusted in God, He was faithful to the promise He had made.

Dr. Evelyn Thompson
Former Missionary to the Philippines

Lord, I do trust in your power; show me the mighty miracles
you can do...

> *"God loves you dearly, and he has called you to be his very own..."*
> ROMANS 1:7 (NLT)

*I*n South Africa, a little girl was born. She was named Joy for the happiness she brought to her family. As time went on, her family realized she was not like other children. She grew to be deformed. By the age of eleven, she had seen many witchdoctors, but found no hope. She covered her face with clay, and hung a bag of bones around her neck. Her family sent her very early in the morning to work in the fields.

One morning she went to the field just as the sun was peaking over the hills. She had been suffering from pain in her back all week. As she bent over, she heard her name, and the voice told her, "Joy, go to the white man's village that lies over the hill five miles away. You will find there an old white-haired man and he will help you." She didn't go at first, and the voice began to say the same thing day after day.

One day Joy was in so much pain that she decided to obey the voice. As she got to the edge of the village, she didn't know where to go. There the voice said, "Go down to the bend of the road to a large tree. You will see an old man sitting on a box—go to him!"

Joy did just that and she met the "white man." She sat down, along with other children, and for the first time she heard the story of Jesus. She learned how much He loved and cared for her, and she asked the white man, whose name was Stan, how this Jesus could come to her.

Stan placed his hand on Joy, and they prayed together for salvation. As Stan continued to pray for her, he heard the cracking of bones, and when he opened his eyes he saw the Master of all things straightening Joy's limbs. Her face was alive with the love of Jesus, and she exclaimed, "How can it be that this one called Jesus could love me so?"

Arlene Ziegler
Former Missionary to South Africa

> *Father, how can it be that you could love me so? There are parts of me that people call ugly, but still you love me...there are parts of my life that need straightening out, but still you call me your own...*

> *"Great is the Lord and most worthy of praise;*
> *his greatness no one can fathom."*
>
> PSALM 145:3

In 1961, I was working with the Choco Indians of Panama, who were very primitive and did not have the Bible in their language.

One of the miracles that God performed was in a man named Jose, whose son Roberto was very ill. Roberto had been so sick that could not even sit up, and he no longer would eat. News had spread up and down the river about a missionary who "put his hands on your head and talked to himself" (prayed!) and people were healed. When Jose heard about it, he decided to send his son. And so, he sent him on ahead with the little boy's grandmother.

Two days later, when Jose arrived, there was Roberto walking around! "What happened?" Jose asked.

The little grandmother told him that they had prayed for him at the end of the church service, then she took the boy home and put him in bed. In the middle of the night, he woke up and said, "Grandmother, I'm hungry!" And she fixed him a big bowl of rice.

When Jose saw that his boy had been healed, he went to the mission station to find out just what happened. The missionary asked, "Do you believe in God?" And Jose said, "I don't know who God is."

The missionary then replied, "Well, he's the one who made the jungle, the river, the whole earth, and he's the one who made your boy well."

"How could I not believe, look at my boy—he's well!" Jose responded.

Then he said, "Do you think that the God who healed my boy could cure me of my drinking habit?" They prayed for Jose and God absolutely took the desire for drink away! What a great God we serve! This same Jose would later become my language informant, the one who would help me translate the Bible into the native Choco Indian language.

Dr. Dick Scott
LIFE Bible College President
Former Missionary to Panama

Lord, I praise you for the wonderful works of your hand...

"Your word is a lamp to my feet and a light for my path."
PSALM 119:105

*I*t took forty years. Forty years to complete a homework assignment that God had given me—to translate the New Testament into the Choco Indian language. I worked with Jose, a Choco Indian that God had saved, delivered, and given as a gift to help perform the task that lay ahead. We took about five years to reduce the language to writing—creating an alphabet, learning the customs, and discovering the grammatical rules—and then we worked on translating the New Testament from that point forward.

I began in 1961, and after forty years, it is finally finished! It is now being formatted and going to press.

It is rewarding to hear the "oohs" and "ahhs" of someone who hears God's Word in their own language for the very first time. When they finally heard us read the Scriptures in their own language, they said, "Finally, God has learned to speak Choco!"

Dr. Dick Scott
LIFE Bible College President
Former Missionary to Panama

God, thank you for your life-changing Word...

"You will seek me and find me
when you seek me with all your heart."

JEREMIAH 29:13

Twenty years ago I was an 18-year-old atheist who was living alone and trying to find meaning in life. One day I was riding a bus when I suddenly saw a bright light, but no one else saw it except me. In the light there was a pillar and a cloud. I heard a voice say, "I am God and I exist." I don't know why, but I believed Him, and I praised Him in a Muslim way.

Later I asked myself, 'Who is this God? Is He the God of Islam or another God?'

So I began to search for Him and I read Islamic books and the Quran, but it didn't satisfy me. I looked into New Age groups, but still I didn't find Him. One day I bought a Bible at a book fair. I started reading the New Testament. As I read the book of Romans, three things really struck me: Jesus is the Sacrificial Lamb, He loves me, and I am a sinner. At that moment, I realized I had found Him. There was no missionary around, but the Holy Spirit was there and I accepted Christ.

Pastor Ihsan Ozbeck
National Pastor in Turkey

Father, thank you that you reveal yourself to those who seek
you. Reveal yourself to the nations and to the individuals
that I lift before you today...

> *"I tell you that in the same way there will be more rejoicing in heaven over one sinner who repents..."*
>
> LUKE 15:7

A couple in a small village lived in a typical native hut of woven walls, grass roof and dirt floor. There was a Foursquare church in this village and many were coming to know Jesus as their Savior.

One Sunday morning the wife was walking by the church when she heard the pastor say, "If anyone here today is sick, Jesus will heal you." This caught her attention, as her husband had a large sore on his thigh that the witch doctor had been unable to heal, and she stopped to watch as the pastor went on to tell the people, "Lay hands on those near you and Jesus will heal them."

The woman saw several whom she knew being healed, so she turned and ran back to her husband. Waking him up, she said, "I know how to make you well."

"Only the witch doctor can heal. Go do your work in the garden." was his response. But the wife quickly laid her hand on his sore and said the prayer she had heard.

He angrily rebuked her, saying, "Get out of here and go to the garden!" She knew she had better go.

After her day's work in the garden, she saw a man running toward her. It was her husband. "Where did you learn to do that?" he demanded. Her husband showed her his thigh. The sore was completely gone.

It was a day of rejoicing in heaven as this couple made their way to the pastor's home, where they received the Lord! If there is great joy when even one comes into the kingdom, imagine the excitement of heaven when these two said "yes" to Jesus, their healer!

Mason and Virgene Hughes
Former Missionaries to Papua New Guinea

Father, I rejoice with you over the work you are doing in my life and the lives of my friends and loved ones...

"Bring the whole tithe into the storehouse...and see if I will not throw open the floodgates of heaven and pour out so much blessing that you will not have room enough for it."

MALACHI 3:10

After being in Colombia for about two years, we went to a small island off the coast of the historic city of Cartagena. Boca Chica was a fishing village of very poor and proud people. The village was primitive with no cars, and the only "stores" were merchants who sold kerosene for lamps, blocks of brown sugar, matches, bananas and other meager necessities out of small rooms in a house.

We planted a church and it began to grow. We hesitated to teach about tithing because the people were so poor and because of the spirit of "Americans grabbing everything." So we prayed. God told us He wanted to bless these people and that we were responsible to teach them to give.

As the people began to tithe, they began to prosper. Their corn and coconut crops increased. The store needed to be enlarged and a cement floor was added. One woman even began selling butter and other products that the people could now afford.

These "poor" people became "rich" in both material and spiritual things because of their obedience to the Lord.

Nearly forty years later when I visited in Boca Chica, I was overjoyed to see how God had blessed these people. They had built a lovely church building and a parsonage for their pastor. Great is His faithfulness!

Virginia Martin
Former Missionary to Colombia and Bolivia

Father, I thank you that there is a great promise connected with tithing. I ask you to remind me and those in my church to be faithful to your words regarding giving, so that we may receive those precious promises...

> *"The god of this age has blinded the minds of unbelievers,*
> *so that they cannot see the light of the gospel...*
> *For God who said, 'Let light shine out of darkness,'*
> *made his light shine in our hearts..."*
>
> 2 CORINTHIANS 4:4,6

*I*f you walk down the well-trodden path to the African village, off to the right you will see a thatched-roof shrine. In that shrine, you will find a god made of two pieces of clay and a handful of monkey teeth. Ears of corn, bowls of rice, pieces of fowl, and other offerings are placed at its base in order to secure favor or a blessing from this man-made deity.

The god of this world blinds many West Africans, but we nevertheless preach Christ, even though it costs us sometimes. The West Africans were so serious about worshipping this idol that they have burned our church down because it was built within one-half mile of their god. They wanted no foreign religion near their god's dwelling.

The good news is that West Africa is experiencing an encounter with Jesus Christ! This encounter is bringing healing to her people. Samuel Nyann, a polygamist with five or six wives, was converted from cultism, which was a mixture of paganism, Bible teachings, and satanic practices. Sixteen months after meeting Jesus Christ, he spiritually matured to the point where he became the pillar of our work in Ghana.

Another man, who was crippled with arthritis to the point where he could not walk, was healed in a crusade. He returned the second night and appeared on the platform where he danced with joy and sang a song. This was the first time he was able to move in this manner for years!

Mitchell Belobaba
Former Missionary to Nigeria

> *Lord, I pray that you would lift the darkness that holds so*
> *many in captivity. May your word be preached in power, and*
> *may you accompany the preaching of your word with signs*
> *and wonders...*

"I will tell of all your wonders..."
PSALM 9:1

M r. Perla was the head chief of thousands of Mansaka tribal people in southern Mindanao, Philippines.

While working in the jungle area, Mr. Perla's ax slipped and cut him deeply in his leg. Gangrene set in and his life was in jeopardy. Several fellow tribesmen carried him from his town to a primitive logging truck road, where he was picked up by a logger who was also a lay pastor. En route to a clinic, this servant of the Lord talked with Perla and he received Jesus as his Savior. Just after arriving at the medical facility, he was declared dead. But then a miracle happened—God raised him from the dead and he was completely healed!

When Chief Perla went back to his tribe, he told them about Jesus and several received Him as Savior. Two pastors were later sent to minister to the tribe and more than 1,200 Mansakas received Christ as Savior in the first two weeks of ministry. More than 800 were baptized in water and 400 received the baptism of the Holy Spirit.

In talking with his people, Chief Perla said, "All of you know the miracle God did for me. Many of you have experienced the miracles of God in your lives. Beyond our tribe is another tribe that has not heard about Jesus, and beyond that tribe is another one that knows nothing of God. Let us not waste the miracles of God."

Dr. Leland Edwards
Former Missionary to Panama,
Missions Director, 1965-1988

Lord, help me to remember those people nearby who have not believed in you. I lift up the names of neighbors and those near to me who need to hear about you..

*"In the morning, O Lord, you hear my voice; in the morning
I lay my requests before you and wait in expectation."*

PSALM 5:3

The pastor and members of the Dunkwa-on-Offin Foursquare Church in Ghana began praying for the villagers of Wasa Gyapa and the Holy Spirit began preparing their hearts. After three days of hearing the message of Jesus, 85 converts received water baptism and many were healed. These new converts began telling surrounding villages about Jesus. Praise the Lord!

In a village near Wasa Gyapa, a local chief heard about Jesus, but not in the traditional way. He simply could not escape a voice in his ear, telling him to surrender his life to God. He didn't understand the message, so he consulted with some of his advisors. Someone suggested he visit the Foursquare pastor at Wasa Gyapa; perhaps the man of God could explain this strange occurrence. The chief and his entire family were converted and baptized, and now want a Foursquare church in their village.

In another village, a local "Imam" (Muslim religious leader) had recurrent dreams in which he was told to serve God. Because he thought he was already serving God, he was greatly troubled. The dreams caused him to think deeply about his life. He was directed to speak to a local Foursquare pastor and as a result the Imam gave his life to Jesus. He then led the people at his mosque to Christ. The mosque is now a Foursquare church! When you attend this Foursquare church, you bring your own prayer rug and take off your shoes before worshipping the Lord who is "the same yesterday, and today, and forever."

Greg and Margaret Fisher
Missionaries to Uganda

*Lord, I thank you that when I wait upon you, you always
show up. Teach me to wait upon you only...*

"And the prayer offered in faith will make the sick person well...
The prayer of a righteous man is powerful and effective."
JAMES 5:15-16

We were invited to preach and minister in a small independent church. After the service, we were all eating lunch together when a little girl named Ariathna fell about 13 feet to a solid concrete floor, landing on her head. When we arrived below she was in bad shape. I embraced her and prayed for her healing immediately. She was in pain, but conscious. Later her head began to swell and she began to writhe in pain and vomit blood.

We took her to the hospital and I carried her into the emergency room and laid her on a table. Five minutes later she was unconscious and shortly thereafter stopped breathing. The doctor informed us that she would probably die, or remain a vegetable. We continued to pray and believe God for a miracle as the doctors forced air into her lungs with a simple hand held pump connected to a plastic tube. That evening we sent out emails to hundreds of friends in Mexico and the U.S. to pray and believe with us.

Twenty-four hours later Ariathna was fully conscious, could see and hear, and began to eat. Forty-eight hours later she was at home with her parents in perfect health. As a result her mother received Jesus Christ as her Savior and the church is considering becoming a part of our movement. God is good!

Dennis and Kathy Pendergast
Missionaries to Mexico City

Lord, you are a good God, full of mercy and miracles.
Thank you for hearing and answering our prayers...

*"Why spend money on what is not bread, and your labor on
what does not satisfy? Listen, listen to me, and eat what is good,
and your soul will delight in the richest of fare."*

ISAIAH 55:2

"Next time you come, if you don't bring rice we'll kill you!"
Missionary Ted Olbrich understood that the man who stood before
them wanted rice. However, as he was still learning the Cambodian
language, he did not fully discern the threat. Even so, Ted noticed that the
facial expression of the Foursquare pastor with him had changed for the
worse. When he asked his friend what else the man said, the pastor simply
and wisely said, "I'll tell you later."

The man who demanded the rice, whose name was Van Saveth, was a
landowner, but he still struggled along with his fellow villagers to make a
living and feed his family. He felt justified in making his death threat to
Ted and the Foursquare pastor for rice. After all, at the time he thought,
"What is more important than food?" He would soon find out.

The greatest miracle of all soon happened to Van Saveth—a
Foursquare evangelist told him about Jesus and he believed and was radically saved. The missionary he threatened, Ted Olbrich, sensed his leadership potential and sent one of his most trained leaders to live with Van
Saveth for months of intense discipleship. The training paid off. Today
Van Saveth is a Foursquare divisional superintendent with 15 churches
under his care.

And Ted tells us, "We never did take the rice."

Foursquare World ADVANCE, 2000

*Lord, help me to pursue not only rice and earthly food, but
also the true Bread of Life that has come down from heaven
as a blessing to all mankind...*

"You intended to harm me, but God intended it for good..."
GENESIS 50:20

Spontaneous revival broke out on the Willowvale Mission in Transkei, South Africa, where we were based. Hundreds came to know the Lord through daily meetings in the Foursquare church and at homes in the community. Among those being saved was the mayor, the deputy mayor, and some local witchdoctors.

The spiritual clash was so great between light and darkness that the non-Christians of Willowvale organized a public march down the main road with banners proclaiming: "Down with Salvation, Down with Faith!" Their intentions were evil, but God used this to serve as a great witness to the entire community that salvation and faith was being preached at the Willowvale Mission. Many more became Christians as a result of the publicity of the march! What Satan meant for harm, God used for His good purposes!

Howard and Terry Manthe
Missionaries to South Africa

> *Lord, I give thanks to you! Even when Satan tries to harm us, you are able to turn it into a blessing...*

"I was hungry and you gave me something to eat, I was thirsty and you gave me something to drink, I was a stranger and you invited me in...I tell you the truth, whatever you did for one of the least of these brothers of mine, you did for me."

MATTHEW 25:35,40

On Sunday morning, November 1, 1998, Hurricane Mitch held parts of Latin America, and especially Honduras, in its death grip. It not only left scars on the landscape but it also penetrated the soul of the Honduran people. As the news reached the Christian world and the call for help came, the response by many of our Foursquare churches was immediate. An outpouring of supplies, food and finances followed in a way that no one could have foreseen.

It was not long before Pastor Glen Grove (New Life Center Foursquare in Everett, Washington), Pastor Tim Talbott (Eastside Foursquare in Bothell, Washington), and Pastor Russ Schlecht (Mill Creek Foursquare in Lynnwood, Washington) gathered together to help rebuild this devastated nation. They committed to the immediate need for food and to help rebuild Masicales, a small village completely destroyed by Mitch. It was the team effort between Foursquare and the villagers of Masicales that brought relief to many people who had no homes and no hope.

Today, the newly built village has a new name as well—Rio de Agua Viva, Nuevo Masicales (River of the Living Water, New Masicales). The village now has two wells operating, a water tower, paved streets, sewers, plumbed and wired homes, and a new 400-capacity church! Twenty new homes are currently in various stages of development.

The rivers of love and service that have flowed from a heart of team-work and compassion have replaced the rivers of mud. The job is not yet done, but what the Lord has begun, He will be faithful to complete.

Foursquare World ADVANCE, 2000

Lord, show us what needs to be done, and give us the heart of compassion that you had for those who need relief. May our deeds and our actions preach your word...

"Then Jesus said to his disciples, 'If anyone would come after me, he must deny himself and take up his cross and follow me.'"

MATTHEW 16:24

As a one-time missionary to China and the founder of The International Church of the Foursquare Gospel, Aimee Semple McPherson's vision was to give the gospel to every nation. The following portion of an article printed in a 1932 Crusader magazine gives a glimpse of her insight into the kind of sacrifice it will take to win the world to Christ...

A man asked me "Why was Christ born in a manger?" and I told him the story of the Moravian missionary who, upon getting to a certain country, found that the people were all slaves and that there was no chance to work among them. They worked very early in the morning and came home too tired in the evening.

The missionary saw he could not minister among them and, after much consideration, realized that it was a hopeless condition. He went to the master and owner of the slaves, and he deliberately sold himself into slavery. He laid aside his garments of the Western world, put on the old rags that the others wore, and went to work in the field. He knew what it meant to have the whip come down in searing blows upon his back. His stomach knew the pangs of hunger like the other slaves, and they respected him, saying, "He has done this for us so that he might be one of us. Let's go and hear what this man has to say."

That missionary led twelve thousand slaves to Jesus in three years."

Aimee Semple McPherson
Foursquare Founder

Lord, help me to identify with people in their human condition, just as you did. Let me have the same attitude...

> *"For the word of God is living and active..."*
> HEBREWS 4:12

W ay up in the interior of Panama in the village of Jaguito we were holding a week of Intense Bible Studies for pastors who had families and were farmers. We also needed a photo to go with an article we were writing, and that is when we met Hermana (Sister) Cuca.

Hermana Cuca was a beautiful little lady about 70 years old. She was dressed in the typical interior dress—long skirt with a loose white top—and her white hair was in two long braids down her back. We sat her down for the photo at a little table with a kerosene lamp and a Bible.

All of a sudden, she placed her bowed head on the Bible and started to cry. I put my arm around her and asked if we had done something to offend her.

"No, Sister Barbara. I am crying because this is the Palabra de Dios (the Word of God) and I cannot read it!" She continued on saying that God had been so good to her—He had saved her, He had healed her, and her family had come to know the Lord.

It was then I remembered that the Bible is "alive," it is the living Word, and that as her pastor gave her the Bible's message, he became the living word as the Holy Spirit whispered to her heart that this was Truth. What a wonderful God we have!

Barbara Edwards
Former Missionary to Panama

> *Father, what a privilege it is that I can read your word. I thank you for that privilege, and ask you to make me a faithful student of your word...*

> *"If you make the Most High your dwelling...*
> *then no harm will befall you."*
>
> PSALM 91:9-10

The strange man who came through the door was dressed in black. In his hand he carried a pint-size canning jar about half full of liquid. At first, he sat near the door, but as missionary Jerry Poppe began to preach, the man changed seats, moving to various parts of the room. Finally, he found a seat directly in front of the preacher. Because of his unusual behavior, one of the church leaders stopped him.

The man informed the elder that he was looking for the "white preacher." Having been involved with witchcraft, the stranger had come to curse the missionary by throwing the black liquid at him. Though Jerry had been standing in front of the congregation all the time, God had blinded the man's eyes. He could not see Jerry! Thwarted in his quest, the man went peacefully on his way.

What a powerful God we serve! Not only does He open the eyes of the blind, but He blinds the eyes of those who are looking to harm those whom He loves.

Jerry and Betty Poppe
Former Missionaries to Haiti

> *Lord, I worship you. You are so mighty, so powerful, so awesome. You keep me safe from all those who would seek to harm me in any way...*

> *"...some people have entertained angels without knowing it."*
> HEBREWS 13:2

The engine just stopped dead. I barely had time to carefully steer the car off to the narrow shoulder. My friend Loretta and I had driven over to a neighboring city to take two of my sons for dental work. It was mid-afternoon and we were another hour outside our town of Jos, Nigeria.

My sons jumped out of the car, unconcerned about our fate, only happy to have time to stretch their legs and chase lizards. Loretta and I were less cavalier. We had no phone, there was no house immediately visible, and there wouldn't be any phones in any of the houses near us. We opened the hood, looked in, and waited.

Suddenly another station wagon appeared and pulled over. It was full of men. We could only pray that their intentions were honorable. A very tall Nigerian man climbed out in an all-white northern Nigerian outfit. If he spoke English, he didn't offer it to us. He bent over the engine and called his driver to bring a tool. After tinkering with the engine for a few minutes, he unfolded himself from over the engine block and shut the hood. He motioned for me to try the ignition. The engine started immediately.

This man gave his driver the tool, wiped his hands on a rag and climbed back into his car. He left as quickly as he had appeared.

As he drove off, Loretta and I looked at each other and said, "Who was that masked man? NO! Who was that angel the Lord just sent us?"

Kathy Kieselhorst
Former Missionary to Nigeria, now serving with her husband, Bill, in South Africa

> *Thank you, Lord, for the angels that you have commanded to keep us safe. We know that they have ministered to our needs...*

"Show the wonder of your great love..."
PSALM 17:7

*A*s the rhythmic beats of the witchdoctor's drums and the croaking of the giant bullfrogs grew louder with the setting sun, a messenger came to our tent. "It's time," she said.

We were in the bush of Gazankulu, a portion of South Africa bordering the Kruger National Park and Mozambique, and a young Shangaan refugee who had fled from war-torn Mozambique was about to give birth.

Lying on a grass mat in the dirt, leaning against a poorly made mud-brick, grass-thatched hut, the girl was relieved to see Terry, who had come to assist her with the birth of her baby. As Terry swaddled the newborn infant, she was reminded in her spirit that even in the midst of dire circumstances—war, famine and sickness—new life could still come. It was a reminder that the love of Jesus takes us from the clutches of death and gives us new life. A reminder that His love is shown in places that we might least expect it.

Today, take a moment to look for the wonder of HIS GREAT LOVE!

Howard and Terry Manthe
Missionaries to South Africa

> *Thank you, Lord, for the wonder of your great love, which is made manifest to us in the midst of our pain, sorrow, and suffering. You have given new life to me, and I praise you for that...*

> *"And the prayer offered in faith will make the sick person well; the Lord will raise him up. If he has sinned, he will be forgiven."*
>
> JAMES 5:15

Susana was devastated when she heard the news. After many tests, it had been discovered that she had cancer in her uterus.

Susana was the daughter of one of our church members in Monterrey, Mexico. She came to the church looking for hope. She did not know the Lord, but wanted someone to pray for her. As we spoke with her, she received Jesus as her personal Savior and we prayed for her healing.

The following day she went back to the hospital requesting another test. The results came in—she no longer had any trace of cancer! The doctors could not believe it and told her to go back for another test. They were sure that there was a problem with the equipment used in her tests. She agreed to go back, and once again she had the same result—no cancer! One more time she returned and received the same answer.

God had wonderfully healed her! Today, she is a walking testimony of God's salvation and healing.

Humberto and Teri Paz
Regional Coordinator to Central and South America

> *I praise you, Lord, for your healing power. I lift before you now my needs for healing and I pray for those who need your healing touch...*

> *"You are blessed, because you believed*
> *that the Lord would do what he said."*
> LUKE 1:45 (NLT)

Susana had come to the altar at our church in Madrid, Spain, asking for prayer. She had miscarried several babies. Doctors had told her she could never carry a baby to term as her uterus was not properly shaped. A group of believers gathered around her and prayed fervently.

Susana's brother had had a jail-house conversion while doing time for drug trafficking. Her mother and sister-in-law had been saved as a result of his testimony and witness. Now Susana had also received the Lord as her Savior. Her husband thought they were all crazy.

Susana believed she was healed and would soon conceive. Out of concern over the emotional strain another miscarriage would cause his wife, Susana's husband forced her to go to the hospital for an ultrasound. He went with her, and could not deny the Lord's divine intervention when the nurse, very familiar with Susana's painful losses, said, "I don't know what has happened, but your uterus is normal!"

Seven months later, Susana and her husband had a beautiful baby boy!

Stan and Molly Doland
Missionaries to Spain

Thank you Lord, that you and you alone are the giver of life...

"I am the way and the truth and the life..."
JOHN 14:6

Recently a medical team went to Nepal to conduct a M*A*S*H* clinic in the city of Bharatpur. While there, they served some of the nation's poorest people. Team members prayed for many to receive salvation and to be healed. One little girl was brought at the end of a very long day of ministry and work. The little girl was paralyzed and had not walked for three months. The doctor examined her and reported that nothing could be done for her medically.

The pediatrician then asked the father for permission to pray for the little girl. The father explained that he was a Hindu priest and believed there were thousands of ways to God and that Jesus Christ was only one of many. But finally he agreed to allow the team to pray for his daughter.

So the doctor, nurses and others laid hands on the young girl and prayed. Immediately, she got up and started to walk across the room! After seeing the dramatic healing of his daughter, the Hindu priest at once received the Lord Jesus as his one and only Savior.

Ralph and Novella Hawk
Former Mission Team Specialists to Nepal

Lord Jesus, you are the only way to the Father. Help me to be steadfast in communicating who you are to those who do not yet know you...

"...he who wins souls is wise."

PROVERBS 11:30

One Sunday morning there was a knock at our door. There stood Sam, our interpreter and helper, along with a man we had never seen before. The man said to us, "I have prepared a big feast for my village today and I told them I would have a special treat for them. I have heard about this thing called salt and I want to buy some."

Mason replied, "Oh, this is Sunday and we don't sell from our trade store on Sunday." We could see the deep disappointment on the faces of both the man and Sam.

"Matrapa (Mason's New Guinea name), this is Tamaseo, my Chief. Can you make an exception?" pleaded Sam.

Feeling prompted by the Spirit, Mason said, "Tell him I don't want to sell him the salt. But I will give it to him, if he will come to church next Sunday." The Chief smiled and agreed. He held out his two big, brown hands and Mason filled them with salt.

Next Sunday as Mason started out to church, he saw a long line of people coming down the mountain. Mason thought, "If they turn left that means there is a tribal fight; if they turn right, well, we'll see."

They turned right and Mason thought he had better see what was happening. As he got near, he recognized Chief Tamaseo. He had kept his part of the bargain and had brought his entire village.

That morning when the call for salvation was given, Chief Tamaseo beckoned for all of his village to come forward to accept Jesus. He said, "Matrapa, you were so kind that we have all come to follow your teaching." Later Chief Tamaseo built a church in his village and became a great leader for the Lord.

Mason and Virgene Hughes
Former Missionaries to Papua New Guinea

> *Lord, I want to follow the leading of your Holy Spirit, and see those around me won to you. Help me to hear your voice and obey it...*

"He is a dear brother, a faithful minister and fellow servant in the Lord."
COLOSSIANS 4:7

Since 1929, when the first Foursquare missionaries arrived in Africa, the Foursquare church has played a large role in winning the lost and planting churches on this continent. Many anointed African leaders have played a role in bringing this continent to Christ. One of these was Severine Kacou Kouame from Cote d'Ivoire (Ivory Coast).

As a young man, Severine gave his heart to the Lord and began sharing his faith with others. In 1998, Severine attended the Foursquare national convention in the Ivory Coast. During this time, God called him to be a prophet to the nations. Severine, a very humble man, soon began to be used mightily of God. The Lord opened doors for him to conduct large crusades in many places, including France, England, and the Caribbean.

When God confirmed His Word with signs following, Severine would joyfully say, "God works too much." God used him mightily to help bring revival to this poor nation. He was considered to be the person responsible for uniting the evangelical churches in the Ivory Coast.

But Severine's appeal was not only to the masses, he was uniquely able to make those with whom he spent time feel as though he had given them a personal part of his life. In fact, one of the people he influenced and led to the Lord was the President of the Ivory Coast.

On Good Friday, 2001, Severine was killed in a car accident. He was 34 years old. Thousands gathered to mourn the loss of this gifted man. But the fruit of his simple faith continues in the many changed lives and churches he left behind him. It certainly was a "good Friday" for Severine, for on this day he heard his Father say, "Enter in, my good and faithful servant."

Dr. Daniel Lucero
Missionary to France and the Francophone Nations of Africa

Thank you, Lord, for Godly men like Severine. May my life
also produce healthy fruit for Your kingdom...

"but you give us victory over our enemies..."

PSALM 44:7

"Who are you, little pastor?" mumbled the 14-year-old demon-possessed girl. We were ministering in Brazil at a youth camp of 150 young people when in the middle of our worship time the young girl fell to the ground and began to blaspheme God. I took the girl aside and began praying for her. The demon, which was controlling her, said, "Who are you, little pastor?" At that very moment the Lord brought six verses to my mind about who I was in Christ Jesus. I quoted God's Word and proceeded to cast out the demon. The Word of God is powerful and the young girl was delivered. Jesus was once again victorious!

For eight years we ministered to the youth in Brazil and time after time young people gave their lives to the Lord and were delivered. Youth camps were used powerfully of God and many times on the last day of camp young people would bring their drugs, needles, cigarettes and other vices to the campfire and throw them in. The enemy lost over and over again!

Many of these same young people today are pastors and leaders in our Foursquare churches in Brazil. This same God desires to bring deliverance and healing to your life. He is a mighty God who gives us victory over ALL our enemies!

Gary and Leslie Royer
Former Missionaries to Brazil

> *Lord, I pray for the young people that you have placed around me. I pray that they would receive the healing and deliverance that they need in order to follow and serve you. Show them who they are in Christ...*

> *"Great is our Lord and mighty in power;*
> *his understanding has no limit."*
>
> PSALM 147:5

*C*limbing the ladder into the house, which stood on stilts several feet high, my husband and I saw a beautiful young woman who was chained to a bamboo floor. Her long black wavy hair was matted and unkempt. She was writhing and twisting in a very unseemly manner. When we prayed, nothing seemed to happen.

Not knowing what else to do, I prayed again, and as I did, out of my mouth came another language. It felt like a ball of fire from the middle of my stomach. It was one I had never spoken before in the Spirit, and certainly a language I had neither learned nor heard. I saw there was a change on the face of the woman for whom we were praying—I saw that her eyes were listening and I began to understand that the language I was speaking was her language.

As this change came over her, I saw the muscles in her face begin to relax and her hands ceased beating the air as though she were trying to strike me. The writhing stopped, as well as her hysterical laughter. Then the most wondrous thing happened. I saw that not only did she understand the language that I spoke, but I also understood it!

Then, with this language I had never learned, I told her the story of Jesus, His life and crucifixion. In the following minutes I led her to Christ with a perfect awareness of every word I was speaking and with full understanding of the language. I did not call the demons out of her body. When Jesus moved into her heart the demons left.

Dr. Evelyn Thompson
Former Missionary to the Philippines

Lord, you are amazing! You speak all languages and under-
stand everything! I pray that you would give me a desire to
use my prayer language to see bondage broken and captives
set free...

*"So the churches were strengthened in the faith
and grew daily in numbers."*

ACTS 16:5

One Sunday morning in Frijoles we were going out on the train when the lady who interpreted for my parents said, "You know, there is something I want more than anything in the world. I want God to baptize me in the Holy Spirit." Up to that time there had not been an outpouring of the Spirit. This was during the very early days of the work.

My father had a service and after a few songs he called on her to pray. She started out in Spanish and all of a sudden she began to speak in a language she did not know. And let me tell you what happened next! That large crowd of people all got up from their seats, turned around and knelt down on the floor, and they lifted their hands and they began to cry out to God, and scores of them received the baptism of the Holy Spirit that day!

From that time on people began to visit other people—friends and relatives in other towns—to pray for them and give them the gospel. The church grew and the work began to spread just like in the book of Acts!

Dr. Leland Edwards
Former Missionary to Panama
Missions Director, 1965-1988

*Lord, I pray that in my life many would be touched by the
power of your Holy Spirit...*

"It is more blessed to give than to receive..."
ACTS 20:35

In my briefcase there is a simple little peanut. Why is there a peanut in my briefcase? Because this is a very special peanut. It's a reminder of a very important person and some very important lessons which that special little person taught me.

I was in the Portuguese colony of Macao, where our Foursquare church operates an orphanage. In one room, I found several of these precious Chinese orphans sitting at their desks with their hands full of peanuts, happily enjoying them.

I felt a little hand take hold of mine and quickly slip something into it. I looked down and found a little chubby fellow looking up at me with a slight smile. In my hand was a peanut. I thanked him and for quite a while we walked around the orphanage together, his hand in mine.

Later that day, I slipped the peanut into my briefcase. That simple little gift from my little friend is still in my briefcase today. Whenever I see it, I am reminded of that little smiling face and his tiny chubby hands in mine.

But that peanut also speaks of other things. It says so simply yet so powerfully, "I want to show you that I love you. I don't have much to give, but I'll share what I do have." That little peanut is a constant reminder that it doesn't take much to touch the heart of another person, and that touch can have a lasting effect. I don't believe that peanut was given just to me. It was given with love to Foursquare people like you who have given to missions.

Larry Six
Former Missionary to Hong Kong

Lord, it is more blessed to give than to receive. Let me respond to every opportunity to give, especially to overseas missions...

"For what is our hope, our joy, or the crown in which we will glory in the presence of our Lord Jesus when he comes? Is it not you?"

1 THESSALONIANS 2:19

During our very first service in Puerto Rico, Dr. Gonzalo Gonzalez was on his way to commit suicide. Although he was well-known in the community, he no longer had any desire to live. His doctor had just reported to him that his swollen earlobe was an early sign of leprosy. In addition to that, he was an alcoholic, his wife was very ill with tuberculosis, and his children were malnourished. He did not see any reason to live.

But when he passed by our first service, he was so intrigued that he stopped to listen. He could hardly believe what was being said, "There is healing in the name of Jesus Christ!" He thought, "If what he says is true, then I can be healed of this leprosy." So, instead of walking on to his suicide, he walked home and prayed for healing.

He woke up the next morning and looked in the mirror to see his earlobe perfectly normal. He had been healed! That night he went down to the altar to receive Christ as his Lord and Savior. Shortly thereafter, he became one of the greatest servant leaders of Puerto Rico and many came to Christ as a result of his powerful witnessing on the street corner. Dr. Gonzalez passed from death to life and now brings that same life to others who need the hope he found in Jesus!

Dr. Nathaniel Van Cleave
Former Missionary to Puerto Rico

Lord, when I feel so hopeless and am struggling with discouragement, bring me back to the message of your gospel: There is healing in your name, Lord Jesus...

> *"Blessed are those who are invited*
> *to the wedding supper of the Lamb!"*
>
> REVELATION 19:9

The king of the Buganda people was married recently. What a celebration! There was free food and drink for everyone. Singing and music all night long for a week could be clearly heard three miles away. Up and down the king's royal road people walked and rejoiced. They were dressed in their finest clothes to honor the king

I was a bit disappointed about one thing: I did not find my name on the invitation list. The name of the president of Uganda was there. The members of parliament, the king of the Zulu people, even the royal family of England were invited. I was not invited.

Today I am thinking about the wedding feast of another great King that will take place soon. What will it be like to attend the wedding feast of the King of Kings? If the music in honor of a worldly king resounded for a week, how much more for the King of Kings? If the wedding of a worldly king brought the commerce and industry of an entire nation to a standstill for a day, then the wedding of the King of Kings will bring the entire universe to a standstill forever!

I can hardly wait to walk on the King's royal highway, wearing the brilliant attire of the Kingdom of God. I can hardly wait to feast at the Royal table. Why? Because I have an invitation to the wedding. The Living God of heaven and earth came looking for me, and found me at the age of six years old, and I was important enough to Him that He included me on that ultimate list, the Lamb's Book of Life!

Greg Fisher
Missionary to Uganda

> *Lord, I thank you that my name is on that list! I look forward to that day when we will celebrate the wedding feast of the Lamb...*

"In your unfailing love you will lead the people you have redeemed."
EXODUS 15:13

Mr. Span was a trader who lived in South Africa during the 1920s. Being a believer in Jesus Christ, he was deeply moved to pray for the spiritual gloom that had come to rest on the people and culture that surrounded him.

In a vision, God showed Mr. Span the face of a man who was to be the answer to his prayer. Sometime later, during Mr. Span's prayer time, God clearly directed the trader to immediately rise up and head for the nearest train station. He had no idea why.

In another part of South Africa, a young family had just arrived from the United States to begin missionary service. They had obeyed God's call to "go," but they did not know just where that call would ultimately lead them. God instructed them to go to the nearest station and "catch the next train out of town." Like Abraham of old, they caught the train with no idea what to do next.

A few hours later, the father heard the Lord say, "Get off at the next station." They did, and standing there was Mr. Span who recognized the man whom he had seen in his vision. His new friend was Rev. Frank Ziegler and that moment signaled the beginning of the Foursquare Gospel Church in Africa. Today, the Foursquare Church in Africa is a vibrant and victorious movement in 27 nations.

That was nearly eight decades ago, but the principle remains the same: through men and women who are willing to obey His call, God is still shining His light into peoples' darkness. And, by the way, others are still waiting for us to come!

Dr. Paul Risser
ICFG President

Thank you, Father, for speaking into the lives of your people. Direct my steps today and give me ears to hear your voice and faith to obey your leading...

> *"How great is the love the Father has lavished on us, that we should be called children of God! And that is what we are!"*
>
> 1 JOHN 3:1

"When we returned from the mission field, we brought with us one of the greatest treasures the Philippines could offer—our Filipino daughter. The Lord had told me He was going to give us a little girl, and that through this adoption He would teach me something about my relationship with Him.

By the time we went to court to finalize the adoption, Michelle had been in our home for seven months. We were somewhat frightened, knowing that if we did not answer questions appropriately, we could lose this little girl.

I was called first and answered questions for nearly one hour. After I stepped down, Johnell took the stand. After asking questions for several minutes with some hostility, the interrogator asked Johnell one final question: "How would you express your love for that little girl?"

Johnell answered by quoting a short poem that was embroidered on a pillow that had been in Michelle's room since she was six weeks old. When she finished, tears were streaming down the face of the court recorder. The interrogator backed off, saying, "No more questions." And the judge brought down the gavel, "It is obvious these people really love this child. I declare her to be legally their own."

These are the words to that poem:

> Not flesh of my flesh, nor bone of my bone,
> But still miraculously my own.
> Never forget for a single minute,
> You didn't grow under my heart, but in it.

The Lord reminded me that the same thing happens when we are born into His family. We are born into His heart of immense love.

Gary and Johnell Loop
Former Missionaries to the Philippines

Thank you, Father, for making me your child. I love you...

"Come, follow me," Jesus said, "and I will make you fishers of men."
MARK 1:17

Raul lived in southern Chile. One day he was passing our church and heard us singing "The Old Rugged Cross." He was carrying a basket of shellfish that he had gathered from the ocean. He would sell them to provide for his family. Though he wanted to enter the church, he did not know what to do with the basket. He finally decided to go in anyway and push the basket under the back seat where he was sitting.

The message that morning touched his heart. He wanted to go to the altar and give his heart to God, but what would he do with the fish? Finally he decided that "fish or no fish" he had to go forward. He took the basket with him!

A few days later we went to visit a church near Puerto Varas. When we drove up to the church, Raul ran up and said, "Pastor, would you please do something for me?" We asked him what he wanted, thinking he was going to ask for money.

"Pastor, would you please let me win souls for God?" Of course, we gave him permission. About two months later we returned to Puerto Varas. Again Raul came running out to the camper all smiles.

His first words were "Pastor, will you do something for me?" We asked what he wanted. He said, "Would you come and dedicate my church?" We did not know about the church, so he told us about it. He said that every day when he went out to sell his fish, he would tell them about Jesus and he now had a church of 60 people. We were thrilled to dedicate his church! Raul had become a fisher of men!

Marjorie McCammon
Former Missionary to Chile

Lord, help me be a fisher of men today...

"Then a voice said to him, 'What are you doing here?'"

1 KINGS 19:13

*G*rowing up and living in the Los Angeles area, I was accustomed to talking about "The Big One." But now I was thousands of miles from home, and although I had experienced many earthquakes in the past, nothing could have prepared me for the morning of August 17, 1999, when the powerful, 7.4-magnitude temblor struck Turkey.

As I rolled out of bed, the floor felt as if it would give way. I found myself crawling on hands and knees towards the bathroom door. The severity of the quake was such that I couldn't help but think the building was going to collapse, and standing under my bathroom doorjamb on the ninth floor wasn't going to help much. Then, out of the depth of my being—holding on to the wall as the building swayed—I cried out in spontaneous praise to God. My heart was pounding in fear, and yet I had an incredible sense of peace in His presence.

Just two days before the earthquake I had been reading in 1 Kings about Elijah's experience in the cave. I was reminded of the story and how after the earthquake the Lord had asked Elijah, "What are you doing here?"

I began to ask myself, "What am I doing here?" And it wasn't "Why was I in this earthquake?" or "Why has this happened to me?" Instead, it was "What is your plan for my life, Lord? What am I doing here?" But even as I asked these questions, I knew God had already been answering.

Whatever our situation—peace or war, calm or quake—may we know in our hearts that we are where the Lord would have us to be. May the Lord speak to all of us with the answer to the same question: "What are you doing here?"

Michael Larkin
FMI Director

> *May I live my life, Lord, in that safe place in the center of your will...*

*"The people were amazed when they saw the mute speaking,
the crippled made well, the lame walking and the blind seeing.
And they praised the God of Israel."*

MATTHEW 15:31

I finished preaching at a conference of about 500 people and gave an invitation for any that would like to be saved. Many responded. Praise the Lord! I then asked if there were any that wanted prayer for healing. Several people came forward, among them a mother carrying her small daughter who was about eight years old.

The little girl was skin and bones. She had never walked and her legs were drawn up to her stomach. I asked some of our pastors to gather around and help us pray. I began talking to the mother and asked her to put her daughter down on the ground. As I was speaking, the little girl was listening and began to respond—she began to extend her legs to the ground as her mother put her down. She started walking with the help of two pastors. Then she walked on her own very slowly and then, to everyone's amazement, she began to run! She was healed!

Several months later, we came back to this same area. When we arrived, a woman and a child came running to meet us with a special gift. The woman thanked me for praying for her little girl. Only then did I recognize her as the same woman who had brought her daughter who was healed. I asked how she was and she said, "This is my daughter!" Amazingly, the little girl was strong and healthy and there was no sign that she had ever been crippled. God had completely healed her! What a powerful God we serve!

Shirley Walker
Former Missionary to Central America

*Lord, it is by your stripes that we are healed. I thank you for
being willing to heal us, and today I bring before you those
who need a healing touch from you...*

"Jesus said, 'I tell you the truth...she put more into
the treasury than all the others.'"

MARK 12:43

"Education by extension" is not new to Foursquare Missions. Throughout the world leaders have taken Bible teaching and ministerial training to remote regions. Panama was no exception.

Many of the pastors in the province of Veraguas had never had the opportunity to study the Bible in a formal way. They couldn't move to the city, so we took the Bible training to them. One Saturday I was in that province for one of our periodic meetings with these student-pastors. They were so appreciative of this program and the opportunity to study in their own homes.

After the sessions, Pastor Sixto Quiroz, usually quite shy and backward, approached me and said he wanted to give me something. He handed me a bag. Later when I looked inside, I found some small green peppers and a cornhusk with string around it. I didn't realize that wrapped in the cornhusk were two brown eggs.

Pastor Sixto lived in a small adobe house with his wife and five small children. They did not have much in this life, but he wanted to show his gratitude for the Bible correspondence program. He had carefully carried this gift down the mountain, and caught a bus on the highway that brought him into the city of Santiago where we had met.

I confess that I kept those eggs for a long time. I have seldom been so honored.

Bonita Schwartz Sanchez
Missionary to Panama

Lord, I pray that my small gifts would honor you. May I cul-
tivate a 'heart of gratitude' toward you for all you have
taught me...

*"The Lord is good, a refuge in times of trouble.
He cares for those who trust in him..."*

NAHUM 1:7

God cares! This is evident when you visit the Foursquare church in the Philippines. The church is alive with the presence of God and we had opportunity to participate in many of the ministries that flow from that beautiful church.

On one occasion we were privileged to hold a four-day crusade near the city of Olongapo. When the invitation for salvation was given, people literally ran to the front. More than 600 responded to receive Jesus as their Savior. We prayed for the sick for several hours each night and witnessed many miraculous healings. Blind eyes were opened, legs lengthened, goiters and cysts disappeared, arthritis and diabetes healed. We encountered so much sickness and disease among these people, but we also encountered the GREAT physician who healed many!

Foursquare Philippines cares for children. It is estimated that there are more than 3,000 abandoned street children in Olongapo. The Foursquare Church (I Care Fellowship) has remodeled its building to provide an orphanage to minister to many of these children.

One woman had a three-year old son, Christopher, born with only one leg, and she was expecting another baby soon. She had no contact with the father and could not support both children. She wanted to give away her baby. She found hope when she walked into the I Care Fellowship.

Don and Sharon Nicholson
Former Missionaries to the Philippines

*Lord, I thank you for the many changed lives in the
Philippines and for the wonderful work you are still doing
there. Bless the people of that nation with a great move of
your Holy Spirit...*

> *"We are confident, yes, well pleased rather to be absent*
> *from the body and to be present with the Lord."*
>
> 2 CORINTHIANS 5:8 (NKJV)

ursing my newborn and having everything to live for, I still wept. I had come so close to being with Jesus. The experience had been brief, but it had left me with a deep sense of longing for heaven and being in the presence of the Lord. I am one of those people who have had a near-death experience.

It happened in San Jose, Costa Rica, during the birth of our third child by caesarean section. The experience was sacred and I told almost no one, not even our children.

Seven years later and curled up in a Madrid, Spain, hospital bed with our cancer-stricken 15 year-old daughter, I confided in her.

"Holly, what is the worst thing that can happen to you? You know that the worst thing for you is really the best thing that can happen to you, because you have put your trust in Jesus Christ."

She listened intently, looking at me with her big beautiful dark eyes. For the first time, she heard about my near-death experience.

A few days later, standing beside her lifeless body, I was greatly comforted, knowing that without a shadow of a doubt, Holly was in the presence of Jesus. She was in that beautiful place that I too had experienced—if only for a short moment—and I knew that Holly did not want to come back.

Molly Doland
Missionary to Spain

> *Father, thank you for the hope we have in Jesus Christ. I*
> *long for the day when I see you face to face, and there will*
> *be no more crying and no more pain...*

"Let the peace of Christ rule in your hearts...And be thankful."
COLOSSIANS 3:15

*B*elow is a journal entry written by Holly, the beautiful 15-year-old daughter of our Missionaries to Spain, Stan and Molly Doland. Holly went to be with the Lord in April of 1993. Holly's life was not abbreviated, but simply accelerated. And she lived it to the fullest, and for Jesus. The entry from her journal below speaks so clearly of the assurance of a Heavenly Father that "above all else is a good God, and we can trust Him."

Dear Daddy,
I thank You for loving me and caring for me;
I thank You for dying for me and forgiving me;
I thank You for making this world and my family;
I thank You for giving us your Word and talking with me;
I thank You for my wonderful friends, especially Lorrie and our smiles;
I thank You for making me and letting me live eternally with you;
And most of all, I thank you for being You in all Your awesome love and power.

Today, may we too find ourselves thankful. Holly may not have lived a long life, but she truly understood what living was about—being thankful for a heavenly daddy who did not spare even His own Son to show us how much we are loved.

Stan and Molly Doland
Missionaries to Spain

Thank you, Father, for sending your Son so that I too can be your child. Give me a pure childlike faith, trusting you completely and talking to you continually...

"I will sing of your love..."
PSALM 101:1

" *I* can't read or write," wept this elderly lady, a member of the Tegucigalpa, Honduras Foursquare Church. She wondered what she could do to share the Gospel with others.

Her sadness turned to great joy when she realized she could pass out tracts. On her first great adventure in sharing the gospel, she knocked on the door of a home. When the woman of the house saw she was passing out Christian literature, she slammed the door in her face.

Feeling a complete failure, this believer sat down on the step and softly began to sing, "Jesus, yo te amo, porque me has salvadao, me has sanada." Later she wandered off.

Several weeks later, a woman responded to the invitation of the pastor to receive Christ as her Savior. She then testified that some weeks ago a lady from the church had come to her door with tracts. She wouldn't listen to her, but the woman had sat on the step and began singing a song about loving Jesus. The words said, "Jesus, I love You, You have saved and healed me."

"I couldn't get the words out of my mind," said the woman. She received Jesus as Savior and many of her family followed her in making decisions for Christ.

Dr. Leland Edwards
Former Missionary to Panama
Missions Director, 1965-1988

I praise you, Father, that you take our feeble efforts and use them to change lives and bring you glory. Use me today and lead me in every situation...

"I have seen your face as though I had seen the face of God..."
GENESIS 33:10 (NKJV)

*F*ear accompanied every step Jacob took toward his brother Esau. The man he had deceived might now take his life. Instead, Esau embraced Jacob. Receiving forgiveness, Jacob said: "I have seen the face of God."

In our case, the man who feared for his life wasn't named Jacob—it was Captain Carriaga, a police officer and dedicated Christian who was committed to sharing his faith and bold in apprehending criminals.

Captain Carriaga had been instrumental in bringing a violent, evil criminal to justice. This man had one last word for Captain Carriaga: "The next time I see you I will kill you."

In the following months, the criminal was incarcerated at the infamous Muntinglupa Prison near Manila where inhuman conditions existed and life was cheap.

Captain Carriaga visited the prison and, as he crossed the exercise grounds, there was instant recognition as he caught the eye of the man he had sent to prison. The words "The next time I see you, I will kill you." rang in his ears. Without hesitation, the prisoner walked straight towards Captain Carriaga.

As the prisoner approached, he grabbed the Captain, threw his arms around him and said, "Jesus has come into my heart; I am now a Christian." Forgiveness and Christ-like love began to flow through them.

No doubt the captain thought, as did Jacob, that he had "seen the face of God." The healing, restoring power of forgiveness is amazing.

Allan Hamilton
Former Missionary to the Philippines

Lord, so often I struggle with unforgiveness, both toward others and myself. Today I forgive all those who have injured me, as you forgave me in Christ...

"You are the salt of the earth..."
MATTHEW 5:13

When my wife, Joni, and I first entered the virgin territories of Western New Guinea's Una cannibals, we used salt and brightly colored glass beads to barter for vegetables and to pay the local people for constructing an airstrip. They loved the white salt.

One day, having shared the Good News with the Unas around the fireplace in the sacred men's house, filled with human skulls, magical paraphernalia, and bows and arrows, they explained why our salt was so precious to them. To get salt, they had to go to the ocean, which took two full weeks of hazardous and backbreaking work as they climbed across 12,000-foot mountain ranges. Once there, they inserted dried banana stalks, brought from their gardens, into the salty water. When the stalks had absorbed the water, they were burned. The black ashes from these were packed into fresh banana leaves and taken back as precious cargo for the village.

The value of salt to the Unas is not much different from Biblical times. In many tropical countries, salt was, and still is, a crucial ingredient in the curing process of perishable foods. The Unas used salt as offerings to appease the rain spirits to stop the incessant downpours. In the Old Testament, salt was offered as a pure, acceptable sacrifice to God (Ezekiel 43:24). God sealed many of His promises with Israel with salt.

Jesus' challenge to us, living in today's broken world, is to be "the salt of the earth." Our lives ought to be a pure, acceptable sacrificial offering to God, demonstrated in the preserving qualities of the love of Christ.

John Louwerse
Former Professor at LIFE Bible College

Lord, let me be that salt in my community today. May my life speak to those around me and bring them to the knowledge that will preserve their life in you...

> *"Let us not become weary in doing good, for at the proper time
> we will reap a harvest if we do not give up. Therefore, as we have
> opportunity, let us do good to all people, especially to those
> who belong to the family of believers."*
>
> GALATIANS 6:9-10

One evening as I entered the Stephen Center, I was confronted by a frustrated waiter. "I cannot deal with the demands of this customer," he said. "He is unreasonable." When he showed me who this upset customer was, I realized the problem.

Seated at one of our tables was a man and his wife who had previously told me they were from Egypt and that he was a "missionary for Islam" in Albania. I approached the man with my best "Christian" smile and apologized for any problems he might be having. He immediately began complaining about everything, "The food was cold…the service was bad." I finally told him we had opened the restaurant as a place to "serve people with the love of God," and if he was not happy he would not have to pay. I took the bill and walked away. He insisted he would pay; I refused his money, and again informed him that as Christians it is our desire to serve him.

Inwardly, I was irritated by his unreasonable behavior and assumed we wouldn't see him again. However, we did see him again a few days later. I thought, "Here he comes for another free meal." I was surprised when he waved to me and said, "Everything is perfect, just perfect!"

Laura and I were able to help this family during their frequent visits to the restaurant. I learned that his initial response toward us was the result of what he had been taught about Christians and their hatred toward Muslims. We were able to show him, without saying it, that we loved him and his family. Truth again defeated the enemy's lies.

Chris Dakas
Missionary to Albania

> *Lord, help us to do good to all people, even when we are
> tired and they are being unreasonable. Give us eyes of faith
> to know that as we keep doing good, we will reap a harvest…*

"How, then, can they call on the one they have not believed in?
And how can they believe in the one of whom they have not heard?
And how can they hear without someone preaching to them?"

ROMANS 10:14-15

Upon the invitation of a new convert, we went to the island of Jintotolo in Masbate, to carry the gospel to people who have never before heard it before. We went throughout the island preaching. Sometimes we met under the coconut trees, sometimes we were in a house, and once we even went to the lighthouse for a service. Many responded and we had the privilege of baptizing some of the new believers before we left the island.

One particular day when we stopped under the coconut trees, a crowd gathered as we began to sing. They listened with eagerness and responded with joy. Then it was time to go to the next place.

As I looked back to see them looking after us, my heart cried out for them. They were so hungry to hear more; it seems we had just been able to give them a few crumbs and they had been so thankful. I thought of how often I had heard the gospel and how many more villages and towns had not yet heard it even once.

Mollie Chaves
Former Missionary to the Philippines

> *Lord, there are still so many people who haven't heard*
> *about you, and the workers are so few. Call and send work-*
> *ers out into the harvest fields...*

*"A wife of noble character who can find?
She is worth far more than rubies."*

PROVERBS 31:10

My wife, Edith Catherine Sumrall, was born a genuine southern belle. When she was only four years old, she was taken to the Panama Canal where she grew up and took a job by the Panama Railroad as a cashier in the Gatun Canal Zone Commissary.

One day a minister of the Canal Zone came to her office and told her about American missionaries in Panama City that he thought she should meet. On Labor Day 1929, Edith and her mother took the one-and-a-half hour train ride to Panama City to meet us. We became friends and continued visiting each other for three years. It was then that I realized I had fallen in love with Edith. I proposed one night overlooking the Canal Zone. Her reply was, "I will have to think about it and make it a matter of prayer." After a considerable time, she finally said yes. I ordered an engagement ring from the Sears and Roebuck catalogue, and one day while out on a country road, I stopped the car by a waterfall, asked for her hand, and put the ring on her finger... her face lit up!

My father, Dr. Arthur F. Edwards, married us on June 21st in Edith's quarters in Gatun, Canal Zone. Edith Catherine Sumrall Edwards has been my one and only girlfriend for 69 years and my one and only wife for 66 years. At the age of 89, she is still the most beautiful lady in ALL THE WORLD.

Donald D. Edwards
Former Missionary to Panama

Father, you will help me with every life decision if I allow you to guide me. Give me wisdom and direction as I live my life in service of you...

"...you will know the truth, and the truth will set you free."
JOHN 8:32

iving in the Andes Mountains, we encountered many people who
had firm beliefs in superstition. The "evil eye" was one such
belief. It was said that if someone had anything wrong with their eye—
such as a crossed eye—then that person could give the "evil eye" to a child
and that child would become very ill. Since there was no cure for it
(although sometimes the witch doctor could help), many children died.
We began teaching our Christians that the blood of Jesus would cover and
protect them and break the bondage of fear of evil.

One day while walking with our little girls, we neared a home where
we saw the people push a girl back into the doorway. This happened each
time we passed. On another day, I was by myself and stopped to ask why
this was happening. They let me see this girl who had a very deformed face
and eye and explained they did not want my pretty little girls to get the
evil eye. This opened the door for many wonderful opportunities for us to
witness to this family.

Before we left Venezuela, that same girl was seated with all our children, singing and worshiping God. No one was paying the slightest attention to her deformity.

There is power; power in the "truth" of Jesus Christ!

Darlene Coombs
Former Missionary to Venezuela

*Lord, thank you that you free me from the bondage of all
superstition. Help me to see you as the One who has the
ultimate power and truth...*

"Stand up...and walk!"
JOHN 5:8 (NLT)

uring a Wednesday night service in Tegucigalpa I noticed Juana, a member of our church, coming in with a woman, man and a teenage boy who was dragging his legs between crutches. After the message, Sister Juana came to me and told me that she told them if they would go with her to church that her pastor would pray and that their son would be healed. No pressure!

Five or six of us prayed for him. The doctors had told him that he would be paralyzed from the waist down and would never walk again. His speech was almost gone and he could only pronounce one syllable at a time. It took only a few minutes to lead them in a prayer of salvation.

Afterwards, I told them that the same Jesus that had forgiven their sins could heal their boy. We prayed. Nothing seemed to happen but I asked the boy, "Do you think God has healed you?" He said yes. I told him get up and walk. With a great effort and the help of his mother he was able to get up on his feet but still with the use of his crutches.

I yelled at him "No! If you are going to walk, do it in the name of Jesus!" and I jerked the crutches out from under his arms. He started to walk normally. He took about ten steps and turned and raised his hands and began to praise the Lord in a normal voice. He grabbed his crutches and ran out into the street screaming, "I am healed, I am healed."

The first week back in his village he won 52 people to the Lord.

Dean Truett
Former Missionary to Honduras

Lord you are my healer. You created and made my body, you alone can fix those things that are wrong with me...

*"For my thoughts are not your thoughts,
neither are your ways my ways, declares the Lord."*

ISAIAH 55:8

"This is Mahmood. Make him a Christian."
    That is what the young Muslim lady told me as she brought Mahmood to the ministry center from which I ministered. He was confused and depressed to the point of being suicidal. His father, a strict Muslim, had tried to force Mahmood to go to the mosque and to do his daily ritual prayers along with the other obligations of Islam. This father's heavy-handedness was pushing Mahmood away from Islam.

The young woman who brought Mahmood to us was a fellow university student. She had more faith in Freud than in Islam. She had taken this young man as a test case for her Freudian philosophies. Her diagnosis was that although she did not put much stock in religion, she thought it would do Mahmood some good. Because of his negative experience with Islam, she decided to find him a different religion. So when she came to us, she said, "This is Mahmood; make him a Christian."

As we spoke to Mahmood he opened his heart to Jesus and was filled with the Spirit. God did a wonderful work in him right at the moment he received the Savior into his life.

Many times God uses people or situations to bring us closer to him and sometimes the tools he chooses to use might surprise us! So we just had to praise God for choosing to use a very unlikely tool—an agnostic Muslim woman—to bring another Muslim to Jesus.

Scott Winter
FMI Missionary

*I praise you, Father, that your ways are not my ways and
that you answer prayers and move in the hearts and lives of
people in ways that I couldn't even imagine. I acknowledge
your sovereignty and lordship, and I give you first place in
my life today...*

"I will remember the deeds of the Lord;
yes, I will remember your miracles..."

PSALM 77:11

One day as I was in the office of the Bible institute in Guayaquil, Ecuador, a mother from the island of Puna came, asking for prayer and financial help. Her daughter was in the hospital, very ill and in need of several thousand sucres to pay for medication. All the money I had at the time was 200 sucres, and I gave them to her. Then we prayed.

As I closed our prayer, I said, "Lord, I wish I had all the money our sister needs, but if I could give her that much she would need the same amount again next month. What we need, Lord, is a miracle of healing for her daughter."

Several months later a woman came into the office. Smiling, she came toward me, but I did not recognize her. It was the woman whose daughter had been ill. She said, "The Lord healed my daughter. I remember what you prayed that day and God gave us a miracle of healing for her."

Jack and Aline Richey
Former Missionaries to Ecuador

Just as the psalmist wrote, Father, I will remember the deeds
of the Lord and remember the miracles you have done in
my life...

> *"All you who fear the Lord, trust the Lord!*
> *He is your helper; he is your shield."*
>
> PSALM 115:11 (NLT)

While I was serving as a missionary in Ecuador, I attended a Ladies Missionary Conference. The speaker shared with us a funny story about a new missionary in Ecuador.

It seems that the new missionary was warned that she must be careful of robbers, who will quickly take your wristwatch from you before you even notice it is missing. With this knowledge, she decided to take a bus trip in the city of Quito. She had her bag, an umbrella and was wearing a sweater. As she got on the bus, and was standing there in the crowd, a very suspicious man stood near her.

At the same time, she looked down and noticed her watch was gone. Being very brave, she decided to get her watch back from the man. So she took her umbrella and put it behind her sweater and poked it into the ribs of the man. She quietly said "Put the watch in my bag." He looked at her and she repeated it again. He responded by dropping the watch into her bag. He moved away, and she got off the bus.

When she returned to her apartment, she noticed that on the table lay her watch. She looked in her bag, and found a man's watch. She quickly realized that she had robbed the man.

From this true story we learn that we must not act too quickly nor rely on human methods. Instead, we must trust the Lord and look to Him to be our help and shield. A heart filled with trust looks up through threatening clouds to see the hand of God reaching down with love.

Jackie Coppens
Former Missionary to Ecuador

> *Lord, help me to not be too quick to take things into my*
> *own hands. Let me trust that you will take care of me and*
> *that you are my help and shield...*

> *"Delight yourself in the Lord
> and he will give you the desires of your heart."*
>
> PSALM 37:4

*I*t was in the shower on a Saturday morning that I began to pray, "Oh Lord, in order to serve our family of nations, churches and missionaries in Europe, I ask you for an assistant who is a strong believer, who speaks fluent English, who is professional in office skills, who is dedicated to her work and leaders, who is honest and full of integrity, and who is a joy to work with."

As I prayed, a certain person came to mind. This person was Helga Koenig, the office manager of a multi-million dollar firm near Frankfurt. I continued praying, "Lord, someone just like Helga."

The next morning in church, I was sharing with the believers about some of my new responsibilities. At the end of the altar call, a woman came to me, and I thought it was to receive prayer. It was Helga. She imparted to me that while I was speaking that morning the Lord very clearly nudged her spiritually and said, "He's going to need some help." At that very moment, her husband Kai nudged her physically and said, "Helga, he's going to need some help. I think you should pray about it." Then she asked if I would be open to that idea. I just about fell over! You can't get more "just like Helga" than Helga!

Helga is not only all of the things I asked God for, but much, much more. I constantly receive comments from national leaders, representatives and missionaries around Europe about what a delight and a joy she is—truly, the Lord is faithful.

Marc Shaw
Regional Coordinator to Europe

Thank you, Lord, that you give me the desires of my heart, especially when it relates to the people around me and doing your work...

"Let the children come to me. Don't stop them! For the Kingdom of God belongs to such as these. I assure you, anyone who doesn't have their kind of faith will never get into the Kingdom of God."

MARK 10:14-15 (NLT)

Recently, as Mike was traveling through East Africa, he became very ill and was bedridden for close to 36 hours. When he called home asking for prayer, he said, "I can't remember ever being this sick." Mike felt that the cause was probably something he had eaten, but because he was traveling specifically to confront corruption and demonic forces, he knew that his battle was spiritual as well.

Several hours after Mike's call, our five-year-old son Kellen came into the bedroom. I told him that he needed to pray for daddy, because he was very sick in Africa and he had missed his airplane because he couldn't get out of bed.

I walked out of the room, and when I returned Kellen was lying on his back with his arms in the air, saying, "Yes!" I asked him what he was so excited about and he said, "While I was praying for daddy, Jesus told me that He already did what I asked!"

Later that day Mike called to say that he was feeling better and was finally able to keep fluids in his system. He told me that at about 6:30 p.m. his fever broke and he was able to sit up without a headache and to drink liquids.

That was the exact time that Kellen had prayed!

Roxanne Larkin
Wife of Mike Larkin, FMI Director

Lord, I thank you for the faith that little children have. Give me that child-like faith and lead me as I pray for the children I know...

*"So pray to the Lord who is in charge of the harvest;
ask him to send out more workers for his fields."*

MATTHEW 9:38 (NLT)

While all missionaries have the same assignment—to share the love of Jesus and bring people to Him—each missionary does this in a slightly different way, according to the local need and the gifting of the missionary. God always gives direction and the ways to share His love, many of which no one could imagine.

We participate in evangelism and discipleship classes for those involved in outreach ministries. Our students already possess the zeal to lead someone to Christ; they just need the scriptural and spiritual tools.

My joy at teaching young women is growing. After the four week class, these women expressed an interest in learning about first aid, self-defense, and women's health. With the constant threat under which they live, it is not hard to see why these are pertinent topics. We arrange for speakers who specialize in these areas to come and share their expertise. By doing so, we are able to share the Lord with other interested women.

John met a young man whose heart had been hardened by years of involvement with a violent, anti-white organization. Themba was at first hostile to John when he visited. Within a few months God miraculously softened Themba's heart and the message of reconciliation to God and to others touched him. He received Christ and recently burned all his materials from the anti-white group—he truly was a changed man!

There is so much more to do. The harvest is truly plentiful. God is looking for those who are willing to go! Is that you?

John and Dianne Shober
Associate Missionaries to South Africa

Lord, thank you for the creative ways in which you bring people to yourself. Give me new ways to serve you and ideas that will bring glory to you...

"There is neither Jew nor Greek, slave nor free, male nor female,
for you are all one in Christ Jesus."

GALATIANS 3:28

O ne day as I sat on the floor with Pastor Oh Pyung Hawan, he looked straight into my eyes and said, "Sometimes I forget that you are a foreigner." We had just spent time laughing, crying and praying together about his church. I felt very rewarded, as we had worked so hard to identify closely with our Korean brothers and sisters, spending hundreds of hours learning and using their language.

One of the stories he told me was how he was called to ministry. Mr. Oh was a bookkeeper who also raised pigs. He told me that one day he read the story of Jesus giving permission to the "legion" of evil spirits to enter a herd of pigs. The whole herd ran down an embankment and drowned in the water, while the man in whom the spirits had dwelt was set free. The Lord used this story to speak to him that a soul was more valuable than many pigs. It was then that Mr. Oh decided to begin training in Bible College and later entered church ministry as a pastor.

Christ has made us one—uniquely bonded together in Him!

Ron and Charlotte Meyers
Former Missionaries to Korea

Lord, I thank you for my precious brothers and sisters in the
faith; those whom I know, and those I will meet in heaven,
who even now are in countries far away. Bless them today...

"Yes," he told them, "I saw Satan falling from heaven
as a flash of lightning! And I have given you authority
over all the power of the enemy, and you can walk among
snakes and scorpions and crush them. Nothing will injure you."

LUKE 10:18-19 (NLT)

My husband, Arthur and I had heard about the tree houses of the tribal people. Now here we were face to face with them. We saw the houses of bamboo and palms perched on stilts six to eight feet high.

There was a man coming toward us. He had an enormous goiter on the side of his neck, and pieces of bone in both ears and in his nose. The first day we were there God healed the goiter. The people were so excited that everyone came to our meeting place. Among them was a woman who was carried into the shelter. People were shouting and crying out in fear of her. When we looked into the face of the woman we saw many demons. We were told she was a voodoo witch.

God reminded us that we had fasted and prayed for this time. He let us know He would deliver her. She spit on us, cursed us and would have harmed us if the people had not tied her so that she could not strike us. We formed a circle and spoke the name: Jesus, Jesus, Jesus.

The natives on the outside of our shelter heard it and began to copy us. The woman relaxed, opened her eyes, and stood up. We untied her and saw the jerking and twisting of her body as the demons came out. We saw Satan defeated. The next morning, very early, the woman went up and down the barrio declaring her salvation.

Dr. Evelyn Thompson
Former Missionary to the Philippines

Lord, Satan has fallen from heaven like lightning. You are
victorious, Lord, you are always victorious...

"He will yet fill your mouth with laughter and your lips with shouts of joy."

JOB 8:21

The Cantonese language is one of the most difficult languages in the world. While the grammar is simple, the nine intonations are demanding. The same sound may have nine different meanings, depending upon the intonation used. For example, the sound "foo" can range from being "sour" to "suffering" to "father" to "pants." Imagine praying to your "hole-ly pants" rather than your Holy Father.

Also, as in every culture, there are special colloquialisms which are unique. As I discovered, attempts at humor do not always translate well.

Weighing over 300 pounds at the time, I wanted to share with the members of the Hong Kong headquarters church that I was not "fat," but that I just had a "large capacity." The response was even funnier than I thought, with many of the Chinese folk doubling up in laughter. Restoring order, I asked my interpreter just what had happened. His face blushed bright red and he responded, "Ask your language teacher."

The next morning during my lesson, my instructor informed me that I had just announced to the congregation that I was "pregnant."

For over 20 years, that guffaw has remained vivid in my memory and in the memories of the members of that church.

Dr. Ron Williams
Former Missionary to Hong Kong

Lord, thank you for filling my mouth with laughter, and in the midst of everything, giving me great joy...

"...He gave them power over unclean spirits, to cast them out, and to heal all kinds of sickness and all kinds of disease."

MATTHEW 10:1 (NKJ)

In February 2000, during eight days of evangelistic outreach in Cotonou, Benin, I was asked to alternate doing altar calls with the former national leader of Foursquare Benin, Rev. Christopher Dewanou. These altar calls were after the tremendously intense testimonies of two former voodoo witch doctors who had been converted from their evil ways to become followers of Christ. Their testimonies were intense and gruesome as they depicted the horrible and unimaginable acts in which these men had participated in order to obtain powers from the dark and occultic world of voodoo.

By the fourth night, faith was rising and people were turning from evil. A number of people were healed of sicknesses of the skin and hair, and of other problems related to demonic bondage.

It was on the last night that we prayed for a high voodoo priest who came forward to repent and be freed from his dark bondage. I rejoiced over the miracle of salvation based on repentance. The next day as we gathered in his home to burn and dispose of the voodoo paraphernalia (skulls, dolls, daggers, body parts and excrements, etc), I was struck by the power of the gospel to turn lives around. The chains of bondage could be seen falling from his face! What a miracle to see this man translated from the kingdom of darkness to the kingdom of light!

Dr. Daniel Lucero
Missionary to France and the Francophone Nations of Africa

Thank you, Father for bringing me into your marvelous light. Use me to bring others out of darkness and into your light...

"See, I am doing a new thing!..."
ISAIAH 43:19

Karl Williams was a successful businessman whose love for Gospel literature and seeing souls won to the Lord was central in his life. He was most alive when he was sharing the Gospel with someone who had yet to hear.

At the age of 70, Karl was unable to go to church because he was recovering from surgery. Although he had a successful business and many fruitful years of ministry behind him, he was feeling old and passed by. After telling the Lord of his hurt, the Lord clearly spoke words to him that gave him direction for the last years of his life, "My son, the next ten years will be the best years of your life."

Karl believed he had heard from the Lord, and he had seen firsthand the need for our missionaries to have free Christian literature. So in 1981, we started Foursquare Missions Press in a rented garage with a one-color printer and a very used "stitcher." To date FMP has produced and shipped over 140 million pieces of free gospel literature to over ninety countries.

Many years later, Karl went home to be with the Lord. He was never happier than those last years of his life, watching the presses run, seeing the shipments go out and hearing how God's Word was winning souls.

Leona Williams
Cofounder, Foursquare Missions Press

Lord, whenever I am feeling 'passed by,' help me to look to you to give me direction and to show me how you want to use me...

"For since the creation of the world God's invisible qualities—
his eternal power and divine nature—have been clearly seen,
being understood from what has been made,
so that men are without excuse."

ROMANS 1:20

*W*e traveled 54 hours toward the south of Chile by train and boat, and then rode another 12 hours by horseback before arriving at La Junta, in the far south of that long, slender country. The next day we rode the horses another three hours to a large lake. As the pastor and I dismounted, a couple with a lovely home nearby invited us in for sopaipillas and mate, a strong, warm herb drink.

As we visited, I asked if they were Catholic. The answer was that the Catholic Church had not come that far. They said they were "believers."

As I continued to probe, I found Romans chapter one coming to life. This couple had truly seen the Creator at work and felt that anyone who had gone to the effort to create all this would also provide all they would ever need to answer the questions of their soul.

One evening they "happened" upon a radio station all the way from San Francisco, California, in the Northern Hemisphere. This short-wave program was Evangelist Paul Finkinbinder, on the Voice of Friendship, and he was explaining the way of salvation. They both said, "This is the way; this is what we believe has been provided for us by the great Creator."

Even though they had never read the Bible or any Christian material, they could clearly see that there was an obvious reason to believe in an awesome God who created all they could see.

Glen Pummel
Former Missionary to Chile

Thank you, Father, that you have revealed yourself through
your creative powers. Reveal yourself to these that I bring
before you now...

> *"... for he guards the course of the just and protects*
> *the way of his faithful ones."*
>
> PROVERBS 2:8

*W*e all have read about the New Testament martyrs, men like Stephen who were literally stoned for their faith, but nothing can prepare us for the possibility that we too might follow in some rather saintly footsteps.

Traveling in a boat down one of the tributaries of the Amazon River in Brazil, our evangelism team arrived at a remote village in the middle of nowhere as dusk fell. We had visited many similar villages with hundreds of salvations with signs and wonderings following. As I greeted the village chiefs with my leaders and the full-time missionary, the Holy Spirit clearly spoke to me that something was not quite right. I instructed my leaders to go back to the boat and prepare the team to leave immediately. The missionary and I continued speaking to them, but began to walk back towards the boat slowly, never losing eye contact with the large group that stood before us. Although these village leaders didn't say anything to let me know what was about to happen, the Spirit did. Once everyone was in the boat, I walked down the path still keeping my eye on the leaders, smiling and waving, but aware something was very wrong.

Just as I turned my back I heard something fly right past my ear, then another and another. Soon a barrage of stones came crashing toward the boat and we were under attack from the villagers. Although dozens of large rocks were thrown, no one was hurt and we escaped rejoicing in the privilege of serving the Savior and knowing that God was with us.

We learned that day there is no safer place to be than in the perfect will of God, no matter what the circumstances.

Robert Hunt
Director of Foursquare Missions Press/FMI Communications Coordinator

Thank you, God, for your protection that keeps us safe when
we walk in obedience to you!

> *"...but when we cried out to the Lord, he heard our cry..."*
> NUMBERS 20:16

Our group of youth went on a three-day retreat to a little village called Avellana. One afternoon we boarded small boats and traveled down the canal to the Pacific Ocean.

As the youth headed for the water, Irv warned them to be careful of the riptide. Fourteen-year-old Carlos was having a good time when suddenly he was caught by the tide, which began carrying him out to sea. Being a strong swimmer, Irv told himself ,"No big problem. I'll dive in and pull him out."

The sea proved stronger than the swimmers. To make matters worse, Carlos had become very frightened and struggled with Irv. They both became exhausted.

"Everything turned blue and I quit struggling," Irv said later. "I gave myself up to die, wondering what complications Florence would have, living in a foreign country. Then a peace came over me."

Meanwhile back onshore, Florence called the youth to prayer and ran to find help. The only man nearby said, "There is nothing I can do. They will come back in three days when the sea washes them ashore."

Florence returned to pray with the others, with her eyes open, trying to see Irv and Carlos. Suddenly, she heard someone say, "Isn't anyone going to help us?" There stood Irv and Carlos ankle-deep in the water. They were too tired to walk.

Our youth recognized God had brought us a miracle. They had seen the power of God that day.

Irvin and Florence Espeseth
Former Missionaries to Guatemala

> *Lord, when I am desperate, I know you hear my cry. Thank you for protecting me when I was in danger, and for redeeming my life in those times when I faced troubles too great for me.*

> *"I tell you the truth, anyone who will not receive the kingdom of*
> *God like a little child will never enter it."*

LUKE 18:17

Elva Melendez is only nine years old, but she has great faith in God. While crossing the street she was struck by a car, and her leg was crushed under the wheels. At the hospital the doctor told Elva's mother that she would probably never walk again and that her leg might have to be amputated.

Elva looked directly into the doctor's eyes and said, "No, Doctor, you are mistaken. God is going to heal my leg." The doctor smiled indulgently at this child who spoke so seriously and convincingly about something that seemed so impossible.

"You will see," Elva said, "When you come tomorrow morning, I will be walking all around this room!"

The doctor walked away shaking his head, but the next day he found Elva hobbling around and talking to the other patients in the ward! Today she doesn't even have a limp or have any scars!

Child-like faith. Jesus demands it. He knew exactly what He was talking about when He challenged us to have this kind of faith. As a matter of fact, God's Word says we have to believe like a child to enter into His kingdom.

Charles and Nelwyn Gosling
Former Missionaries to San Salvador

> *Lord, make me like a child today. Give me that sincere*
> *child-like faith that trusts you in every situation...*

*"Then your light will break forth like the dawn,
and your healing will quickly appear..."*

ISAIAH 58:8

Taichung Park is not one of your typical parks in Taiwan, although it's the largest one in the city of Taichung. There are few couples strolling, kids playing or dogs barking. Instead, you find many homeless men and women wandering the grounds, collecting whatever they can use as bedding material or food.

I met Shing, a 28-year old woman, at this park. She was talking to a man who had one limp leg. I later asked her who this man was and she told me it was her husband. They had come to Taichung in hopes of finding a job. Since her husband was disabled and had no vocational skills, the couple had no money. They lived in the park with no means of support.

I also learned that Shing had given birth to a baby boy just a week earlier. The child was their second; however, doctors expected him to die just as their first one did, when he was three months old. The couple had nothing left, and no hope. I asked Shing if she wanted to receive Christ, who was able to heal her child. Desperate and without any other alternatives, she agreed. I prayed with her for the healing of her soul, the healing of her baby boy, and the employment of her husband.

I saw Shing one month later. "I've been trying to find you!" she exclaimed happily. She then told me that her baby was completely healed—confirmed by the doctors—and that he was perfectly healthy. In addition, her husband had found a job as a vendor in the night market. What a mighty God we serve!

Ken Hong
Missionary to Taiwan

*Thank you, Father, that as we give our lives over to you, your
light comes and dispels the darkness in our lives, bringing
healing and restoration and hope...*

"Praise the Lord, O my soul, and forget not all his benefits—who forgives all your sins and heals all your diseases..."

PSALM 103:2-3

After I spent some time ministering in the area, the Lord directed me to purchase three acres of land in Granja Ceclia, Mexico. A large cement block building was built to provide for both the church and a training institute.

Shortly after the facility was completed, Ernesto Santiago was leading a revival meeting there. One night after the service the Lord impressed upon our hearts to visit the delegado (mayor) of the area. I took four other men with me, and when we arrived very late in the night, we found the mayor's deputy had blood poisoning in his right arm. The doctor had said it must be amputated immediately, but the deputy had refused and returned home. He was now suffering great pain.

We began talking with this man about Jesus and His saving grace. The deputy accepted the Lord and then the men prayed for his healing. The next day when they stopped by to see how the deputy was, they found all the swelling had disappeared, and he was completely healed.

Later that same deputy directed traffic at our revival meeting. Praise the Lord!!

Ludwig Mantei
Former Missionary to Mexico

Lord, I thank you for all your benefits in my life. There are so many – healing, forgiveness of all my sins, peace, joy...

"A man's steps are directed by the Lord..."
PROVERBS 20:24

*R*afico was a nine-year old Otavala Indian boy in Ecuador. One night, in a drunken stupor, his parents tied him to the railroad tracks, muttering they had eight other children and didn't need so many. Rafico managed to wiggle free, except for one leg that he lost above the knee. Neighbors saved his life and eventually Rafico came to live at the Houses of Happiness.

Miraculously, God opened doors for Rafico to get medical treatment in the States. When the day arrived to be fitted for his artificial leg, the AP wire services became aware and the story spread.

A copy of the Miami Herald found its way to the small shack in the jungle of Brazil where an oil man was eating his lunch. The Lord touched his heart as he read Rafico's story. Six months later his company transferred him to Ecuador to build a pipeline over the Andes Mountains. That line "just happened" to cross our property. One day this man proceeded to tell Henry about the story he had read. Henry smiled, "Would you like to meet that boy?" He wept when he met Rafico.

With their equipment we carved out a soccer field, built a 50,000 gallon water reservoir and did thousands of dollars worth of grading. We realized God did this; He provides every time we have a need.

Rafico is now a fine Christian man and an optometrist in Ecuador.

Dorothy Davis
Former Missionary to Ecuador

Father, direct my steps this day. Your understanding is far beyond my own; come and lead me and those around me that our lives might intersect for your glory...

"You, dear children, are from God and have overcome them,
because the one who is in you is greater than
the one who is in the world."

1 JOHN 4:4

The town of Escazu in Costa Rica is the center of witchcraft for that nation. The satanic spirit in that place was very strong. Often we would go to this town for services.

One Sunday afternoon, Juan and our son Jim started out for services in Escazu. The leading witch had pronounced a curse on them and had sprinkled powder on the bridge they had to cross to get there. He told many people in the city that before "those Christians" reached the other side of the bridge, something terrible would happen to them. He had invoked the spirits to put a curse on them.

When Jim and Juan came to the bridge, Juan became fearful and hesitant about crossing. Jim assured this new believer that God's power was much stronger than that of Satan. They began crossing.

There were many people standing on the far side of the bridge, waiting to see what would happen. As they crossed over, they sang a chorus about the blood of Jesus. When they got to the other side and nothing had happened, the people thronged around them.

God used this opportunity to show these people His love and great power. Many turned from witchcraft to Christ that day because of what they saw.

Marjorie McCammon
Former Missionary to Latin America

> *Father, thank you that He who is in me is greater than he*
> *who is in the world. Help me to understand and walk in that*
> *power, so that you might be glorified and others might come*
> *to know you...*

*"But you will receive power when the Holy Spirit comes
on you; and you will be my witnesses in Jerusalem,
and in all Judea and Samaria, and to the ends of the earth."*

ACTS 1:8

As I stood in front of the congregation of the Kampala (Uganda) Foursquare Church in Bakuli Market, I paused before the Lord, wondering how the promise of Acts 1:8 applied to the impoverished people of this great church on the outskirts of Kampala. And then the Lord showed me the faces of the miracles, the stories that have been told through FMI videos, the FMI Today newspaper, the ADVANCE magazine, the Global REPORT bulletin inserts, the Prayer Force emails, and other communiqués of FMI.

I think of people like George, who had been deaf and dumb, but today is completely healed and is training to be a pastor. Or Miriam, who was set free from the enemy of her soul on Christmas morning. Or David, a political Marxist from Ethiopia who found Jesus and refuge at the Kampala Foursquare Church. Or the lady in the village who was healed from partial paralysis when missionaries George and Margaret Fisher went to her home to pray for her. And finally Suzanne, who has been dying of AIDS but the Lord continues to sustain her life, raising her from her deathbed no less than five times.

In remembering their witness on that Sunday morning as I stood before them, I realized they too will receive power when the Holy Spirit comes upon them and they will be witnesses for Jesus in Bakuli Market, in Kampala, in Uganda, in Africa, and to the ends of the earth. May the world hear and read their witness.

Michael Larkin
Missions Director

> *Lord, help me to be a witness for you in my own community
> and to the ends of the earth...*

"For we are God's workmanship, created in Christ Jesus to do good works, which God prepared in advance for us to do."

EPHESIANS 2:10

What an honor for the Lord to allow us to live long enough to see sweet fruit from our labors! Today is such a "Day of Great Honor" for me as I write from Japan. It's hard for me to contain it all, the "joy down inside!"

I was reminded today, over and over, the impact of one person's obedience on the world. It all began when I answered God's call to Japan 43 years ago. I was 23 years old and, as I landed in Japan after a 10 days ride across the Pacific by ship, I had never been happier. I can remember that day as if it were yesterday. It was a dream come true!

Today, 43 years later, a 26-year-old girl name Rae—whom I've never met before—thanked me for coming to Japan and changing her life. She thanked me for obeying God, for serving in Japan and beginning a church where her pastor got saved. It was her pastor who led her mother to the Lord, and it was her mother who led Rae to the Lord, and Rae is determined to serve God and to lead her newborn child to the Lord.

During the "Dedication Message" of the new church, the Lord touched Rae and it struck her how one person's obedience has a domino-effect—the surrounding people are impacted and they pass that impact on to the next and the next until countless people and future generations are changed for the glory of God. With this in mind, Rae dedicated her life anew to Jesus and asked Him to use her in that same way. She gave her life to God to make an impact on the world.

When we obey God, our feeble attempts turn into real masterpieces. That's just what God does!

Jack and Shirl DeBay
FMI Associates, Hong Kong

Father, thank you that you take our acts of obedience and weave them into a masterpicce of intertwined lives. Lead me in those works that you have prepared in advance for me to do...

"Who gives him sight...is it not I, the Lord?"
EXODUS 4:11

*T*OTALLY BLIND...what a terrible diagnosis. Francisco de Oliveria, only 26 years old, would never see again. He lives in the city of Tupa, in the state of Sao Paulo, Brazil. He has been a member of the Foursquare Church for six years.

For almost four years Francisco suffered—he was totally blind, unable to see to even eat the food set before him. Then, in the last months of 1965, Francisco began to suffer severe attacks of pain in his head. They were almost too much to endure.

It was during this season of time that he went to an evening service at the Foursquare Church and, as he was singing Somente pela Fe ("Only by Faith"), the pain became even more intense in his head. After he went home, it became even worse. He called the national pastor, Guilherme Rodriguez Pereira, to come and pray for him.

The young man was suffering so greatly that it was difficult for Pastor Guiherme to keep Francisco from gouging out his own eyes. The battle continued and they prayed fervently until four o'clock in the morning. Then the pain was relieved, and wonder of wonders, Francisco's sight was completed restored in both eyes.

Here indeed was a miracle wrought by God! To Him be the glory!

Foursquare World ADVANCE

Lord, I thank you that you have power over every evil Spirit, even those that cause sickness and infirmities...

> *"Do not be afraid of those who kill the body but cannot kill the soul. Rather, be afraid of the One who can destroy both soul and body in hell."*
>
> MATTHEW 10:28

"When the guests arrive, the chicken gets nervous!" This is probably one of my favorite African proverbs. I am not a great meat-eater but chicken is the meat of choice in most African countries. In visiting remote churches it is required that you have a meal with the pastor. In a three day period we visited thirteen churches and had chicken in each place. This proverb was shared with me by one of our African pastors when I told him that the three of us had probably decimated the chicken population of the entire region in three days.

In fact the pastors gave my pickup a name. In Kiswahili it is known as Mla kuku. It translates as "chicken eater." The majority of surviving chickens got real nervous when they saw Mla kuku heading their way.

So here's my question: What makes you nervous? Probably the things that make you nervous are the things that can't really hurt you. The chickens of Africa know what can kill them and they get nervous—and they should! As Christians we must remember that God is all powerful and that we can walk in peace knowing that HE is in control of our life. He has power to kill both body and soul, yet He chose to give us Jesus so that we could live forever!

Glen Mickel
Former Missionary to West Africa

Father, thank you for your mercy and salvation. I want to serve you today boldly, without fear or stress or anxiety over worldly matters, and with a reverent fear and healthy respect of you...

"Follow my example, as I follow the example of Christ."
1 CORINTHIANS 11:1

*W*hile our English-speaking congregation in Hong Kong was meeting in the Cultural Center, two Chinese men joined one of the services. After the service we discovered they were from mainland China and had entered the "wrong" room. They had planned to attend a seminar about immigration to Australia. Nevertheless, they enjoyed the service and asked if they could return the next week.

That following week, one of the men, Karlson, did return. After the service Carolyn discovered he was a teacher but had never heard anything about the Bible. Carolyn decided to begin with Adam and Eve. When she got to the part about being tempted to eat the forbidden fruit, Karlson asked, "Did they eat it? Did they eat it?" Of course, she had to give him the "bad news" that they did. But then she gave him the "good news" and he accepted Jesus as his Savior.

Shortly thereafter, we did not see Karlson for several weeks. He had been in China visiting his mother who was very sick with a heart condition. He was told she would probably die the night he visited her. He immediately began fasting and praying through the night. By morning she was well. When he returned he gave a wonderful, but matter-of-fact, testimony of her healing.

Since we had not taught about divine healing while he was with us, we asked him how he knew what to do. He said, "I just did what I saw you do."

Gary and Carolyn Cooper
Former Missionaries to Hong Kong

Lord, help us today to be an example to others, teaching
others the Good News in our words and in how we live...

> *"Always be prepared to give an answer to everyone who asks you to give a reason for the hope that you have."*
>
> 1 PETER 3:15

A great thing occurred in one of our churches which meets on a farm. The farm is near Marondera in the area known as Theydon. The owner of the farm has been under threatened lately and war veterans have been terrorizing his workers. They accuse them of being opposition members because they come to a "white man's church."

To make a long story short, 13 of our church members were kidnapped at gunpoint from the farm. Eleven of them were later released and I went to the farm to pray for them all and lead a service. The two remaining brothers who were kidnapped were taken away for more than two nights. No one had heard from them and we did not know if they were dead or alive.

When they finally returned, the older of the two brothers reported that he had begun to sing praises to Jesus and testify of his joy in front of the kidnappers. They then became agitated and asked, "Why are you so happy? Don't you know that we are going to kill you?"

The brother replied that if it was God's time for him to go he wanted to be happy when he died. After two days of capture, the kidnappers could not bring themselves to kill the man that they had taken. They actually told him that they liked him and were glad he told them about his God!

Alan and Anneke Frank
Missionaries to Zimbabwe

> *Father, give me the boldness to testify for Jesus even in the most dire of circumstances. Help me to be ready to give an answer in season and out of season, and give me the faith to speak boldly...*

"Train a child in the way he should go,
and when he is old he will not turn from it."

PROVERBS 22:6

Many children in Uganda are not able to attend school. For some, their caretakers prefer to keep them as house girls and boys, while for others, the fees involved prevent them from attending. Whatever the reason, many children grow up illiterate and therefore are often unable to rise above the poverty into which they were born.

God put it on my heart to help these children to learn to read. We began literacy classes for school-age children who are unable to attend school, and God gave us a leader who is assisted by volunteers from the church to run this program. The children come every day for two hours for a three-month period. Then we begin a new group.

People in the community are recognizing what is happening, and adults are asking for classes. God has used the literacy program to show our community that the church, the Body of Christ, cares about them. In addition, it helps the children to gain a new perspective on who they are and who they can become. It is an effective way to fight poverty in both the physical and spiritual realms as they become empowered to read the Word of God!

Sarah Adams
Foursquare Missionary to Uganda

Lord, I thank you that many are being taught to read, and
I pray that they would become great students of your word.
Raise up pastors and teachers from those who are being
taught...

"How great are his signs, how mighty his wonders!"
DANIEL 4:3

A student at Aselapura School in Sri Lanka was demon-possessed. The school principal requested that Foursquare Pastor Kingsley come to pray for her. As he was praying, the local witchdoctor arrived and demanded that Pastor Kingsley leave immediately. Then the witchdoctor began his chants and incantations, but soon declared that this demon could not be driven out by anyone. He walked out of the school and left the girl in the condition he had found her.

The principal sent the young girl home where members of the Foursquare Church gathered to pray for her. The demon manifested itself and said, "Because the witchdoctor has tied a knot in her hair, I cannot leave her body." The knot was cut and further prayer was offered. The girl was healed and set free! Her deliverance became a powerful testimony to the students and faculty at her school.

In Sri Lanka, pastors are trained to believe that God confirms His Word with signs following. And He does!

On another occasion a leper was covered with a white cloth and lying on the floor when the Sri Lankan pastor visited him. He had lost the use of his hands and the sores on his legs had almost completely paralyzed him.

As the pastor laid his hands upon the leper and prayed with compassion, the man began to stretch out his hands, bend them, and then swing them around. Next, he stood up and began to walk! Within two days the wounds were dried up and he was able to return to work. The following week, he came to church riding a bicycle!

Foursquare World ADVANCE, 1994

Lord, I thank you that when we declare your word, you confirm your word with miraculous signs. I ask you to reveal yourself today by your mighty works...

"Ask the Lord of the harvest, therefore, to send out workers into his harvest field."

MATTHEW 9:38

*P*rayer makes a difference and God is true to His Word.

After returning from furlough one year, I had prayed and asked God for direction concerning my ministry in Chile. The Lord spoke to my spirit about the Biblical plan to raise up leadership. Purchasing maps of Chile, I cut them into the 12 regions and distributed these maps to the Foursquare women's groups over the length of Chile. We asked them to pray for that region for one year, praying that the Lord would send laborers into His harvest. These women did pray, from one end of the country to the other—an expanse of 3,000 miles.

Within one year we witnessed the answer to those prayers. Our Bible Institutes were filled with new students whom God had called to ministry. These men and women went out and planted new churches; from that time till now more than 75 new churches and preaching places have been established.

I was reminded of the importance of prayer in the life of a missionary, and in the life of each and every one of us. When we pray, God moves!

Sheila Ransford
Missionary to Chile

Lord, thank you for the power of prayer. I pray now for you to raise up laborers for your work...

"O Lord my God, I called to you for help and you healed me...Your right hand, O Lord, shattered the enemy."

PSALM 30:2...EXODUS 15:6

Shortly after arriving in Manila, we were sent to the city of Iloilo. The Lord directed my husband Al to conduct a two-week series of meetings. Although it was raining very hard the whole two weeks, people came, and God met us in a powerful way! This did not make the enemy happy.

Early on the last morning of the meetings, I heard Al call out in a weak voice, "Mollie, please come and pray for me." I found him lying on the floor, too weak to get up. We began to pray and he was immediately healed. Later that morning, he preached to a full church and many received Jesus as their Savior. During the two weeks of meetings, 52 were saved and many were healed.

God is awesome! No matter what the enemy tries to do, we serve a victorious and powerful Savior!

Mollie Chavez
Former Missionary to the Philippines

Lord, thank you that when I need to be healed, you are there to heal me. Thank you for your power to heal which is greater than the power of the enemy...

> *"A man's steps are directed by the Lord."*
> PROVERBS 20:24

*P*astor George and two fellow pastors were traveling through the tea estates to visit several who had received Jesus as their Savior through a Foursquare church correspondence course.

After several visits, they were passing a store when the van suddenly stopped and would not run. It was hot and they were tired, so two of the men went across to the store to get a cold drink. As they entered the store, they noticed one wall was covered with shelves of small figures. This was the god shelf and each object was for sale.

The pastors noticed that among these gods was a statue of Jesus. They asked the proprietor about this and were told that statue was for sale, just like the other gods. When they began to tell the man that Jesus was the son of the Most High God, he listened with interest. That day he received Jesus as his Savior. He begged the men to return to tell him more. They promised to come to hold a Bible study in his home if he would gather some people. He eagerly agreed.

When they returned to the van and turned the key, it started right away. God had an appointment they might have missed if the van had not stopped.

Eloise Clarno
Former Missionary to Philippines

> *Lord, I know you will guide my steps today if I allow you to do so. Teach me not to have my own agenda, but to fully rely on you to schedule my days, that I might have 'divine appointments"...*

"Come, follow me," Jesus said, "and I will make you fishers of men."
MARK 1:17

As Evangelist Nathaniel Donkor walked into Afransie, a Wasa village in Ghana, he noticed a group of men sitting near the bus stop. As he looked over the group, one man seemed to stand out. He approached that man and simply said, "Follow me. God has something special for your life." The man left the group and followed the evangelist.

The two men located several people in the village who had been treated at a clinic set up by the team that had visited Ghana. Nathaniel shared the gospel with each one. Before the day had ended, he had met many of the important people of the village. As he left the village, Nathaniel left behind some printed tracts and booklets. He instructed his new disciple to continue sharing the gospel message.

Some time later Nathaniel invited missionary Greg Fisher to join him in visiting Afransie. To their surprise, as they entered the village the people greeted them as "Foursquare ministers." Many people began following them, saying, "Please, put my name on the list!" Neither knew what that meant, but the people persisted. Finally they found Nathaniel's disciple who quickly produced "the list" of 62 names. These were people he had shared the gospel with and who wanted to know more about Jesus Christ. To top it off, they discovered the village chief had already donated a large plot of land for a church building.

At their first Sunday morning worship service, the new church had over 80 people in attendance.

Foursquare World ADVANCE, 1995

> *Lord, make me a good 'fisher of men'. Lead me to those people whose hearts have already been prepared by you to receive...*

"I love the Lord, because he hath heard my voice and my supplications. Because He hath inclined his ear unto me, therefore will I call upon him as long as I live."

PSALM 116:1-2 (KJV)

*W*hen we arrived in Greece we needed a student visa to stay. When I went to enroll at the University, they told me I needed a student visa first. So I went to immigration to get my visa. The immigration officer told me that I needed to be registered in the University before I could get the visa. I was stuck in the middle of a real life "Catch 22!"

I went back where we were staying and prayed something like this, "GOD, WHAT ARE YOU DOING? YOU TOLD US TO BE MISSIONARIES, WE SOLD EVERYTHING AND LEFT HOME, AND NOW WE CAN'T STAY? I NEED TO HEAR FROM YOU NOW! NOT TOMORROW! NOT TEN MINUTES! NOW!"

I was not at my spiritual best at the moment so my wife, Marlys, went out to the living room to pray for me. During her prayer, a woman named "Joy" called to tell me about a missionary who had solved the same snag. That call set in motion everything we needed to stay in Greece.

God answered me in exactly the terms I was praying. He answered me immediately, not tomorrow, not even in ten minutes. He heard my voice and answered me according to my cry. And He used Joy to do it!

Brooks Bryan
Former Missionary to Greece

Lord, you give me what I need, exactly when I need it. You are so good! Thank you for answered prayer...

"Jesus Christ is the same yesterday, today and forever."
HEBREWS 13:8

From the hour we started the church, it grew as God confirmed His Word with signs following. With a knowledge that He was with us and people were hungry for the Gospel, we waxed bold in the faith. We only preached salvation to begin with, but knowing that in the precious atoning blood of Jesus Christ there is provision for both soul and body, we began to preach Christ in His finished work. It was nothing to see the deaf receive their hearing right while the preaching was going on. Multitudes of hungering and thirsting people came to hear and see. How we thank God we had this opportunity to see these thousands come to the Lord.

Then, while the Word was being preached one time, we were literally forced to tell them about the baptism of the Holy Spirit because they began to receive it without having any preaching on the subject. Without being told about tongues, interpretations of tongues, or prophecies in the New Testament way, they began to speak in tongues and to interpret! We had to explain these things to them afterwards!

Further, as hands were laid upon the sick, they recovered. The lame, the blind, the deaf, those with cancers, goiters, tumors, and leprosy came and God healed them before our very eyes.

The gospel hasn't changed, friends. The gospel is just the same. It still works. There still is nothing impossible!

Dr. Evelyn Thompson
Former Missionary to the Philippines

Lord, you are the same yesterday, today and forever! Just as you were in New Testament days, so you are today! You are everything to me...

"If you believe, you will receive
whatever you ask for in prayer."
MATTHEW 21:22

Fernando Salvatiera grew up in Ibiato with his parents who worked faithfully for the Lord for many years, helping me train the Siriono Indians that I brought out of the jungles to Ibiato.

One day, Fernando became very ill and was rushed to the hospital in Trinidad where the doctors put him through a complete examination to find out what caused his illness. Several weeks passed before they told him that he had a very serious lung infection and would die if he did not have the regular blood transfusion treatment. They also told him that he could not leave the hospital.

The church was praying for the Lord to heal him because he did not have the money to pay for the treatment. One night when he was praying, Fernando felt that the Lord had touched him. He told the doctors he was healed and wanted to go home, but they would not allow him to leave. However, when Fernando kept on insisting, the doctors made him sign a document saying that they would not be responsible for his death. He was very happy to sign it.

Fernando was released after 40 days in the hospital and he came to church praising the Lord for his miracle! Everyone praised the Lord with him for answered prayer.

Jack and Darlene Anderson
Former Missionaries to Bolivia

Lord, I want to have faith in you! Help me to believe in your
power to heal the sick today...

"Enter through the narrow gate. For wide is the gate and broad is the road that leads to destruction, and many enter through it."

MATTHEW 7:13

The church in Oizumi, Japan, was the first Foursquare church to be pioneered in the nation. Kay Kamiya was one of the students in our Sunday school class. As a teenager, her father asked her to give up her faith in Jesus Christ or leave his house. She said she could never give up her Savior because He was her only God and Savior. He beat her and she retreated to our house. The next day, she sneaked back home, packed her clothing and other possessions, and returned to our house. Soon she was living in the dormitory of a Bible college in Tokyo, where she began studying.

Another student in our Sunday school at that time was a beautiful and very talented young woman who was a friend of Kay's. Unlike Kay, though, she made decisions that led her away from the Lord. And although these girls studied together in the same Sunday school class, they chose very different roads for their lives.

As the years passed, Kay's friend left the church. She became a famous movie star, and her face appeared on the cover of many Japanese magazines. One night she phoned Kay. She was rich and famous, but so very unhappy. She asked for prayer.

Like all of us, Kay and her friend made choices that affected their lives here on earth as well as their eternal destinies. There are many paths that lead to the wide road of destruction, but there is only one narrow road that leads to life. Whether you choose the broad road or the narrow path is up to you.

Billie Charles Francey
Former Missionary to Asia

> *Lord, I know I will make choices today that will have consequences throughout eternity. Help me to always choose your right paths...*

"Though he slay me, yet will I hope in Him..."

JOB 13:15

"*I*f you don't know beyond a doubt that God has called you to Nigeria, you won't last six months. The stories alone will paralyze you with fear." Those were the wise words of the man who mentored us onto the mission field.

We went "feeling" God had called us to be missionaries and somehow feeling that God had special grace or anointing that allowed missionaries to stand in the face of hostile, dangerous circumstances.

Then, within several months, two missionaries we knew personally were killed. One was a man who had served with his wife in Nigeria for over 30 years. He was shot and killed while trying to prevent thieves from stealing their car. The other was our own Foursquare missionary in Zambia, Edgar Coombs, who was struck and killed by a truck as he crossed a road.

Our response to these events was, "What's with this, Lord? Are You our Protector or not?" We had to ask ourselves, "Is God still God in the midst of tragedy?"

We stayed home for several weeks while we regrouped our faith. Slowly the Holy Spirit adjusted our understanding: we all have the same promises wherever we serve. All Christians are vulnerable to tragedies.

God gave us two Scriptures: Job 13:15,"Though He slay me, yet will I hope in Him…" and Hebrews 2:14b-15, "…so that by His death He might destroy him who holds the power of death…and free those who all their lives were held in slavery by their fear of death."

In the face of any worldly circumstances, all of us choose whether or not we will trust in God and serve Him.

Kathy Kieselhorst
Former Missionary to Nigeria, now serving with her husband, Bill in South Africa

Lord, despite tragedies that come my way let me hold on to you. Even though I don't understand why things happen as they do, help me to put my trust in you...

> *"Greater love has no one than this,*
> *that he lay down his life for his friends."*
>
> JOHN 15:13

R onald Leung was known as "Middle Ronald" to be distinguished from "Big Ronald" the missionary and "Little Ronald" the member of another Foursquare church in Hong Kong.

When Middle Ronald was eight years old, he was asked if he would be willing to "give his blood" as his four-year-old sister Joyce needed a blood transfusion. The young girl was going to undergo surgery and the doctors felt Ronald's blood be the most acceptable. After much thought over the next few days, Middle Ronald decided he would "give his blood for his sister."

The transfusion began and was proceeding normally, when suddenly Ronald became agitated. He called for the nurse, and after he settled down, he asked, "Just when is it that I'm going to die for my sister?" Happily, the nurse informed him that "giving one's blood" was different from "giving one's life."

As we thought back we all realized that, in taking time to make his decision, this young lad had been willing to sacrifice his own life for Joyce.

Sounds like what Jesus did for us, doesn't it?

Dr. Ron and Carole Williams
Former Missionaries to Hong Kong

> *Thank you, Lord, that you gave your life for us. I lay down*
> *my life for you all over again, picking up my cross and fol-*
> *lowing you today...*

"So I now proclaim `freedom' for you, declares the Lord..."
JEREMIAH 34:17

*W*hen 7,000 Christians marched and took part in a rally on Easter Sunday morning in 1992, it was a miracle of God.

We were in Nepal to participate in this historic event. Up to this time in this Hindu nation, it was illegal for a Nepalese to convert to Christianity or any other religion. Anyone caught propagating the teaching of Christianity was subject to arrest. The establishment of a new government brought limited religious freedom, but Christians did not "come out of hiding" right away.

But on Easter Sunday the previously underground church joined together to march through the streets of Kathmandu, proclaiming Jesus as the risen Lord. Banners heralded the Good News of Jesus. Songs of praise rang out boldly to the hundreds of Nepalese who crowded the sidewalks.

On this day Christians rose up from a grave of fear and intimidation with a new strength and determination to make Jesus known to people who had long been held in the bondage of paganism. It was both a privilege and a humbling experience to be part of this unprecedented event in the history of the Kingdom of Nepal.

Don and Sharon Nicholson
Former Missionaries to the Philippines

Lord, I pray that I would be free of fear and intimidation as I serve you. Help me to be bold as I speak to others about you and what you have done for me...

"In everything set them an example by doing what is good."
TITUS 2:7

David, a 14 year old Chinese student in Singapore, was having trouble in school. Anne, a Foursquare Church member, offered to tutor him each afternoon. Before long, she had led David to Christ. His conversion met with a cold reception from his mother, a devoted Buddhist. One day he returned home to find his Bible torn to shreds and scattered across his room.

David's natural reaction was, "You tore my Bible, so I burn your Buddha..." It seemed to David the obvious way to even the score.

Lighting one match and holding it under Buddha's nose did provide a measure of satisfaction. However, David's vengeance quickly turned to panic when he took the match away and discovered that the statue's once white nose was now permanently blackened.

He called Anne, confessing. "I know I shouldn't have done it! Please help me!" Together they scrubbed without success, and it seemed David would suffer the consequences for his mistake. It gave Anne the chance to talk about the importance of honoring parents, showing God's love, and not provoking unnecessary conflict. Finally, Anne tried a bottle of typing correction fluid. That did the trick and when David's mother offered her prayers the following morning, the familiar white-faced Buddha greeted her.

David's family has noticed a definite change in him since then. His mother no longer objects to him going to church. She likes the changes that she's seen in David and both his father and little sister have now become Christians!

George Butron
Missionary to Papua New Guinea

> *Lord, help me to set an example for those around me, that I would be an encouragement to those who are young in their faith or who don't know you yet...*

> *"But God chose the foolish things of the world to shame the wise;*
> *God chose the weak things of the world to shame the strong."*
>
> 1 CORINTHIANS 1:27

We had just finished preaching and were praying for the sick when we heard a great commotion at the door of our church. We saw the parents of a boy about 12, trying to force him to come into the building. He began to scream, curse and spit on everything around him. We stopped and commanded the spirit of disturbance to be quiet.

We needed to discern the spirits living in him. While doing this one of the spirits cried out, "You can't do anything—MANY have prayed for me to come out, but I will not." The boy fell on the floor kicking and screaming. A surge of power rushed into that room. We all felt it. Perhaps God wanted to show how He could use the "weak things to confound the wise."

A supernatural strength came upon me. I became angry at the spirit that was threatening us—I never was one to pet the devil. A river of the Holy Spirit's language poured out of me. I reached down with both hands and lifted him up and set him on his feet. He quickly turned around and yanked all the tracts we had hanging in pockets on the wall and stuffed his pockets with them. We laughed because we knew we had all prayed and wept over those tracts that they would be used for the salvation of souls. At that point we could not say we witnessed deliverance.

The following Sunday morning, a young boy sitting in the front stood and moved toward the pulpit. He said, "Don't you recognize me? I love Jesus now." In one week his whole visage had changed—he did not look like the same boy!

Dr. Evelyn Thompson
Former Missionary to the Philippines

> *Lord, thank you for the deliverance you bring through our*
> *prayers and our petitions, even though we are so weak. Use*
> *me to do your healing and delivering work...*

"Our mouths were filled with laughter,
our tongues with songs of joy..."
PSALM 126:2

O ne of the most enriching and enjoyable things about missions travel is being able to meet our missionaries. Being with them is enriching—and sometimes humorous!

We visited Hong Kong when Gary and Johnell Loop were there. They invited us to stay with them and they moved their three-year old, Tim, into the hall to give us his room. The first night we felt bad about it, for it seemed that he cried himself to sleep.

The next night he started again. My husband said, "Listen to that child! He is not crying; he is singing." Sure enough, he was actually singing the Doxology in Chinese.

Another time, Dr. Courtney and missionary Jack Anderson and several others were en route from the town of Trinidad, Beni, Bolivia, to Ibiato, the Indian camp. They were each riding a large mule through the swamp when suddenly the mule being ridden by Jackie Baker, missionary nurse, stopped suddenly and threw her into the swamp, eye to eye with a large alligator.

Imagine the confusion and fervent prayer that went up to the Lord! The alligator disappeared out into the swamps and Jackie was able to get back onto the mule so the party could continue. We can laugh about it now!

Vaneda Courtney
Wife of Dr. Howard Courtney, Missions Director, 1944-1950

Lord, I thank you for the joyful events of my daily life. Help
me to see each inconvenience from your eternal perspective...

"...they will place their hands on sick people, and they will get well."

MARK 16:18

*D*ue to a family feud, a witch doctor had cast a curse upon an idle parcel of land, which bordered the properties of two feuding families. In her curse, she stated that anyone who would attempt to cultivate this land would be afflicted with a terrible disease.

One day her son, a young Choco Indian, decided to clear the unused strip of land so he could cultivate it. He had cleared several rows with his machete when suddenly he felt a sharp pain near his wrist. It was as if someone had driven a sharp-pointed object into his flesh.

His forearm soon swelled out of proportion. He became deathly ill and was near death for 17 days, but recovered to the point that he was able to seek out the witchdoctors, trying every cure they offered.

After five years of constant suffering, he made his way to the "mission station" and met our Foursquare missionary, Dick Scott. Brother Scott explained how God could make him perfectly whole. He then prayed for the Indian and the very next day the young man was completely delivered!

Foursquare World ADVANCE, 1968

> *Lord, I thank you that you have power over all the power of the enemy, and that you took upon yourself every one of the curses that were pronounced against me...*

"The reason the Son of God appeared was to destroy the devil's work."

1 JOHN 3:8

God is moving powerfully in the Foursquare church in the town of Alicante, which is nestled on the Mediterranean coast of Spain. Stan Doland, FMI missionary to Spain, testifies of God's move among this group of believers.

"Sister Juana, who is the woman in charge of this church, is operating under such an anointing that it reminds us of the book of Acts," reports Stan. Sister Juana's church has seen many delivered from the bondage of darkness. People who suffered from demon-possession are being set free.

One lady's face was disfigured when manifesting the power of the demons over her body. She had even tried to kill her daughter while under the influence of the evil forces. Now she has been completely set free by the Lord.

"If you met her today, you would never know of the former influences that controlled her life," says Stan. Many in the Alicante church witnessed her deliverance and can see the new life of Jesus Christ in her.

God's church is growing all around the world. He is faithful!

Foursquare Global REPORT, 2000

Lord, I thank you that you have power over every evil spirit!
I ask for deliverance for these people who are in bondage...

"They saw what seemed to be tongues of fire that separated and came to rest on each of them."

ACTS 2:3

People came from other islands, cities and even countries to see what God was doing in the Philippines. People received Christ in their homes as well as on the streets. Police were sent to take care of the crowds. Among them was a police captain who came to see the magic we were using to cause people to fall out of their seats. He examined the button near the pulpit that caused the bell to ring for Bible study time. He examined our old-fashioned washing machine, feeling sure he had found the machine that was hooked up to the seats. The captain did not give up. He came back one night and sat behind a post, where he intended to watch carefully without being seen.

The presence of the Lord was very strong. At one point I left the platform to go to the open front doors to speak to the hundreds of people outside. People began to pray and cry out as they felt the power of God. Many were being healed and saved.

Suddenly there was a loud cry from the captain saying, "Get out, get out, the place is on fire!" He started toward the platform but fell to his knees crying, "Fire! Fire! Help her! She is on fire!" That night he became a changed man. Later he told us he believed the building was on fire and that he saw fire shooting from my fingers. While I was praying for the people he also saw my hair on fire. We saw Satan fall as the captain was loosed from his bondage. The consuming fire of God showed up in a mighty way to break the power of the enemy!

Dr. Evelyn Thompson
Former Missionary to the Philippines

Lord, let your consuming fire fall in my life, burning up everything that is not of you. Let the fire of your anointing rest upon me, that I might minister to others...

"But the one who received the seed that fell on good soil is the man who hears the word and understands it. He produces a crop, yielding a hundred, sixty or thirty times what was sown."

MATTHEW 13:23

W hile serving a short-term assignment in Hong Kong, we made a trip to China and wanted to take several Bibles with us. We held our breath and silently prayed as we went through security. We made it through with the "Good News."

On our second day, we asked our guide if he would take us to a church. He obliged and found a government regulated church for us to visit. The pastor was happy to see us, but because we spoke no Chinese, our guide served as our interpreter. We talked about Jesus and the pastor asked us many questions about our faith and the church in America. We didn't realize at the time that the conversation was being interpreted by a Communist. Then the pastor asked us to pray for him. Again, the guide interpreted.

God used the conversation and prayer to plant seeds in the heart of the Communist guide. Before concluding the tour, he very discreetly asked if we would give him a Bible. We were glad we could and had a few minutes to share salvation with him. His last words to us were, "Maybe someday I too will be a Christian."

It may sometimes seem impossible to reach certain people for Christ, but remember God is not limited, keep sowing seeds and believe for a harvest!

Don and Sharon Nicholson
Former Missionaries to the Philippines

Thank you, Father, that you are the one who causes the seed to grow. Help me sow your seeds of truth wherever I go...

"Therefore, my dear friends, as you have always obeyed-not only in my presence, but now much more in my absence-continue to work out your salvation with fear and trembling, for it is God who works in you to will and to act according to his good purpose."

PHILIPPIANS 2:12-13

*D*uring our training to prepare us to live and minister in Africa, a well-respected lady in the Foursquare Church spent a day with the four couples who were missionary candidates. In the times of prayer and worship God began to speak to us through this lifelong servant. Each couple received words of encouragement and confirmation that uplifted us and seemed to be the finishing touch to our training.

My wife and I received a word about our ministry in Africa and at the time neither one of us understood it or had seen it happening in our previous trips to Africa. She told us that God had been doing a mighty work in Africa and some of the work had been covered over with the sands of neglect. Part of our calling was to go and discover those hidden springs of God's work and brush the sand off and remind the people that the awesome work of God must be allowed to continue.

Just as she had prophesied over us, it came to pass. Many times in the months ahead we would identify a work of God, and as we named it or declared it as such, people responded and God was able to finish what He started.

What Scriptures have you marked in your Bible because God spoke through it to you but now, many months or years later, it is just highlighted words? Brush those Scriptures off and watch God do what He wants to do in your life and ministry.

Glen Mickel
Former Missionary to West Africa

Lord, remind me today of those things that I have neglected or forgotten. May all your purposes for my life come to pass...

*"Now to him who is able to do immeasurably
more than all we ask or imagine..."*
EPHESIANS 3:20

Recently I visited a village in Togo and attempted to visit the chief so that I could preach the Gospel of Jesus Christ to him. The closest I got to the chief was to have an audience with one of his senior elders in the village. After I shared the Gospel with him, he asked me to pray for one of his sons, who was suffering from epilepsy. This young man could not do any work because at any time he might go into a fit and begin foaming at the mouth. Somebody always had to be with him for safety. In their culture and society, to be non-productive is shameful to both the person as well as to the family.

Through two interpreters I spoke to the young man about Jesus and led him through the sinner's prayer. I then laid my hand on him and prayed for the healing touch of Jesus. When I had finished there was a large crowd around us who had witnessed all that transpired. After we left the village, we received a report that the young man was completely healed. Not only was he able to cut wood, but he was able to carry it back to the village as well. Now the Chief himself, who was unable to meet with us earlier, has requested us to come back and preach to the entire village!

Manny and Linda Hernandez
Former Missionaries to West Africa

*Thank you, Lord, for your plans for my life! So often I ask
for something and you give me something that is so much
better! Help me to see your hand at work in everything...*

"And these signs will accompany those who believe..."
MARK 16:17

Armando is a retired Brazilian Air Force pilot and airplane mechanic who attends our church. One day while he was waiting to visit a friend in the hospital, he overheard the doctors talking to the mother of the boy in the room across the hall, telling her that there was no hope for her 12-year-old son. After Armando visited his friend, he felt impressed to talk with the mother of the young boy. He learned that the boy had been unconscious for days and was being fed intraveneously.

When she learned that Armando was a Christian, the woman begged him to pray for her son. Armando put his hand on the boy and prayed a fervent prayer for healing. As soon as he finished praying, the boy opened his eyes and said, "Who are you, and what are you here for?"

Armando answered, "I am a servant of Jesus and I have asked Him to heal you."

The boy said, "Then I'm healed."

He sat up and pulled the needle out of his arm and got out of bed. The room quickly filled with doctors and nurses who all wanted to know what had happened. After they examined the boy, they all acknowledged that he had been healed and released him from the hospital the next day. Armando was called to a conference with thirteen doctors, who asked him what he had done. He explained about salvation through Jesus Christ and "laying hands" on the sick. They were dumbfounded and each one of the doctors agreed that the boy's healing was a miracle from God!

George and Jane Faulkner
Former Missionaries to Brazil

Lord, your power to heal is so awesome to me. Let me be used in the lives of those around me to bring your healing touch to their bodies.

*"But our citizenship is in heaven. And we eagerly await
a Savior from there, the Lord Jesus Christ..."*

PHILIPPIANS 3:20

"Where are you from?"
This is one of the most difficult questions for any MK (missionary kid) to answer and one which is often asked when the missionary family is home in the U.S. Our teenage daughter, Holly, was no exception. Her answer often was, "Well, I was born in the U.S. I used to live in Chile, but now I live in Spain."

Holly often felt very Spaniard around American kids and very American around Spaniard kids, a confusing place to be. She did not know exactly what "home" was and how she should feel or even dress.

Psalm 90:1 says, "Lord, you have been our dwelling place throughout all generations." Holly finally came to a conclusion at a young age that her home was not a geographical location. Her home had to do with a heavenly Person and relationship. Earthly homes change; not only where you live, but also who lives with you. However, there is a consistency when it comes to our heavenly home.

Holly came to a place where she wrote in her diary, "It doesn't matter where I call home here on earth as I know that my real home is in heaven. God is my home."

Holly went to her "real home" to be with her heavenly Father on April 13, 1993, at the age of 15.

Stan and Molly Doland
Missionaries to Spain

*Thank you, Father, that my home is with you and that in
my Father's house there are many mansions. I long to be in
my heavenly home, but for now give me joy as I serve you.*

"Praise the Lord...who redeems your life from the pit
and crowns you with love and compassion..."

PSALM 103:1,4

When Pastors Juan and Abigail Reyna opened the door to the dimly lit room, they were shocked by a horrible stench, and in the dark shadows stood a man with leprosy. The man's wife had heard of the miraculous healings that had occurred in the pastor's church in Tampico, and had asked the pastors to come to her house and pray for her husband.

Despite the man's condition, or perhaps because of his condition, God told Pastor Juan to hug him. Pastor Juan obeyed the voice of the Holy Spirit, hugging the man and sharing that Jesus loved him and had died for him. The man asked Jesus into his heart and the pastors prayed for him.

Weeks later during a Sunday service, Pastor Juan saw the man's family enter the church and he instantly recognized the man who had leprosy. God had healed him!

The man testified before the congregation, "I thank God for my healing. But if I had died a leper, I would have been happy because I met the Savior. When the pastor saw me for the first time, he gave me a hug and told me that Jesus loved me. I thought, "It must be true because I don't even know this man and he is hugging me, even with my sickness! My old friends never even came to see me after I became sick, and this man was giving me a hug! I experienced the love and compassion of God through this pastor and that is why I received Christ as my Savior."

Humberto Paz
Regional Coordinator to Central and South America

Thank you, Lord, that you have redeemed my life. Crown
me now with love and compassion, that I might reach out
and embrace others just as you have embraced me...help me
to embrace even those that seem unlovable...

"Then he said to the man, 'Stretch out your hand.' So he stretched it out and it was completely restored, just as sound as the other."

MATTHEW 12:13

While holding a series of meetings in Jaffna, on the northern tip of the island of Sri Lanka, a mother brought her 30-year old son forward for prayer. His right hand was withered. She explained he was right-handed and unable to work to support his family. We prayed for him that night and he left.

Every night the man returned to the services, but there was no improvement in his hand. As we returned home, I thought about this young man and felt sad because he had not been healed.

It was three weeks later that I received a letter from his mother. She wrote to tell us that one morning her son woke up and found his hand had been completely restored!

The Lord reminded me that the disciples preached the gospel and everywhere they went signs and wonders followed them. From that time on I never looked for the signs, I just believed that they would follow, as we were obedient to His Word.

Richard and Betty Kaiser
Former Missionaries to Sri Lanka

Lord, help me to be obedient to what you have called me to do, to be encouraged in you, and not to be overly concerned with the results of my ministry...

"...your young men will see visions, your old men will dream dreams."

ACTS 2:17

A man named Peter had a strange disturbing dream. In this dream a large group of people invaded his bedroom, seeking to harm him. The dream surprised and terrified Peter, as a certain family member led the group. According to African tradition, family members can lead groups of witches for the purpose of killing. This type of killing is not done physically but spiritually, and the victim may sometimes see the group attacking him in a dream. Later, the person would gradually weaken and die.

Because of his Western education, Peter never believed these traditions were real. But when he had this dream, he instinctively knew that something real was happening and he sat up in bed and cried out to God for protection.

Peter learned that the person who appeared in his dream did wish to do him harm. The experience convinced him that the power of darkness was real. He reasoned that if the power of darkness was real, then the power of God must also be real. This realization caused him to begin a search for a personal relationship with God.

In spite of his searching, Peter felt unfulfilled. Then one night, another dream came to him. In this dream he was shown the name of a church. Peter asked Abraham, a man he worked with and knew to be a Christian, if he had ever heard of the church that appeared in his dream—the Foursquare Church!

Peter had asked the right person—Abraham Mantey pastors one of the Foursquare Churches in Accra.

Greg Fisher
Missionary to Uganda

I thank you, Father, that your power is far greater than the powers of darkness. Push back the darkness in my life, and speak to me in dreams and visions....

"Let us fix our eyes on Jesus,
the author and perfecter of our faith..."
HEBREWS 12:2

I was a new missionary of not quite a year and was still squirmy around cockroaches, especially the flying two-inch variety. My husband, Charlie, and I were visiting a small church where the people welcomed us with beautiful smiles and big hugs. As we worshiped, we all joined in, clapping our hands and singing with all our hearts. Somewhere during the second song a nasty cockroach flew into the assembly and came to rest on the cement floor near the feet of the worship leader. Probably no one but me noticed. I went from worshiping to staring at the big bug, in hopes that the singer would stomp on it as she excitedly worshiped the Lord.

I was gripped by the thought that if someone didn't kill it soon, it might fly to where I sat, and then what would I do? My imagination could summon up a whole scenario of what would happen.

Suddenly, my thoughts were interrupted when one of the ladies in the front row removed her shoe, whacked the bug dead, and swatted it out the door. Relieved, I turned my attention back to the worship leader, only to find her looking at me with a big smile on her face! Embarrassed, I managed to smile back and begin to sing again.

Bothersome things can disrupt our lives and cause worry. It depends upon our focus. It's easy to focus on the distractions, but God wants us to keep our eyes on him. I think the next time, I'll keep my eyes closed during worship!

Darla Finocchiaro
Missionary to Dominican Republic

Jesus, help us to fix our eyes upon you, and to not be distracted by the "bugs" of life that can seem so huge...

*"And these signs will accompany those who believe...they will place
their hands on sick people, and they will get well... Then the
disciples went out and preached everywhere,
and the Lord worked with them and confirmed
his word by the signs that accompanied it."*

MARK 16:17,18,20

Roberto was one of our first orphans to come to the Houses of Happiness Orphanage. He was an epileptic. Nine months of the year, Ecuador has a thunder storm just about every afternoon. Each time these storms came, Roberto ran out in the yard, and with a terrified look on his face, cowered under a tree or anything that would give him cover. Often this would be followed many times by a severe seizure.

One afternoon when one of these attacks started, it was worse than the others. A missionary friend working with us told us to put a pencil in his mouth so he wouldn't bite his tongue. Then we got serious with the Lord.

I remember praying, "Lord, I have heard all the stories about other missionaries and about Your miracles on the mission field. If we are to be missionaries, we must have Your power too." I opened the Bible to Mark 16:15-20 and placed it on Roberto's chest. He began to convulse all the more and then sat up and began to vomit.

Soon Roberto laid back, relaxed, and never had another attack. To God be the glory!

Dorothy Davis
Former Missionary to Ecuador

*Father, thank you for confirming your word with signs and
wonders. Continue to reveal yourself in power... give me
boldness to preach your word and to pray expecting divine
healing and miraculous answers to prayer...*

> *"Then Jesus said to the centurion, 'Go! It will be done just as you believed it would.' And his servant was healed at that very hour."*
>
> MATTHEW 8:13

While living in Hong Kong, we taught a class on Foursquare History in the English speaking Bible College. On the day of a final exam, one of our students came rushing into class just in time for the test. She told us that she had been in an accident, was taken to the hospital and told by the doctor she had a broken arm that must be set. She told the doctor, "I don't have time for that now, I'm on my way to take a final exam. I have been learning that Jesus is the Great Physician, so I'll just pray for Him to heal my arm." As she proceeded on to class, she was instantly and perfectly healed!

On another occasion in that same class, we took the students to the graveside of Robert Semple to see the headstone that Sister Aimee had erected there. One of our students was a medical doctor and he had been feeling very ill. As the class members stood around the headstone, they said, "Let's pray that God will heal Dr. Lee right now!" They prayed and Dr. Lee was completely healed of his illness.

God said it. I believe it. That settles it.

Fred and Carol Dawson
Former Missionaries to Hong Kong

Father, today I ask that you would give me rock-solid faith and a child-like trust in you. Help me not to question how you will answer my prayer or doubt your ability to perform even the most amazing of miracles...

"...your young men will see visions, your old men will dream dreams."
ACTS 2:17

While attending LIFE Bible College, my father Dr. Arthur F. Edwards would often arise early in the morning and walk to the school building to spend time in prayer before the classes began. In the spring of his final semester, while in prayer at the altar of the main classroom on the 4th floor, God gave him a vision.

He plainly saw an elderly man in a field with an old horse drawn plow. His hair and beard were white and he was leaning on the plow, with one hand to his brow and looking afar off, as if looking for someone. The vision was very vivid and as dad looked at the man, he could distinguish very clearly every feature of his face and the wind was lightly blowing his hair and beard. There was no message, no words were spoken. The vision faded and the Lord gave no interpretation.

Unexpectedly one day, a few weeks after arriving in Panama, dad was called to the bedside of a dying missionary. It was the elderly man of his vision. He had settled in the town of Chitre, about 160 miles from Panama City, in an area where there was no gospel witness of any kind. Dad later found his diary and turned the pages to the time when he had that vision in Los Angeles, California, about a year before. This is the entry Mr. Latham had made in it: "I am now much along in years and my strength is waning. Lord, please span the miles and put your hand on someone else to come and take up the plow." This experience was a confirmation for Dr. and Mrs. Edwards that they were now in the country to which God had called them.

Dr. Leland Edwards
Former Missionary to Panama
Missions Director, 1965-1988

Father, speak to me in dreams and visions. Show me your will for my life and for this day...

*"His master replied, 'Well done, good and faithful servant!
You have been faithful with a few things; I will put you in charge of
many things. Come and share your master's happiness!'"*

MATTHEW 25:23

Vera Luiza Thomazi Rosa pastors one the most outstanding Foursquare churches in Brazil. But she was not always a pastor.

Raised on a farm near the city of Tatui, Vera was converted and baptized at the same time her father, Antenor Thomazi, found Jesus as Savior. Antenor was diagnosed with a terminal illness and promised God he would preach the gospel if the Lord healed him. God answered that prayer and Antenor began to fulfill his vow by pastoring a small, fledgling congregation. During the next nine years, the work grew significantly and during those years nearly 30 pastors matured in the faith and planted churches under his leadership.

Antenor's 26-year-old daughter Vera led the youth group at her father's church, and the group grew to about 300 members. Vera was also single and had a good job, and she began feeling the call of God on her life, but was unsure of the direction the Lord wanted her to pursue. She kept praying.

When her father died, the Foursquare leaders asked Vera if she would assume the pastorate of the 800-member congregation "for a trial period." This was a turning point in her life. Vera saw the Lord do far more than she had ever anticipated. During that first year of her leadership, more than 600 people were saved and added to the church. Since then, thousands of people have been baptized through the church's ministry.

Foursquare World ADVANCE, 1993

> *Lord, I pray that you would call men and women to be pastors and worker for you. May many be raised up to shepherd your people, bring healing, and give instruction...*

> *"The One who calls you is faithful and He will do it."*
> 1 THESSALONIANS 5:24

*I*t is stressful and discouraging to live in a country and not be able to understand nor speak the language of the people, especially when you are there to communicate the Gospel to them.

When we arrived in Tegucigalpa, Honduras, we did not speak Spanish. My husband, Ed, began taking Spanish lessons right away. I was expecting our second child and too busy at home to attend classes with him. I read my Spanish Bible faithfully, although I did not understand it, and listened intently to people conversing, hoping to pick up a few words now and then. I was praying daily that God would help me.

After about six months, I was completely frustrated. One Sunday night as I was preparing to preach through an interpreter, the Lord spoke to me, "Preach in Spanish tonight." I was overwhelmed and said, "But, Lord, I can't; I don't know that many words." I continued to hear the same message. I said, "Lord, give me a promise from your Word and I will." The Holy Spirit brought to my mind the words of Jeremiah 1:9, "Behold, I have put my words in your mouth." Still doubtful, I said, "But, Lord, are they Spanish or English words?"

That night I did preach in Spanish for about 25 minutes. I did not understand all I was saying, but I felt a unique presence of the Holy Spirit. I knew the anointing was giving me the words. It was like the anointing in book of Acts 2:11, "We hear them speaking in our own tongues the wonderful works of God."

That did not happen to me again, but as I studied Spanish, read my Spanish Bible and wrote my notes in Spanish, the Lord did facilitate it for me and gave me the wisdom, anointing and strength to fulfill His call.

Vonitta Gurney Boylan
Former Missionary to Latin America

> *Lord, I know that as I open my mouth for you, you will fill it. Help me rely upon you for the words to speak...*

"I have learned the secret of being content in every situation, whether well fed or hungry, whether living in plenty or in want."

PHILIPPIANS 4:12

Wherever we live, life has its pluses and minuses. That was true when I lived in Villa Neilly, a little border town between Panama and Costa Rica.

Our town had an electrical plant. When it was working we could do all kinds of things—buy gas for our few cars, keep things cold in our refrigerators and ice boxes, and even see at night during our services and Bible school classes. When machinery in the plant broke, it might take some months to repair it, because it needed to be sent overseas.

Without electricity, life went on. Our meeting place for the Bible Institute was simply a concrete floor with two side walls. The other two sides were open to whatever weather was on the menu. When we had no electricity, we pulled our homemade desks and chairs together under a suspended gas lantern.

With or without lights, I could smell the baking bread from the bakery that was about three minutes from my house. But in this little tropical town, you could buy no bananas.

Shortly after arriving, I tried to buy some bananas. I said to the store-owner, "Why don't I see any bananas?" He responded, "Oh, everyone goes out and gets their bananas in the grove." Stalks of bananas were waiting to be picked and enjoyed.

Life anywhere holds opportunities to see how God will work. Count your blessings today and thank God for His guidance and His provision, no matter how great or how small.

Dorothy Buck
Former Missionary to Latin America

Teach me, Lord, not to complain, but to see the blessing in every situation. Let me see the good side of everything, and discern your hand at work...

> *"...and if they drink any deadly thing...they shall recover."*
> MARK 16:18 (NKJV)

A woman had come into the city of Iloilo and was saved while she was there. She invited us to go with her to her town, Jintotolo, to preach. She said, "No one has ever been there to tell us about Jesus."

As we were about to leave, our son Ron caught a bad cold. The doctor told us it would be okay for him to go with us, as long as he took the prescribed medication. Our trip included first the plane, then a train ride, and finally a lap in an outrigger canoe.

In the house where we stayed, I had put Ron's medication on the headboard of our bed. It was in a brown bottle. In the morning, I gave Ron a spoon from this bottle. Immediately he spat it out and cried, "What was that?" I looked at the bottle and to my horror it said "Carbolic Acid." As I was about to panic, Ron said, "I didn't swallow any." Although the acid made his lips peel, he was fine.

As for who switched his medicine for the carbolic acid, we don't know, but we were told later that it was known throughout the island that this house was filled with many spirits.

We do know that the fruit of preaching remained. Within a few years, two of these converts were studying in Bible college, preparing to return to their island to teach others.

Mollie Chaves
Former Missionary to the Philippines

> *Lord, thank you that I don't need to fear any evil spirit, for you have power over every one of them. Thank you for keeping me safe from all harm..*

"And God will generously provide all you need..."
2 CORINTHIANS 9:8 (NLT)

In San Cristobal, Venezuela, we had outgrown our meeting place and needed to build or secure a bigger building. My husband, Edgar, challenged the congregation to begin a building fund. Some proplr objected; they thought the churches in the States would build it. "Don't you have connections?" some others asked.

Our people were poor, but we continued to challenge the people, "We will build our own building. If help comes from outside, that's fine too. God will provide." They caught the vision; they now knew personally that God would provide.

One evening a lady came for prayer. She was seriously ill, and God healed her instantly. She came back to church so excited. She had a piece of property that the dictator government had taken from her. "Let's pray. If I get that land back, I will give it to the Lord." God worked a miracle and we built our church on a beautiful lot right on a main avenue in our city.

Many miracles were associated with the construction of the church, along with much persecution. One day while listening to the local radio station, directions were given to an event happening in our barrio. The announcer used our church as a landmark to identify the location of this function. I thought God must have smiled; I know I did.

Darlene Coombs
Former Missionary to Venezuela

Lord, I want to thank you today for your generosity. You give to me far above and beyond what I would expect. You bless me in ways I never expected...

"Jesus had compassion and touched their eyes."
MATTHEW 20:34

The children were getting ready for school and I was reading in my home office when suddenly I heard and felt the rattling of an explosion. I heard Patti praying loudly in her spiritual language and ran to see what had taken place.

Patti stood in the breakfast nook, with her hands over her face. She was saying, "Jesus! Jesus! Jesus!" The oven had exploded and blown her across the kitchen into the breakfast room, melting the front of her robe and obviously burning her face and hair.

We decided that I would take the kids to school and as soon as I returned I would take her to the doctor. Thirty minutes passed before I got home and Patty told me that something had happened while I was gone. She told me this story:

"While I was lying on the sofa, half asleep and half listening to a teaching tape by Dennis Easter, the front door opened and three men walked in. Two were angelic and one was obviously the Lord. One of the angels was explaining to Jesus what had happened. Then Jesus said, "Patti, I'm going to place my thumbs on your eyes. You'll feel a warm sensation go from your head to the your feet and back. Then you will be healed."

The Lord then nodded to the angels, stood to His feet and left through the front door. As the door opened for them to leave, Dale walked through the door to find Patti healed. No blisters! No burns! No apparent eye damage! Even the hair that was previously burned was replaced with new hair within three days.

Dale and Patty Downs
Former Missionaries to Brazil

Lord, you are so good to me! Thank you for coming to me, touching my injuries, and healing me. Thank you for your precious healing presence in my life...

"May the God of hope fill you with all joy..."
ROMANS 15:13

Let me tell you about Mamma Abraham, a wonderful Acholi woman from the north of Uganda who is a joy junkie. She is a walking miracle! The victim of a land mine encounter, which filled her brain with shrapnel and removed her left eye, the medical doctors are at a loss to explain how Mamma Abraham is even conscious and coherent—let along walking. Mamma Abraham has seen suffering and trial in her life that most of us will never experience. But, she knows something else as well—the joy of the Lord! Her face—though scarred from the land mine—constantly radiates the joy of the Lord.

Mama Abraham is a great example of someone who finds joy not in her circumstances, but in her relationship with her Creator. Jesus knows our circumstances...let's look to him for our joy!

Greg Fisher
Missionary to Uganda

Lord, I ask that you would fill my heart with your joy today.
Let me see trials through your eyes and not my own...

*"Put on the full armor of God so that you can
take your stand against the devil's schemes."*

EPHESIANS 6:11

"*P*astor, pastor, come, please come." It was a man from the beach barrio forty miles down the coast. A storm was on the horizon, but how could we not go? We were reminded of the sixth chapter of Ephesians where we were told to "Put on the armor of God." Indeed we felt like we were being clothed for the task ahead. The man who came to our house was the father of an 11-year-old boy who had been held captive for several days by the power of a witch doctor.

We soon saw the witch doctor that had caused the boy's right leg to be bent. In due time we spoke to him in the Name of Jesus to let the boy go, but the witch doctor just laughed. We also asked him to leave, but he would not. Arthur and I felt the "chills" of evil. Suddenly we felt God's power in a supernatural way. We sensed God making us strong in Him. My husband reached for my hand, and the power of God surged through our bodies like an electric shock.

Arthur spoke in the Name of Jesus to the boy's leg, saying, "Leg, loose yourself and stand upright on your foot." The witch doctor was working hard to keep control of the boy, but he was losing as the leg began to unbend. We stood aside and watched the battle as God worked. We saw the leg and the boy completely loosed from Satan's power. The witch doctor was screaming words we did not understand. He went out defeated! God had the victory!

Dr. Evelyn Thompson
Former Missionary to the Philippines

*Lord, I pray that I would be fully clothed in the armor you
have provided for me to be protected against and victorious
over Satan...*

"He jumped to his feet and began to walk. Then he went with them into the temple courts, walking and jumping, and praising God."

ACTS 3:8

On March 22, 2001, I was conducting a miracle rally in a town called Nuwara Eliya. Hundreds turned out for this special meeting. A Hindu family came and desired prayer for their son Jeyagaran who was seven years old. He had problems in both his legs and he couldn't bend them. He had undergone surgery three years ago, but the surgery only made it worse.

After I finished preaching, I called for anyone who needed salvation or healing. Immediately, the parents responded to the call and brought their son forward. As soon as we laid hands on Jeyagaran, he was miraculously healed. He ran up and down the stairs excitedly and began to do things he had never done before! The following day his parents brought Jeyagaran's sister, along with some relatives and friends, for the meeting.

God once again did the miraculous! Many of them were delivered from demons. We started a church in Jeyagaran's house the following day.

Leslie Keegel
National Leader in Sri Lanka

I promise you, Lord, for you are a miracle-working God!
Move in power in my life and in my pastor and church body.
Hear our prayers and do miracles like you did in the book
of Acts...

"So they began their circuit of the villages, preaching the Good News and healing the sick."

LUKE 9:6 (NLT)

God is manifesting His power! Even when we are on our way to another town for a meeting or to pray for some dying person, people stop us, asking us to be merciful and come and heal one of their people who are sick.

We prayed for a young man who had been badly injured in an automobile accident. He was almost dead, but God heard and answered prayer. His neck was broken, along with a number of his bones, and his hand was also badly torn and bleeding. We prayed for him and the Lord healed him.

"What sort of doctors are they?" people asked. I told them that Jesus is the Great Physician. The accident happened on Friday and, on Monday, when I went to his house to see him, he was completely well.

His whole family gave their hearts to the Lord, and the news of his healing spread all over the island. Automobiles filled with people came to our house all the time, seeking prayer. God is answering our prayers—many are healed instantly! What a joy it is to serve such a loving, compassionate God!

George and Tony Illauan
Former Missionaries to the Philippines

> *Lord, you and you alone are the Great Physician. There is no one like you. I bring before you these people who need healing...*

> *"Don't harm yourself!...Have faith in the Lord Jesus*
> *and you will be saved."*
>
> ACTS 16:28, 31

Born into a prestigious Iranian family, John (his last name is withheld for security purposes) was raised as a strict Muslim. However, the carnage of the Iran-Iraq war forced John to flee through the mountains of Turkey, finally reaching safety in Germany as an exhausted and injured young man...

I was eighteen years old and away from my family for the first time. I was feeling very lonely and was in bad shape mentally and emotionally. So I decided to commit suicide. But as I made up my mind to take my life, a German missionary came to my apartment and started talking about Jesus.

I told him, "In the morning I have an appointment with my doctor. I don't want to go there. I want your God to finish me off!"

This brother told me, "Jesus Christ is not going to take away your life. He is going to heal you." He prayed for me and immediately I felt warmth going from my knee down to my toes.

The next day I went to the doctor for my appointment for surgery. After the doctor checked my foot, he asked me, "What did you do?"

I said, "Nothing, but a missionary came to my apartment yesterday and prayed for me. Now is my foot worse?"

The doctor answered, "No, you have been healed! You do not need surgery!" I jumped out of his office as a bird would fly out of his cage. I went to my friends and told them about my healing. My life changed completely. My friends noticed the change in me and they knew that it was because of the things the missionary had told me.

John
Missionary to a Muslim Nation

> *Lord, I pray for those internationals living near me who suffer from loneliness and despair. Help me to reach out to those I know with your words of truth and power...*

> *"Lord, even the demons submit to us in Your name!"*
> LUKE 10:17

At least 75 people crowded into the large room of the house in the remote village. No one pushed or complained; everyone sat cross-legged on the hard floor. The team of Americans fidgeted, unused to sitting this way, as they tried to find comfortable positions. The team had come to help with evangelistic meetings in the island nation of Sri Lanka.

When the preaching was over, people came forward for prayer. The American team sensed the presence of evil as one woman began to moan and cry out in a loud and unnatural voice. They watched as Leslie Keegel, the national leader, prayed for the woman, who had fallen to the floor. In a strong voice, he commanded the demon to leave the woman. She became quiet and peaceful.

Leslie asked her if she wanted to commit her life to Jesus Christ. The team watched as she replied that she did. She received the Lord and became part of the new church that was planted that day.

Julie Brockett
Former Short-term Missionary to Sri Lanka

> *Thank you, Lord, that you set the captives free! Teach me to walk in the authority you have given me over all the power of the enemy...*

"...for all have sinned and fall short of the glory of God."
ROMANS 3:23

Our first glimpse of the Philippines wasn't what I had expected. After a 14-hour drive to Northern Luzon in our jeep, which we air-conditioned by rolling down the windows, we were greeted with a refreshing drink of coconut milk and a warm coke.

The small church building soon filled to overflowing with many more on the outside looking in the open windows. We elicited considerable curiosity with our light hair and white skin. They would start with a handshake and then their hands would go up your arm to feel your face and hair. The first one called out to the others "Corn-silk!" This brought others to see and touch.

I had gone to the Philippines with a very wrong concept. I thought if the people there could only be more like Americans, with our proper hygiene and our ways of living, they would be better off. I thought about how much we needed to teach them, as if we were better than they were. I was thinking these thoughts when they began to sing and worship the Lord without inhibition. You could see and feel the love of God on their faces.

Then the Lord spoke to me about how He had sent His spotless and pure Son from heaven to earth, where He had no home, lived in the filth of our world among people who hated and resisted Him, and yet He gave His life for us. We all need Him. We were all sinners. From that moment I felt the love of God flow through me to these people we had come to serve. I no longer felt like I was above them but rather that I was one of them.

Donna Howse
Former Missionary to the Philippines

Lord, show me where pride and arrogance have kept me from ministering to people you want me to touch. Let me have your love for people and give up my own agenda...

"For my thoughts are not your thoughts,
neither are your ways my ways," declares the Lord.
ISAIAH 55:8

God sometimes works in ways we would never expect...

A letter came into the ICFG (International Church of the Foursquare Gospel) offices from Samuel Young, a church planter on St. Vincent in the south Caribbean. Samuel desired to connect with Foursquare to plant churches in his local area. The return address had "WI" in the return address so the letter was given to Ann Roth, who works in the national church office, who then forwarded the letter to the Great Lakes district office that oversees church planting in Wisconsin.

Glenn Bleakly of the Great Lakes District read the letter and realized that the church planter was wanting to plant Foursquare churches in the West Indies, not Wisconsin, so he sent the letter to FMI offices in Los Angeles. He also put a note with the letter indicating that he wanted to talk to someone from FMI.

FMI Director Mike Larkin then had FMI Regional Coordinator Ted Vail call Glenn since the West Indies is a part of the region he coordinates. It turns out that Glenn has planted churches in the West Indies and has many contacts there. Now Ted and Glenn can network with the future Foursquare planter Samuel to establish a Foursquare church-planting network in the West Indies.

These connections might never had been made had the letter not been divinely routed to the Great Lakes district instead of FMI.

Michael Larkin
Missions Director

Thank you, Lord, for sovereignly ruling over all the details of my life...

> *"The man went away and told...that it was*
> *Jesus who had healed him."*
> JOHN 15:5 (RSV)

After six months of being in Panama, my father took us out of Panama City to a little town called Frijoles. We started a service under a mango tree and the whole town came. While preaching, my father mentioned just one sentence in his sermon that God could heal. After the service, when he gave the altar call, out of the crowd came a 20-year old young man. He pulled up his pant leg and showed a horrible ulcerated sore that went from his leg to his foot. He said he had been to many doctors, including witch doctors.

The young man said to my father, "Heal that!"

My dad said, "I don't heal, but my Dad does. If you want us to pray, we will." So a short prayer was offered up and we announced that in a few hours we would be back for another service.

At the beginning of the next service, this young man came out of the crowd and pulled up his pant leg. What had been a horrible oozing sore had dried up—a miracle had taken place in a short time!

The man brought his brother and he was healed of stomach trouble. These two young men said, "If you'll come back, we will tell the whole area what we have seen and heard." The next Sunday we returned, and for many Sundays after that. Eventually a church was built there.

Dr. Leland Edwards
Former Missionary to Panama
Missions Director, 1965-1988

Lord, I thank you for your ability to heal any kind of sickness! Today I ask you to heal those who suffer from chronic illnesses...

> *"...for I am the Lord that healeth thee."*
> EXODUS 15:26 (KJV)

Though I am careful as I can be, I had picked up "something" while traveling through Africa. A battery of blood tests revealed that malaria was the probable culprit, yet I needed one more blood test before final treatment could be prescribed.

I was becoming so weak I could hardly walk, but I knew I had to keep a lunch appointment the day of the final blood test. It was with a couple who had a long and event-filled life. The man had just responded to the altar call that Sunday, his first time in church, and they wanted me to meet with them though they no longer lived together.

I made it through lunch as discreetly as possible. Wiping the perspiration off my face and having successfully kept my head from falling into my soup, we moved to the living room for tea. Quickly God began to deal with issues and the couple cleared a major hurdle for reconciliation.

We next found ourselves huddled tightly together in prayer—arms around each other's backs with tears flowing. Unnoticed to them, I was about to pass out but was being kept upright by their arms locked around my back. Being in the presence of God like this was so new to them I don't think they could see what was happening!

Then I asked for prayer for me. Instantly I sensed the presence of God heal me in response to their heartfelt and sincere prayers! The blood test an hour later confirmed the wonderful touch of Jehovah-Rapha!

Dr. Daniel Lucero
Missionary to France and the Francophone Nations of Africa

> *Lord, you have promised me enough strength to do the work you have called me to do. I thank you for the healing you have brought to my body, that I might proclaim your works...*

"...give thanks in all circumstances..."
1 THESSALONIANS 5:18

We often encountered interesting creatures while serving overseas. I laughed about the spiders, cockroaches, bats and lizards; Johnell was genuinely frightened. As time passed, she learned to cope and could kill a cockroach as nonchalantly as she could swat a fly. She could kill a mouse with a single swing of a stiff broom. She even learned to watch without flinching as small lizards ran down our walls to eat mosquitoes. But the big gecko lizards were a different story. She never quite adjusted to seeing them jump from wall to wall or to hearing their eerie calls of "TEE-COO" echoing through the darkness.

One summer, Johnell went by herself to speak at a camp. She was in her hut, just about to smash an unwelcome beetle with her shoe, when a gecko leapt out and ate the beetle. Should she be grateful that the beetle was gone or terrified by the lizard?

She thanked God for the mosquito net above her bed and managed to fall asleep, but was suddenly jolted awake by a suspicious thud. Johnell sat up and was horrified to see the lizard sitting in her open suitcase. After sticking his head into her cup and licking her toothbrush, he jumped on top of the mosquito netting and stayed there for the remainder of the night.

Although she was unable to sleep, she did count her blessings. I asked her what blessings she had listed. She told me that one of them was that I was not there to laugh and sing; "I'll Go Where You Want Me to Go, Dear Lord!"

Gary and Johnell Loop
Former Missionaries to the Philippines

Lord, I will go where you want me to go. Please help me to count my blessing in the midst of unpleasant or uncomfortable situations...

"How beautiful are the feet of those who bring good news!"
ROMANS 10:15

ctavio Brenes is the Costa Rican missionary to the Cabécar Indian Reserve. When he was a commercial pilot, Octavio had prayed for these Indian people as he flew over their region. Now in his retirement, he led thirty people from our church in San Jose, including Linda and me, to the Cabécar Indian Reserve to build a Foursquare church building.

We brought an electric generator, power and hand tools, and building materials. While the men and women worked to clear the site and build the church, Linda and a group of trained children's workers ministered to the Cabécar children.

In spite of the pouring rain, we built the structure and put up the tin roofing in a day and a half. On Sunday morning we dedicated this new church to God. Mario, the Cabécar pastor, led us in worship in his language. To us, this had been a missionary endeavor to help build a church; to Mario it was a place for his tribe to worship and hear the preaching of the gospel. He was so thankful and as he worshipped, we were deeply moved.

God has given us this responsive community of Cabécar people. And God has chosen to use Octavio, a Costa Rican who has special love for a very special people.

Lewis and Linda Richey
Missionaries to Costa Rica

Lord, I want to thank you for the people who travel far to bring your good news to others. May you protect and guide them and help them be effective for you...

*"With man this is impossible, but with
God all things are possible."*

MATTHEW 19:26

nyone who wants to live and work in a foreign country needs a
visa. And the type of visa needed depends upon what the new resident will do. Missionaries need visas too, and since some countries are not
favorable to Christians, God often uses miracles to secure such residency
and remind the missionary that He called them to that specific nation.
The Lord did this for us in Malaysia.

When well-meaning friends learned we were trying to receive a missionary visa in the Muslim country of Malaysia, they thought it was a
ridiculous idea! We had prayed as we prepared to move to Malaysia. We
believed we were in the will of the Lord in making this move, and God
had impressed upon our hearts that we should apply to receive missionary
visas. Now was the testing time.

Soon after arriving in Malaysia, Michael attended a pastor's luncheon.
At this meeting he heard there was a new breakthrough with the government that may allow for the processing of missionary visas. Other pastors
didn't seem too interested at the time, but we were. Our family had made
one trip out of the country already to renew our visitors' visas, and Michael
believed the Lord would make a missionary visa a reality.

After three months of diligent work, a major financial deposit, and
hours of sitting in the immigration office, we were awarded the first long-
term missionary visas granted in nearly twenty years. The Lord had proven
once again that with Him nothing is impossible.

Jannie Stubbs
Missionary to Malaysia

*Lord, your ways are wiser than ours. Help me not to listen
to the wisdom of the world, but to hear your voice and do as
you direct me...*

"The Lord is... not willing that any should perish,
but that all should come to repentance."

2 PETER 3:9 (NKJV)

I was 19 years old, a new single missionary, and not prepared for what I saw. After arriving in Bolivia only four days earlier, we started for Ebiato, a jungle village in the "green hill country." We had traveled two or three days on horseback, and I had never ridden a horse before. The trip took us through dense virgin jungle, pampas and swamps. There were animals of every description, snakes everywhere, and mosquitoes by the millions!

The first Indian I saw was an old man who felt very dressed up—the extent of his dress was a purple string around his ankle. As we neared the village I saw a thatched roof held up by twisted tree trunks. These people were naked and sometimes acted more like animals than human beings.

I began asking God, "Do You really care about these people? Is it worth it?" After about three days, God spoke to me. "If these had been the only people on the face of the earth, I would have died for them. I love them; they are mine." I wept.

Before leaving Bolivia, I had the joy of seeing many of these Indians saved, healed, baptized with the Holy Spirit, and reaching further into the jungle to bring fellow Indians to Jesus.

Virginia Martin
Former Missionary to Bolivia

Lord, I thank you that you know each of us by name. You
know me and you love me, and you sent your own Son to
die for me...

"But he was pierced for our transgressions, he was crushed for our iniquities; the punishment that brought us peace was upon him, and by his wounds we are healed."

ISAIAH 53:5

For years Violeta, a pastor's wife, suffered one sickness after another. She was a woman of faith and prayer who had experienced many healings in her hospital ministry. Violeta was very ill and it seemed that her husband would need to leave the ministry so he could take care of her.

One day Violeta was rushed into emergency. Tests showed a large tumor on her heart and major damage calling for immediate surgery with the hope of saving her life. Just before the surgery, her physician and 10 other doctors gathered to observe her heart on a monitor. Suddenly the black masses over and around the heart began to quiver and move around. Her doctor trembled and cried out, "What is happening?"

Violeta said, "Oh doctor, all I know is that I told you my Jesus would heal me." Then suddenly, with one great swish, all the black masses were removed, showing a perfectly normal heart. The entire hospital staff was called to observe the tests taken prior to the miracle as well as the newly cleansed heart.

Since that time, the ministry of Violeta's husband has grown, and a door has opened for them to begin a radio station for the Mapuche Indians in southern Chile. Once again, the Lord is true to His promise—by His stripes WE ARE HEALED!

Sheila Ransford
Missionary to Chile

Thank you, Lord, that it is by your stripes we are healed. I bring before you today those who need your healing touch...

*"For they heard them speaking in tongues
and praising God!"*

ACTS 10:46

The train from Colon, Panama, brought several passengers to the village of Frijoles one Sunday morning. Many had heard of the miracles of God in this church and came for physical healing. One was an elderly woman known as Mama Mecha.

That morning Mama Mecha received Jesus as her Savior. After the service, the congregation went to the inlet of Gatun Lake, which is a short distance from the church, to baptize the new converts. Her testimony of her conversion that morning stirred many hearts.

As Mama Mecha came up out of the water, she lifted her hands in praise to the Lord, and suddenly she began to speak in another tongue. Standing in the crowd was a man from Spain. He had been an archeologist in Egypt for several years and also served as a Roman Catholic priest in Spain and Panama. Late that afternoon, while on the train returning to Panama City, he said to missionary Arthur Edwards, "After her baptism, that elderly woman spoke in an ancient Egyptian language and quoted a psalm of praise from the Old Testament. There is no way she could even speak one word of that language which I learned in my work as an archeologist in Egypt. That had to be God."

Dr. Leland Edwards
Former Missionary to Panama
Missions Director, 1965-1988

Lord, I thank you for giving me a prayer language. Let me use my gift to glorify you...

"Therefore go and make disciples of all nations, baptizing them in the name of the Father and of the Son and of the Holy Spirit..."
MATTHEW 28:19

*B*aptism is an important part of a believer's life. We understand that to be true, but in dry and dusty India it was not always easy to find enough water to baptize new converts. It took some creativity, but with a little imagination and a lot of help from God, it was possible!

On one occasion all we could find was a concrete irrigation canal about 20 inches wide with about 18 inches of water running through it. We decided that if the candidate sat down in the canal and folded their arms over their chest, I could simply lay them down flat in the canal. It worked!

The Lord reminded us that the way we did it was not the important part. It was the testimony of the work of Jesus in the life that was important.

Richard and Betty Kaiser
Former Missionaries to India

> *Lord, thank you for the new life that you have given me! I come to you again, confessing my need of your saving and cleansing grace...*

*"I have come into the world as a light, so that no one
who believes in me should stay in darkness."*

JOHN 12:46

"Kuru" is a word that has several meanings in the Melanesian Pidgin language. First, it describes a rare disease, which has only been found in Papua New Guinea. Also know as "the laughing death," Kuru destroys the central nervous system, reducing its victims to spasms and convulsions, which often resemble laughter in the final stages. Today, the disease is disappearing because it can only be contracted through eating human brains. Although cannibalism is a thing of the past in PNG, instances of the disease still occur because it can lay dormant in the body for decades. There are also reports of people getting the disease when a spiritual curse is pronounced against them through a form of black magic.

"Kuru" is also the name of a remote village in the rugged Eastern Highlands Province where the disease was first discovered. This village is the site of a new Foursquare church and it provides a picture of the change that the gospel brings. Stories of tribal warfare, cannibalism, and a dreaded disease are reminders of a past that has been transformed by the gospel of Jesus Christ. This is just one example of how Jesus is still winning victories over the powers of darkness and death.

George Butron
Missionary to Papua New Guinea

*Lord, I thank you that you have brought me out of darkness
into your marvelous light. Now, Lord, I pray for those people in my life who are still in darkness...*

> *"I will praise the Lord for all he has done...*
> *according to his mercy and love."*
> ISAIAH 63:7 (NLT)

Tachilek, Burma, is the center of the Golden Triangle and the battle-ground for government forces who fight against the drug-lord tribes-men who manufacture heroin. In the middle of it all, God is at work in the Foursquare church in Tachilek, which is just across the border from Thailand. Pastor Pa Khim ministers faithfully in this church. When we visited with them one Sunday morning, we were told two miraculous stories of God's love and protection.

Forces belonging to the drug-lord armies were walking through the town one night when a Foursquare member crept in the dark to a second-floor window to look out. His wife was unaware and turned on the light, silhouetting her husband. The soldiers saw the light and the resultant shadow in the window and fired their automatic weapons at the man. He jumped back as something cut into his face. His wife switched off the light and the soldiers walked on.

God had protected him! He had only a cut on his eyebrow. The bullet that he found on the floor at his feet had struck the iron grille of the window just where his face was. A piece of the bullet had come off and struck his eyebrow.

In this same city a young woman gave birth to twins. During the delivery a nerve was injured, paralyzing her from the waist down. She was not a Christian, but when the church prayed for her, she was healed. Two weeks later, she responded to the Word and came forward to receive Jesus as her Savior.

Phil and Diane Franklin
Former Missionaries to Thailand

> *Lord, your love and mercy are so great! There is no end to your goodness toward us. I thank you for your protection over my life...*

> *"Blessed are those who are persecuted because of righteousness,*
> *for theirs is the kingdom of heaven."*
>
> MATTHEW 5:10

*P*apua New Guinea is a Pacific island nation composed of the main island of New Guinea (just above Australia) and dozens of smaller islands that are often only accessible by boat. On a recent trip to the island of New Ireland I came to the area where the Foursquare work began about nine years ago.

Today, with no visits from leaders or missionaries, with fierce persecution and almost no outside input, there are a dozen churches and several more in the process of forming. The spiritual atmosphere of this island is steeped in traditional practices of spirit worship and witchcraft, and the infrastructure is badly neglected, with roads, schools and health care suffering an almost complete breakdown in some areas. In spite of these challenges, we found a vibrant work.

Every single pastor has been physically threatened and beaten at one time or another. One young pastor named Greg was attending school in another part of the country when he came to Christ and started fellowshipping with a Foursquare church. As he went back to his village to start a church, he was beaten several times by people who wanted to put a stop to his message about Jesus. He showed me where five or six of his teeth were broken out from the beatings, then smiled a gap-toothed smile and said, "It's all right because I've got plenty more teeth and I still love Jesus and will never turn back!" His persecutors realized they were not going to quench the fire that was burning in his heart and several have now given their lives to Jesus and are part of his church.

George Butron
Missionary to Papua New Guinea

> *Lord, I want to follow you no matter what it costs me. It is*
> *such a small price to pay for so great a salvation...*

"The righteous will live by faith."
ROMANS 1:17

*I*n the Philippines ministers and Christian workers return from annual conventions excited and fired by the anointed ministry of the Word and the Holy Spirit. They work very hard to get to these conferences too. Every year they raise pigs and chickens so they can get to the convention. By faith, they believe for God to bless their project.

In 1994, Rev. and Mrs. Henry Braganza who were ministering in Masara Thompson Christian School bought a piglet dedicated for their convention fund for 1995. They were to be ordained that year. After ten months their pig had grown big, but before they could sell the pig it got sick and died. They were tried and tested in their faith. They were disappointed, discouraged and frustrated. It was too late now to buy another piglet to raise for their convention fund.

Little did they know God had a plan! I had been collecting computer waste paper, plastic bottles and aluminum cans for recycling. When I had saved $100.00, I sent it to the Philippines to Masara Christian School for any special needs. The money came a week before the convention. It was enough to meet their convention needs. God honored their faith and answered their prayers!

Derly Suan
Foursquare Philippines

Thank you, Father, that as I live by faith and trust in you, you provide my every need...Help me to look to you in all things...

"He shall give His angels charge over you, to keep you in all His ways."
PSALM 91:11 (NKJV)

*W*hile in Tegucigalpa, Honduras, we learned one evening that our missionary Mattie Sensabaugh was ill. We felt very strongly that we should go to her, even though it meant starting out over a narrow, mountainous, and rocky road at night.

When we shared with the congregation about Mattie and our need to go, they very kindly asked us to reconsider. It was not safe to be out on that road at night, especially with a new jeep. They then prayed for our safety and one lady gave us the words in Psalm 91:11.

We had traveled about four hours when we saw three men standing in the road ahead, blocking our way. They each had a machete. We quickly checked that the doors were locked and rolled up the windows before we stopped. One of the men walked to the window and asked, "Are you alone?" The Holy Spirit brought to mind the words of the Psalm and I answered, "No, the angels of the Lord are here in the car with us." He quickly stepped away from the jeep and left with the other men. We wondered why.

Our curiosity was satisfied three months later when we were holding a house meeting in the village near where we had been stopped. Several came to accept Jesus after the teaching. One of the men who came forward said to Ed, "Maybe you don't remember me. I am the man who stopped your jeep and asked if you were alone. When your wife answered that angels were in the car, your car filled with a fire so bright we were blinded and fearfully ran away."

Not only did we thank the Lord for His angels that protected us, but for the salvation of these souls as a result of that incident.

Vonitta Gurney Boylan
Former Missionary to Latin America

Lord, I praise you for the protective angels that you have commanded to keep me safe as I go about your business...

> *"Looking unto Jesus... who for the joy that was set before Him*
> *endured the cross, despising the shame..."*
>
> HEBREWS 12:2 (NKJV)

There is a scene in a movie where a pastor comes upon the scene of a serious accident. He climbs out of the car and runs across a field to find two badly injured young people. Quickly, he prays with the driver to receive Jesus as his Savior. On his way back across the field, Sonny is expressing his joy by singing and shouting a bit of praise to the Lord.

I'm sure people who lack a relationship with Jesus Christ found that scene an entertaining caricature worthy of a few chuckles, but not me. I doubt the fallen world can understand the joy there is in serving the Lord Jesus Christ. I doubt many people know that rush of joy filling your soul as you see someone change their eternal destiny from hell to heaven, but I do. I live for that joy. I am addicted to that joy.

Is "addiction" too strong, or too negative a word to describe this feeling? Possibly, but how else would you describe an attraction to something so strong that one would willingly suffer any humiliation, any torture, any shame in order to gain it? That is exactly how the writer of Hebrews 12:2 describes it: "Looking unto Jesus... who for the joy that was set before Him endured the cross, despising the shame..." Certainly there is an echo of this same thought found in Romans 1:16: "For I am not ashamed of the gospel of Jesus Christ."

Greg Fisher
Missionary to Uganda

> *Lord, it is such a privilege to tell people about you, to share*
> *the way of salvation in ways they will understand, and to see*
> *their changed lives. Thank you for allowing me this blessing...*

"I am the Lord who heals you..."
EXODUS 15:26

chool breaks were a good time to get out of Manila with the family and travel to the northern provinces of Luzon. Several of our students from the Foursquare Bible College had gone before us to prepare for daytime training sessions and evening evangelism meetings. We were staying in a remote barrio without roads, electricity or telephones.

During the night my wife Sally became very ill with a high fever. By the next day her skin was turning bright red and she became progressively weaker. Our host suspected that she might have hemorrhagic fever (a mosquito-borne disease causing internal bleeding of the blood vessels). After prayer and counsel with the local believers, we decided to return immediately to Manila—a thirteen hour trip.

We took Sally to the Manila hospital where she was given a home marrow test. The doctor confirmed she had hemorrhagic fever and needed a blood transfusion immediately. The doctor was a believer and joined me in prayer. Members of Calvary Foursquare Church in Manila were also praying. I asked the doctor if he would order a second bone marrow test, which he did. He was amazed with the second lab report, and said she didn't need a transfusion as she had begun building back her own blood. The next day we brought her home.

We thank the Lord for His help in time of need and for His promise, "I am the Lord who heals you."

Dr. Don McGregor
Former Missionary to the Philippines
Missions Director, 1993-1995

*Thank you, Lord, that because of your great love and mercy
you have provided healing for me...*

> *"...He got up and rebuked the wind and the raging waters;*
> *the storm subsided, and all was calm."*

LUKE 8:24

When we left the shore, the skies were bright blue and it looked like a good day for a trip. We headed across a strip of ocean to the island where we would minister. When we were quite far from the shore, a tremendous storm suddenly came up. When the wind tore the sail from the boat, the men grabbed the oars and began rowing, but the storm was stronger than the oarsmen.

The downpour continued and the sky turned very black. When the boat began to take on water, we all tried to bail it out with our hands. Two of the men said, "Pastor, we have been fisherman by trade and have been out in many storms, but we have never been in one like this. It looks as if we might go down."

All eight of us in this little boat joined hands and began to pray. The storm continued. Finally we began to sing, "Peace, peace, wonderful peace, coming down from the Father above." It was still dark and the rain kept pouring down.

As we continued to sing, the boat took on more water. When we sang the song one more time, we felt warmth on our faces. We opened our eyes to discover the clouds had disappeared and the sun had begun to shine brightly.

Our ministry on that island that day was very fruitful. While the enemy would like to have seen us destroyed, God again protected us and once again we were reminded that Jesus is Lord of the storm!

Marjorie McCammon
Former Missionary to Latin America

> *Lord, you have power over the wind and the waves of the*
> *sea. There is no problem too great for you. Help me to trust*
> *in you always, even in the midst of stormy days...*

> *"...our gospel did not come to you in word only,*
> *but also in power and in the Holy Spirit..."*
>
> 1 THESSALONIANS 1:5 (NASB)

*M*edellin, Colombia was touched by the mighty power of the Holy Spirit. Reverend Ramundo Jiminez, the evangelist, had been advised not to expect miracles and multitudes in Medellin, but God gave both.

This was the first united effort by Pentecostal groups in Medellin, and the Foursquare organization, led by Lloyd Dickerson, assisted with the planning and preparation. Reverend Dickerson worked diligently to get permission from the city to use the parking lot of the bullring, La Macarena, and to set up a platform and lights.

From the opening night, crowds grew in numbers, from two thousand to four thousand to ten thousand. So many accepted the Lord each night that it was impossible to deal with each convert individually. God continued to move—the deaf heard, the mute spoke, the lame walked. A man brought his wife to the service. She had been accidentally shot in the back and spent her days in bed because the bullet had severed her spine. Her husband carried her forward for prayer and she walked away, completely healed! The power of God showed up in a mighty and unexpected way!

Dr. Herman Mitzler
Missions Director, 1950-1965

Lord, I want to feel the touch of your powerful Holy Spirit. I
want to see you touch my community and heal the sick.
Lord, move in my life and in the lives of those around me...

"My soul is consumed with longing for your laws at all times."
PSALM 119:20

I was teaching the class for the children. We did not have a room, so we met under a tall coconut tree that was surrounded by shrubbery. One little eight-year old boy named Jose was a very faithful student.

After class one day, when he returned home, his drunken father was angry with him for attending church and he beat him severely. Jose was fearful of receiving another beating, so he did not come for a while.

One Sunday as I was teaching, I noticed movement in the bushes. Upon investigation, I discovered it was Jose hiding there. I said nothing, but waited until the rest of the children had gone into church.

I slipped over to the bushes and there was Jose! I put my arms around him and said, "Jose, your father will beat you again!" He threw his arms around my neck and began crying and said, "But I just had to hear about Jesus one more time!"

What a hunger for God's word!

Marjorie McCammon
Former Missionary to Honduras

> *Lord, I pray that you would give me such an intense longing for your word that I would be willing to suffer in order to hear about you...*

"...let your light shine before men, that they may see your good deeds and praise your Father in heaven."

MATTHEW 5:16

The Sakhalin Islands lie north of the Japanese Island of Hokkaido. Over the centuries, these islands have been the focus of intense international conflict. Today, the cities that dot the islands are catching up with the rest of the world in business and education. The islands are also the site of a fresh move of God.

During my visit, I was introduced to a lady who had never heard the gospel. In her despair, however, she was intrigued by many people in her community whose faces revealed a different light and were full of smiles. They seemed to have peace, regardless of their circumstances. The worse things became, the more they were at peace. She wanted to ask them why, but was afraid to do so.

One day, she was invited to visit a church in the town. Arriving at the church, she was shocked to discover that all those happy people she had admired were there at the church. She asked them if she could get what they had, and their answers were all about Jesus.

Today, to others who ask her, she happily gives the same answer—it's all about Jesus!

Dr. Paul Risser
ICFG President

Thank you, Lord, that it's all about you. Every good thing about me is a gift from you...help me to allow your light to shine through me today...

*"Give all your worries and cares to God, for he cares
about what happens to you."*
1 PETER 5:7 (NLT)

I had just remarked how good these dirt roads were out here in the middle of nowhere. As I crested the hill and slowed down to cross the
bridge, reality struck. There was no bridge. There was only water rushing
over the banks of the river. A local pastor riding beside me said, "Hakuna
matata." (Kiswahili for 'no problem,' as those who have seen The Lion
King already know.)

Dismounting from my trusty four-wheeler, I surveyed the situation.
There was a bridge. It was about a foot beneath rapidly moving water.
People on foot were not going across. To go back and find another way
would take about six hours. Should I trust the truck and my suspect driving
skills or should I go with the gut feeling inside of me that screamed, "This
is indeed a problem, a big problem!"

1 Peter 5:7 came to mind: "Give all your worries and cares to God, for
He cares about what happens to you." (NLT)

So I did that. I gave my worries to God. However, I was still on the
wrong side of the river. The best way to prove that I believe God's word is
to act upon it. So, I acted upon it and drove across the submerged bridge.

Glen Mickel
Former Missionary to West Africa

*O Lord, help me to give every problem to you today. As I
commit them to you, may I receive your reassurance and
act upon the words you give me...*

"Then my soul will rejoice in the Lord..."

PSALM 35:9

Revival services were held in the Pagaduan area of Davao in the Philippines. Rev. Evelyn Thompson, Foursquare missionary and evangelist, reported that it was one of the most successful campaigns since the beginning of the work in Davao.

Nightly attendance averaged four thousand except on Saturday when the crowds swelled to over ten thousand. There were between three and four hundred decisions for Christ every night. On Saturday, thousands responded to the message of salvation.

Miracles abounded and God worked in both the hearts and lives of the people. Blind people received their sight. Those who suffered from diabetes, paralysis, and many other diseases received prayer, and God performed wonderful miracles.

One blind woman caused a great deal of excitement as she cried out, "The light is so bright!" Later she could see perfectly.

One man ran and jumped on the platform. Sister Thompson asked him what he was doing. He shouted, "Look, my leg—it walks!"

My soul rejoices in the goodness of our God!!

Dr. Herman D. Mitzner
Missions Director, 1950-1965

Lord, I rejoice in your awesome power and your gentle healing touch. May I see your hand at work in and through me today...

"...He has sent me to bind up the brokenhearted,
to proclaim freedom for the captives and
release from darkness for the prisoners..."

ISAIAH 61:1

*T*wo hundred men live in a prison near my small village church in Uganda. We recently started a prison ministry there and I gave an evangelistic message. As a result, forty men gave their lives to Christ. Many of the men who gave their hearts to the Lord have been healed and some have been released from prison. About eighty percent of the inmates now profess to be born again.

In addition, they have selected leaders from among themselves to teach the Bible. Since they have only three Bibles, they use study materials that my pastor and I have either scrounged or designed for them. Each "dorm" has appointed someone to lead evening prayers.

All this in a prison that grows its own opium for the prisoners to smoke, and has traditionally rewarded the most evil, drug abusing men with leadership positions!

God is moving among these inmates...to Him be all the glory!

Margaret Nelson
Missions Team Specialist in Uganda, Africa

O Lord, I pray for those who are in prison right now.
Though they are incarcerated, I know that you are able to
set their souls free...

"I will give you a new heart..."
EZEKIEL 36:26

*J*orge Ferrufino was a Sandinista commander in Nicaragua during the war that ravished that nation. During the time of the revolution he was a military trainer and taught young Nicaraguans to handle weapons.

When the revolutionaries won the war and overthrew the government of Somoza, Jorge Ferrufina continued training military personnel. One day when someone witnessed to him about the love of the Lord, Jorge received Jesus Christ as his Savior.

A few months later, Jorge resigned from the military. As he began reading the Bible, this strong atheist's heart was changed. He became a man with a strong, vibrant testimony of faith in Jesus Christ. Five years later he became a Foursquare pastor.

Jorge continues to faithfully serve the Lord and preach the Good News. Today he is a strong leader in the Foursquare Church in Nicaragua. He is still training men and women to win Nicaragua, but now he has a new Commander.

Serafin Contreras
Missionary to Panama and Nicaragua

> *Lord, I want to serve you and teach others to serve you. Help me to be someone who brings others into your kingdom and shows them how to follow you and win others to you...*

"God is our refuge and strength, a very present help in trouble."
PSALM 46:1 (KJV)

"God is our refuge and strength, a very present help in trouble." One dark night in Nigeria this verse took on a new meaning for three lady missionary teachers.

They were returning to the Foursquare mission station one evening after teaching in the night Bible school in Yaba, about 20 miles away. The road to Ikorodu was lonely but they did not mind the long drive as they were enjoying a good conversation.

As they started across the one-way bridge, car lights suddenly flashed on before and behind them, and they were trapped on the narrow bridge. Several drunken men got out of each car and approached them, speaking rapidly in their native dialect and waving their fists. The ladies could not understand what they were saying, but they prayed fervently for God's protection.

Suddenly the men stopped. Turning around, they ran quickly back to their cars and drove off immediately. Unharmed, the missionaries continued across the bridge to their home. The following day, the newspaper gave an account of three robberies that had occurred on the bridge the night before.

What had caused the men to run back to their cars without harming the missionaries? Did they see or hear something which made them stop? God had again revealed himself as a "very present help in trouble."

Audra Sowersby
Former Missionary to Africa

Lord, you keep me safe in so many ways. I thank you that you love me and watch over me. Keep those who work for you in other countries safe as well...

"If you, then, though you are evil, know how to give
good gifts to your children, how much more will your
Father in heaven give good gifts to those who ask him!"

MATTHEW 7:11

There are three things every missionary kid needs to experience during their furlough in the United States: Disneyland, Universal Studios and Christmas with the grandparents. They will also remember how Dad or Mom preached the same sermon over and over, and the places they visited during those months.

When we went to Hong Kong, we had two sons. Our youngest son was "made in Hong Kong." He was four years old when we returned to the US for our first furlough. He had never met his grandparents, nor had he visited the above VIPs (Very Important Places).

Within a week of arriving in Los Angeles, the Williamses went to Disneyland, where we spent 16 hours enjoying the rides, waiting in line, eating all the things we couldn't find in Hong Kong, and waiting in line again. When the park closed that night, we headed back to our car and to the Southern California freeways.

With Mom and the older brothers asleep in the back seat, Derek was wide-awake in the passenger side in front. As I pulled onto the Santa Ana Freeway, this four-year old slapped my leg and remarked, "Thanks, Dad, I needed that!"

Dr. Ron and Carole Williams
Former Missionaries to Hong Kong

Thank you, Father, that you bless our lives with such won-
derful things and experiences. You are so good to us!

"...he who wins souls is wise..."

PROVERBS 11:30

O ne of our lay pastors, who worked for the school district, was assigned to go to a town for several weeks and paint the school building. He began to have services in the city. Many people attended and as he taught them about Jesus, many were saved. He also encouraged them to win souls to Jesus.

One little girl wanted to win someone to the Lord, so she asked the pastor what she could do. He told her to think of the meanest person in town and then to give him a tract.

She decided upon the local storekeeper. She would go to the store and put a tract (supplied by Foursquare Mission Press) on the counter and then run away. She did this several times, which irritated the storekeeper.

One day she had to get some medicine at the store. As the storekeeper reached back to get the bottle, keeping an eye on her so she wouldn't leave another tract, he accidentally gave her a bottle of rat poison instead of the medicine. After she left, he realized that he had given her the deadly poison. He cried out, "If there is a God, please forgive me and do something."

On her way home, she fell and broke the bottle. Upset, she ran back to the store and told the storekeeper. Because God had brought the little girl back, he told her to come on Sunday morning—that he wanted to go to church with her. He became a Christian and now gives out tracts himself!

Shirley Walker
Former Missionary to Costa Rica

Lord, let me have that passion for winning souls to you!
May I lead many into righteousness for your glory...

> *"...He bent over her and rebuked*
> *the fever, and it left ..."*
>
> LUKE 4:39

*D*avid, a four-year old boy, was very ill with a high fever. His family had little hope for his survival, since each morning on the boulevard leading to the cemetery they saw a parade of small white boxes carrying children who had died of this fever.

By the time we were called, David was on his deathbed. As we entered the humble home, we could smell the fever; heat radiated from under the mosquito netting. The father was not there, but had gone to try to get money to buy a box for burial.

I pulled back the netting and laid hands on David. As we prayed I suddenly said, "David is not going to die. He is going to live." Then I asked myself, "Why would I say that since it is obvious this boy is dying?" When we left, I told Marian that the Lord just spoke those words through me.

Shortly after, the mother testified that after we left David began to stir. He woke up and was hungry. He was totally healed.

We were able to see David several years later when we visited Guayaquil. He was doing well and remembered the day God had healed him. What a testimony to the power of our God!

Art and Marian Gadberry
Former Missionaries to Ecuador

> *Lord, you have authority to heal! Thank you for your heal-*
> *ing mercy in my life and in the lives of those I bring before*
> *you now...*

*"For I am about to do a brand-new thing. See,
I have already begun! Do you not see it? I will make a pathway
through the wilderness for my people to come home.
I will create rivers for them in the desert!"*

ISAIAH 43:19

Two weeks ago I was still in the church office well after the Sunday morning meeting had ended, when the public maintenance people from the city called me. People had reported seeing a river of water flowing from our place of prayer (the building we rent). They thought that a water pipe had broken and needed me to turn the water off immediately.

But despite what people had seen with their physical eyes, there was no such flowing of water! This happening is a real spiritual encouragement to me as I feel revival is closer than it has ever been! This sighting comes just as the Spirit has begun to move in our midst like never before!

Is it your desire to see the rivers of God flow? Let's pray together for revival to flood our world, as Jesus proclaimed it would!

Dr. Daniel Lucero
Missionary to France and the Francophone Nations of Africa

Father, let it begin with me. Tear down the walls and take away every obstruction that would hinder the flow of life-giving water into my life. Let your living water flow into my family, my community, and the nations of the world...

> *"...Don't be afraid...God in his goodness has granted safety to everyone sailing with you.' So take courage! For I believe God. It will be just as he said."*
>
> ACTS 27:24-25 (NLT)

Brother Updike and I were holding meeting on the Pearl Islands in Panama. We had just finished the meetings and had to cross over 20 miles of open ocean to the main island in a dugout canoe with a little sail on it. All of a sudden a big storm came. We were bailing out water as fast as we could.

At this exact time, my wife Barbara later told me that all of a sudden she had a great burden. She could hardly stand it. She called Brother Updike's wife Juanita to pray. Both of them were unaware of the storm that was occurring at that time. Barbara later received a letter from her mom telling her the Lord had woken her up to pray for me. She asked if I had been in any trouble. It was during this time we had been in the midst of the storm.

God allowed us to be washed up on a beach of an island that was not our destination. On this beach were six grass huts lined up on the sand. Suddenly out of one of these huts came a fellow hollering at us. As he got closer he used my name. Pointing at me he said, "You know, two years ago I went to your church in Panama City. I visited my family who took me to your church and I got saved. I bought a Bible and a hymnbook. I sing a little bit and read my Bible everyday and since you are here we are going to have a service."

He believed God had caused that storm so that we could come! I believe that too.

Dr. Leland Edwards
Former Missionary to Panama
Missions Director, 1965-1988

> *Lord, I thank you that others are praying for me, for there are many storms in my life right now. Use the storms to lead me to the places you want me to go...*

*"It is the spirit in a man, the breath of the Almighty,
that gives him understanding."*

JOB 32:8

I was returning from Holland and I had a five-hour lay over in Dubai. I was walking around the airport, window shopping and looking around when suddenly my eyes fixed on a man who was fast asleep.

Looking at this man I had a strong feeling that he needed help. I wanted to walk away from him but the inner compelling of the Spirit was so strong—I sensed that he was dying. As I kept gazing at him God began to speak to me.

I felt the Lord tell me that he was suffering of heart failure. He looked like he was fast asleep, but maybe he wasn't. As I felt the Holy Spirit's lead, I naturally resisted, "Lord, this cannot be, the poor guy has had a long day and he is sleeping, why bother him?"

Finally, I gave into the voice of the Holy Spirit and went and sat next to him in obedience. He appeared to be fast asleep and, fearing that I was making a mistake, I did not want to risk waking him up. I did, however, want to obey the LORD, so I decided to do something kind of funny!

I lifted my luggage above my head and dropped it. The heavy luggage came down making a loud noise. The man woke up in shock. I quickly apologized, introduced myself to him and began to talk to him. I told him what the Lord told me. He immediately affirmed that he was having heart pains. I led him to the Lord and prayed for him. God touched him instantly and healed him miraculously! He was a Buddhist man, but now he is a Christian!

Leslie Keegel
National Leader in Sri Lanka

Lord, teach me to hear the voice of your Holy Spirit and be obedient. Make me receptive to what He wants to do that I might be used in a powerful way...

"The Lord himself watches over you..."
PSALM 121:5

*M*oving a family to any new location can be a challenge. Just imagine moving to a totally new culture, where you do not know the language or customs.

Our first months in Cambodia meant getting used to the dust and heat, having people stare at us, being frustrated with language learning, and learning to shop in the smelly markets. We knew we would adjust to these things and we would love living here.

I struggled to learn the language. I remember the laughter when I thought I was asking if pineapple was sold in the market. The word for pineapple is manure; the word for people is manoo. No, they did not sell people in the market.

It is difficult to get used to the frequent stares we receive. Unlike our culture, where it is considered unacceptable to stare, in Cambodia it seems that any time we go out we have an audience of five or six people.

It has been fun to learn how to cook with what I can find. Things grown locally are very inexpensive; imported goods are not. Since they are grown locally, pineapples cost about twenty-five cents. However, a box of cereal (usually covered with dust) is about six dollars.

We try to be mindful of the children's needs as well. They have gone through some of their own challenges. We had a deadly snake slither by the front door. Thankfully, the children were inside.

I am reminded of the promise the Lord gave us before we came. Psalm 121:5 says, "The Lord himself watches over you! The Lord stands beside you as your protective shade." It is a good place to be.

Amy Matteson
Mission Team Specialist to Cambodia

Lord, let me have a positive outlook on inconveniences and adjustments. Help me to be flexibile when I face things or people that are different than I expect...

> *"...your kingdom come, your will be done*
> *on earth as it is in heaven."*
>
> MATTHEW 6:10

When we heard of the suffering of the Iliwas and Yaqui Indians in the Valley of Trinidad in Mexico, we decided to undertake the one hundred and fifty mile trip into the mountains to minister to these disadvantaged people.

The trek, which began with forty miles of dangerous roads through desert sand, was made more difficult by the severe cold. I had invited another man to go with me and we loaded the station wagon and trailer with food and clothing and prayed for a safe trip. I knew if we had trouble on this road, the likelihood that someone would come by to help us was slim.

After we arrived in the village, we located the chief's home. He invited us in and we soon learned that his elderly mother was very sick. The chief allowed us to pray for her. Shortly after we prayed, his mother jumped out of bed, declaring that she had been healed!

God used this healing to open the door to future trips for ministry in this area. Our plan was to minister to these people's physical needs, but God wanted to meet their spiritual needs as well.

Ludwig Manthei
Former Missionary to Mexico

> *Lord, your ways are so perfect. You always know what you*
> *are doing and you do all things so wonderfully...*

"Here am I. Send me!"
ISAIAH 6:8

God is doing miracles through the students of the Center for Advanced Pastoral Studies (CAPS) in South Africa. When you desire to be used by God, anything can happen!

Mrs. Jacobeth, a second year CAPS student, prayed for a fellow employee who had brain cancer. When the employee went to the doctor for a brain scan, there was no evidence of tumors or any other problems! As a result, Mrs. Jacobeth has now been given a regular time for prayer during her employer's staff meetings.

Isaac, another CAPS student, was in a taxi that broke down in a remote area. The people were afraid of being attacked, so the driver went to get help. While they were waiting, Isaac was able to minister to the people in the taxi—three people were healed and five received salvation. When the taxi driver returned, he also gave his life to God!

God desires to use each of us, in every opportunity! Open your heart today to the endless possibilities. Let your response be, "Here am I, send me!"

Howard and Terry Manthe
Missionaries to South Africa

> *Lord, I want to be available today for whatever you want me to do. Open my eyes to see the ministry opportunities you have prepared for me...*

"Summon your power, O God; show us your strength..."
PSALM 68:28

"Show us the power of your God!"

That was the challenge given to the pioneer pastor working among the former New Apostolic cult in Khampong Tong. He asked them what they wanted God to do. They told him that they had just planted their rice and needed plenty of rain, so the pastor prayed with them for rain.

Then he went to the next village about a mile away to work among people who had been in the same cult. They also challenged him to demonstrate the power of his God. Again he asked, "What do you want God to do?" They said, "We have not finished planting our rice. Please pray that God will keep the rain away until we are finished." The pastor felt trapped but he prayed anyway. An amazing thing happened—for the next week it rained regularly on the village that needed rain, but the rain completely missed the village that had not yet planted their rice.

The people were so impressed that they went to the district governor and renounced their affiliation with the New Apostolic group, put it in writing, and had it notarized. Next, they declared themselves to be Christians and prepared an elaborate document, which stated this. More than 100 adults signed the document and added their thumbprint. Many were baptized and added to the church!

Ted Olbrich
Missionary to Cambodia

Lord, that is my prayer: Show me your power! I want to see you at work in the world today...

"...greater is He that is in you, than he that is in the world."

1 JOHN 4:4 (KJV)

A brother and I journeyed through the mountains to investigate a cave to which God had supernaturally led us. This was the location where Venezuelan and Colombian spiritists had united to perform satanic rituals against specific evangelical leaders in Latin America who were damaging the work of Satan. We knew we were in Satan's territory, but we knew our God was greater.

As we entered the cave, we discovered many altars that contained the names of leaders of the Christian Church in Latin America. One altar in the shape of a hammock was tied and supported in five places and attached to the roof of the cave. At each of the five supports, satanic idols had been strategically placed along with the flags of the United States, Panama, Costa Rica, Nicaragua and Guatemala. The name on this altar was my name—Serafin Contreras.

We began destroying the altars, rebuking the principalities that worked through the rituals and asking the Lord to reveal the meaning of the altar erected against me. The Lord graciously showed us that the five points represented the five members of the Contreras family; the flags represented the countries where God wanted to use us. The aim was to bring bondage to us so God could not work through the gifts He had given.

Unbeknownst to us at that time, God was going to lead Alva and I to minister in each of the five nations represented by the flags. The enemy's plan against us was destroyed that day. Greater is He that is in us than He that is in the world!

Serafin Contreras
Missionary to Panama and Nicaragua

Lord, I pray that you would reveal the plans of Satan against your people, that we could break his curses and that no weapon formed against us would prosper...

> *"I have learned the secret of being content in any and
> every situation, whether well fed or hungry,
> whether living in plenty or in want."*
> PHILIPPIANS 4:12

Orlin lived in Ilocos Norte, the northernmost part of the Philippines. He came from a poor family that lived in a one-room nipa hut. Although his lifestyle was very common for that part of the island, Orlin was very different from other young people—Orlin had been born blind.

One year Orlin was able to attend a summer camp in Northern Luzon where my wife Johnell was speaking. As the week progressed, the night of the talent show arrived. Since Orlin could sing and play a guitar, he represented his church in the competition.

As expected the campers became louder and more enthusiastic as the evening went on. When it was Orlin's turn to sing, one of his friends led him onto the platform. He began to strum his guitar and sing, "I have everything I need to make me happy; I have Jesus to show me the way."

The campers became quiet; there was hardly a dry eye. All of those there knew Orlin; they knew he was poor and had been blind since birth. However, they also knew he meant every word he sang. He had nothing as far as the world was concerned, not even his eyesight. But, he felt that because he had Jesus, he had everything he needed to be content.

Many of us have so much more than Orlin ever had and yet we complain and yearn for more.

Gary and Johnell Loop
Former Missionaries to the Philippines

> *Father, help me to find contentment right where I am
> today. You are all I need, Lord Jesus...*

"The blind receive sight, the lame walk,
those who have leprosy are cured, the deaf hear,
the dead are raised, and the good news
is preached to the poor."
MATTHEW 11:5

While a team from Hope Chapel Hermosa Beach, California, was ministering in Kampala, Uganda, the Lord gave a word of knowledge through Pastor Alan Kisaka that there was someone in the crowd who had just lost a family member to AIDS and needed prayer and guidance. After the service, a young man came forward who had lost his father to AIDS four days earlier. After receiving ministry, he begged the ministry team to come to the home of his mother who was very ill.

When Missionary Greg Fisher and a prayer team arrived, they found the woman lying in bed, totally blind and unable to hear or speak. She was completely unresponsive and had been in a deep depression for about two years. The prayer team began to come against the powers of darkness that were operating in that home. Every day for the next three weeks someone from the Kampala Foursquare Church came to pray over the woman. Then, one day when Missionary Margaret Fisher came for a visit, she found the woman sitting up, able to see, hear, talk and understand! A miracle had occurred! Praise the Lord!

Foursquare Global REPORT, 2000

Lord, I thank you that in response to my prayers, you open
blind eyes and make them see. You heal the deaf and lift
depression from those living in darkness. I pray your power
to deliver would come to those who are suffering from
depression right now...

"Nothing will be impossible for you."
MATTHEW 17:20

I learned to love the word "impossible" when we served as missionaries in Central America. It seemed God always did the impossible!

One of these occasions was when we drove with a couple of our Bible Institute students to a place of ministry in San Jose, Costa Rica. To get there, we had to go down a steep hill, cross over a bridge, and then come up the hill on the other side of the bridge in order to get to the church. This was the only way to get there; there was no other way. It was pouring rain and the windshield wipers were going as fast as they could, but it was still very hard to see.

We came to the bridge area and all we could see was a lot of debris, but we paid no attention and went over to the other side. When we arrived at the church and ran in through the driving rain, people began to ask us how we got there. Several people seemed very concerned, so I asked them why they were so upset. They told us that the bridge was gone—completely washed away—and that the floodwaters were so high that it was impossible to cross. We walked to the bridge and to our amazement, it was not there!

I have often thought about this, and I know that God either rebuilt the bridge for us to go across and then destroyed it again, or that angels simply picked up our Jeep and carried us over. Either way, we were filled with gratitude to God.

God made a way when it seemed there was no other way! And He continues to prove that to us daily. Trust Him—even the impossible is possible with God!

James and Shirley Walker
Former Missionaries to Central America

> *Lord, you do the impossible to keep us safe and to glorify your name. I worship you, O Lord; your ways are so amazing to me...*

*"Do not be afraid of what you are about to suffer. I tell you,
the devil will put some of you in prison to test you,
and you will suffer persecution...Be faithful, even to the point of
death, and I will give you the crown of life."*
REVELATION 2:10

*I*n many countries new converts face persecution for giving their lives to Christ. The following comes from an email from a missionary currently working in the Muslim world:

We started our first home group last night. One young man was a Muslim relative of the owners of the home...at the end of the meeting he came to me and we walked through the salvation scriptures in Romans. I knew he was taking it all in. Then I asked him if he would like to become a follower of Christ. He said he did and he prayed to receive Jesus as his only Lord and Savior.

After the prayer, a wonderful peace was upon the young man and he was clear in expressing his gratitude.

Then he said, "There is only one problem."

"What might that be?" I asked.

He responded, "I could be stoned for what I have done."

From a missionary currently working in the Muslim world.

*Lord, my life is so easy and comfortable! I pray for those
who are even now being persecuted for following you.
Protect and watch over them and keep them safe.*

"May the Lord direct your hearts into God's love..."
2 THESSALONIANS 3:5

ri Lanka is entangled in an ethnic civil war, pitting Tamils against Sinhalese. Because of the years of bloodshed, the hatred between the two groups is intense.

While in Sri Lanka, I began a rehabilitation center for drug addicts and alcoholics in a small house on a coconut farm. In our center were Tamils, Sinhalese and Muslims. The history between these groups often erupted into arguments and even fistfights among the residents of our center who were forced to live together in the small home 24 hours a day.

Two individuals in particular were often at each other's throats. One was Sinhalese; the other was a Tamil whose family was almost entirely wiped out by Sinalese army members while they were holding a prayer service.

On my last day at the center, we had a foot-washing ceremony. I washed the feet of each resident and staff member. The Sinhalese man then began to wash the Tamil man's feet. As he did, the Tamil man was set free from a demon. The mere act of humility and God's love broke the power of the demon that entered his life through the bitterness and hatred over the slaughter of his family.

Scott Winter
FMI Missionary

> *Father, keep hatred far from me and let me walk in your love today. I confess any hatred I have in my heart... Show me what I am to do to walk in love and break the chains of unforgiveness in my life...*

*"The Lord watches over you...The Lord will keep you
from all harm— he will watch over your life.*

PSALM 121:5,7

When we arrived in the Philippines in 1964 we were given a vintage jeep to use, which looked like it had been in the war. The exterior was rusted out and you could actually stick your foot through the floorboard, a safety feature in case the brakes went out. We had it restored and it didn't look too bad. I remember that one time I was shifting gears and the gearshift came off in my hand, so I pulled over and put the nail back in that was holding it and drove on.

One day we were ready to leave for church when we discovered our car had not just one, but two flat tires, and the spare was flat too! This was Sunday morning, and we needed to be at the church! After finally arriving at church, my husband, Dan, went directly to the office and found that we had some mail we had not picked up the day before. Included was a letter from one of the churches in the States, saying they felt we could use the enclosed check for some new tires. Praise God!

Another time we had just been to Manila, and we drove our jeep back up the zig zag road to our home in the mountains. Dan took the jeep in to have it checked over and repairs made, something that was done every time we made a trip. The mechanic said, "Don't go down the zig zag." Dan told him we had just come up the zig zag. "You couldn't have, the bolts are worn off, there is nothing left to hold the wheels on!"

A few weeks later a letter came asking if we were in trouble on a certain date as they felt a burden for our safety and prayed for us. It just so happened it was the very day we had gone up the zig zag road. We're so glad that God knows all and sees all, and that He cares and watches over us.

Donna Howse
Former Missionary to the Philippines

Thank you Father, for watching over me and over my loved ones that I bring before you now...

*"O Lord God Almighty, who is like you? You are mighty,
O Lord, and your faithfulness surrounds you."*

PSALM 89:8

ilda helped us in our home while we helped her through high school. She went on to Bible college and graduated to have a very fruitful ministry of teaching Bible in the public schools around the province of Romblon.

While on a bus trip on the island of Mindoro, the bus went off the road and rolled down an incline. Nilda's arm was caught under a supporting beam of the wooden body of the bus, tearing the muscle just below the elbow. Her arm hung by only a small bit of flesh.

When we received word of this accident, Aline went to the clinic where she was being treated. The doctor washed her arm many times to remove the dirt, gravel and bits of grass that clung to that muscle. He then carefully stitched the muscle back into place and we began praying. When he finally finished, Aline said, "We will continue to pray there will be no infection."

"Oh, there will be infection," the doctor replied. "I have left a drain for that purpose."

No infection developed in that wound and Nilda had full use of her arm. In addition to leading thousands of children to the Lord, she has trained many others to carry on this ministry.

Aline Richey
Former Missionary to the Philippines

*I praise you, Lord, for there is none like you, who is mighty
in power and faithful to save. I love you, Lord, and ask that
you go with me in a special way today...*

"...And continue to pray as you are directed by the Holy Spirit."
JUDE 1:20 (NLT)

The baby was already dead when the young couple brought him to Susana, one of our senior students at the Cebu City Foursquare Bible College. Even so, Susana believed for a miracle, and she took the baby in her arms and began praying in tongues.

A doctor came to look at the baby, but Susana was unable to speak to him because of an overwhelming anointing of prayer in tongues. As they all continued to pray, they took the baby to the church of her superintendent. The pastor there challenged the couple to "get things right with the Lord," and the couple repented and tearfully prayed with the pastor. Meanwhile, Susana continued to cuddle the baby and pray in the Spirit over the lifeless corpse.

After the couple repented, the baby suddenly changed color from blue to pink as it began to breathe in response to the healing power of the Lord! Praise God for the power of Spirit-filled prayer.

Fred and Leah Horner
Former Missionaries to the Philippines

Lord, lead me and direct me and give me faith as I pray today, just as you gave Susanna your leading as she prayed in tongues over that little baby...

"...Then they will know that my name is the Lord"
JEREMIAH 16:21

*C*ambodian Foursquare Pastor Daniel Em recently went to a rural part of Cambodia that had been under the control of the Khmer Rouge until earlier this year. Pastor Em had the privilege of being the first to bring the Good News to people who had been completely isolated and cut off from the rest of the world for twenty years.

"When I reached the rural area of Khampong Thom Province and shared the gospel it was warmly received. More than usual, almost like the people were primed and expecting the truth. After I spoke, an old woman told me that 20 years ago, in the "killing fields" of Pol Pot, God did a miracle in that town.

Khmer Rouge soldiers had gathered up the town leaders, including the woman, and forced them to dig their own mass grave. Then, as the soldiers aimed their guns at them, the people began to cry out for help to "any god who could help them." She said some cried out to Buddha, others to demon spirits, but she cried out to "the God who hung on a cross."

They huddled together and closed their eyes—expecting the shots— and then they all "saw" the same thing: a cross. They then heard a voice say, "My sons and daughters, don't be afraid. I have come to save you now. No one else can save you but me."

When they opened their eyes, their executioners were gone. At the time, none of them knew Jesus. They didn't even know his name and from then until now they simply called him the "God who hung on a cross." Now they know Jesus by name and they are starting a church. The old woman is very happy, as she has waited for this day for 20 years."

Ted Olbrich
Missionary to Cambodia

> *Father, thank you that you reveal yourself to people in ways we could never imagine. Reveal yourself to the people who are on my heart today...*

> *"Don't be afraid; just believe, and she will be healed."*
> LUKE 8:50

A woman named Yu Sho in Tainan, Taiwan, became ill and her health began to deteriorate. She went to see the doctors, but they could not diagnose her problem. Yu Sho's mother began to visit many temples to inquire why her daughter had become sick. The mother feared that she had angered the Chinese gods, and the illness was their retribution.

From every temple she visited, Yu Sho's mother brought home an idol she had purchased there. She hoped that by bringing the images home, the gods would be appeased and help her daughter. Eventually, two complete stories of their three-story home were occupied by idols, which cost Yu Sho's mother about $30,000 U.S. dollars.

Even with all the idols, Yu Sho's condition did not improve. Instead, she began talking to herself, and the doctors proclaimed her mentally ill.

Yu Sho's neighbor, a member of the Tainan Foursquare Church, told Yu Sho's mother about Jesus. The neighbor said that if she believed Jesus, He could heal her daughter. Yu Sho's mother, at her wit's end, was curious and took her daughter to church. The church prayed for Yu Sho after the Sunday service every week for three months. They also told her mother to get rid of all the idols and to worship only Jesus.

Gradually, Yu Sho stopped speaking incoherently and her mind became clear. Jesus kept His promise and she was completely healed!

Global REPORT, 2000

Thank you, Lord, for your promise to heal. Help me in my unbelief; give me faith to believe and to see healing in my life and in the lives of those I pray for...

"The godly offer good counsel..."
PSALM 37:30 (NLT)

When revival happens, the enemy is not happy! Many times there are those driven by demons who are bent on stopping what God is doing. This happened in Willowvale recently during a revival. There were violent threats to burn down the churches and homes of the Foursquare pastors in the Transkei.

During this time we decided to fast and pray. I received word from one of the perpetrators that they wanted to meet with me and I gave my word that I would go.

The local elders of the Foursquare Church in Willowvale earnestly pleaded with me not to go, as they feared it was a trap. I felt that since I had given my word I should go. The elders were distressed by this and met privately to pray and discuss the situation. They then met with me and said that I could go, but one day earlier and that they would accompany me.

When the elders and I arrived at the meeting one day early, it became very apparent that the perpetrators didn't want to talk with me after all. They were furious at the surprise visit and they cursed us as they had plotted to kill me the next day, when the original meeting was to have taken place. God used some very wise men to speak godly counsel.

Howard and Terry Manthe
Missionaries to South Africa

Lord, give me a wise heart, that I would listen to godly advice and take heed to it. Keep me from stubbornly following my own way...

"I have given you authority over all the power of the enemy..."
LUKE 10:19 (NLT)

The meetings had created such interest that people came early. By the time we began the meeting, the building was full. Others stood outside looking in. From the very beginning we were aware of the presence of the Holy Spirit as well as strong spiritual opposition. The meeting was suddenly interrupted by demonic demonstrations among the people. We heard loud moans in one area, choking in another, screams in still another.

Each of us on the platform took immediate action. I remember walking across the backs of the benches, praying as I went. In the anointing of the Holy Spirit and the authority of Jesus, each of us commanded the demons to leave those who were under attack. Victory was unquestionable. In a short while, things quieted down and the service resumed.

That was not the end; God had something more in store. Among those who responded to the invitation was a small, gray-haired mother. As we prayed for her, tears began to flow. We knew the Lord had touched her, but we didn't know the whole story.

The next morning she came to the door of the mission house. She told us the reason she had come forward the night before was because she was blind. The tears that flowed from her milky white eyes were, in part, her cataracts. She was healed!

Allan Hamilton
Former Missionary to the Philippines

> *Lord, although the devil wants to disrupt your plans, I know*
> *that you have given me authority over his power and you*
> *will be victorious...*

> *"There is a time for everything, and a season for every activity under heaven... a time to weep and a time to laugh..."*
>
> ECCLESIASTES 3:1,4

Learning a new language is not without its humor, and sometimes its horror. In this regard, I've had my share of foibles.

In Colombia, during one of my first sermons in Spanish, my intent was to encourage the people that the Lord wants to strengthen us in every situation and to give us "support" (appolo). Instead of telling the congregation the Lord would give them "appolo," I told them the Lord would give them "pollo," meaning chicken.

Imagine my surprise when, at the end of the service, an usher came asking, "Where is our chicken?"

"What chicken?" was my response.

"In your sermon you said God wanted to give us chicken."

Then he began to smile.

As I thought back on my sermon, I remembered at one point the congregation had snickered. I thought their laughter was delayed from something I had said earlier. But then I realized I had promised chicken! We all knew what I had meant to say, but the idea of the Lord giving us chicken gave us all a good laugh.

At another time, while ministering in Mexico with Mike Larkin, Mike was asked to dedicate a baby. I was his translator. The translation went smoothly until Mike said, "And now, Lord, we present this baby to you." My translation went, "And now, Lord, we offer this baby to You in sacrifice."

At that point, the father, fear upon his face, retrieved the baby from Mike's arms and stepped away.

Charlie Finocchiaro
Missionary to the Dominican Republic

> *Lord, help me to not take myself too seriously, but to laugh at myself and rejoice in you, my God, who forgives me and sets things right and even uses my efforts to bless others...*

*"So Abraham called that place 'The Lord Will Provide.'
And to this day it is said, "On the mountain
of the Lord it will be provided."*
GENESIS 22:14

My husband, Henry, used to say we were a "low budget operation." But over and over when we had a need, God provided.

While in the U.S., Henry spoke at a men's camp. Earl, a paint salesman, asked him if he could use some paint. "I can't promise anything, but I will talk with my boss. How much paint could you use?" Henry said, "How much do you have?"

Earl talked with his boss who wasn't very interested. The next morning, however, his boss picked up the newspaper and read the story about Rafico, a young Ecuadorian at Houses of Happiness who had lost his leg to a train. When Earl arrived at work, the boss said, "Well, what did that cost you?" Not knowing what he was talking about, Earl glanced down to see Rafico's photo smiling up at him.

We received 5,000 gallons of discontinued paint. The man also called a friend who sent hundreds of brushes and paint pans. And, because of a special governmental privilege, everything arrived duty free! The paint was enough to cover the orphanage completely and then some. Many of our Foursquare churches on the coast of Ecuador were painted "hot pink" and the Ecuadorians loved it!

Jehovah Jireh, the Lord will provide!

Dorothy Davis
Former Missionary to Ecuador

*Father, thank you for providing for my needs. You have not
only provided Jesus to meet my spiritual needs, but you also
provide my every need day by day...*

> *"For the Word of God is living and active.*
> *"Sharper than any double-edged sword..."*
> HEBREWS 4:12

*C*erebral malaria is an exceptionally deadly form of malaria. Often the person loses consciousness, slips into a coma, and dies very quickly. We recently received a report that one of our Sunday school children was desperately ill with cerebral malaria. But when we checked, the father reported that the five-year-old boy was making a rapid recovery.

The mother said that as the child was slipping into the twilight of unconsciousness, he began to repeat over and over again the memory verse from his last Sunday school lesson: 'For God so loved the world that He gave His only begotten Son, that whoever believes in Him shall not perish but have eternal life.' The parents were amazed that their son had memorized that Scripture and credit the Word of God for saving their son's life.

Greg Fisher
Missionary to Uganda

Father, help me to hide your Word in my heart and to memorize Scripture so that I can bring it to mind in the day of trouble...

"He is your praise; he is your God, who performed for you those great and awesome wonders you saw with your own eyes."

DEUTERONOMY 10:21

There was a young man whose job took him to the northern coast of Honduras. After about a year, he gave us a call. He said, "Pastor, can you come? I have 60 people and I don't know what to do with them."

So we went and held a service under a big tree. After the preaching was over, a lady began to call from the group. She said, "Brother Dean, there is a man who wants you to pray for him." They opened up a pathway for him and the man came forward. His leg was stiff, and he was totally bent over at the waist and his arm was bound up against him. He was obviously in bad shape.

I asked him what had happened to him and he said, "If I told you, you wouldn't believe me!"

"Try me!" I responded.

He then told me the story, "Ten days ago I was at the railroad track and I stopped to wash my hands in a creek that ran under the railroad bridge. While I was bent over, a train went over the bridge and a cow fell off a flat car and landed on top of me."

The man was all busted up because a cow fell on him!

We prayed for him, and in an instant and in the presence of about 100 people, we could all hear and see his bones go back into place! In a matter of seconds he was completely healed!

Dean Truett
Former Missionary to Honduras

Thank you, Lord, that you perform wonders before our very eyes. Help me to keep my eyes on you today in every circumstance, and to trust in you no matter what happens...

> *"And if God cares so wonderfully for flowers
> that are here today and gone tomorrow,
> won't he more surely care for you?"*

LUKE 12:28 (NLT)

A very devoted and religious lady lived in the village of Amiri-Orlu. She was well-known in the town and very influential. In God's providential plan one day she met a Christian who was a part of our Foursquare church in Nigeria. She told her about Jesus' love. Right there the lady accepted Christ and within a short time was filled with the Spirit. Her conversion and evidence of Jesus' continued work in her heart caused a great stir in that village. It was proclaimed a miracle, and she became a walking testimony of how God cares for people and changes lives.

In that very same village lived a mentally ill man who was very known throughout Amiri-Orlu. He lived at home because there was no place for him to get help. Only those who were violent were institutionalized. One day a Christian witnessed to him about the power of God to deliver and heal. This man responded to the love of Jesus and prayed the sinner's prayer. Not only did Jesus save him, but He also completely restored him to full mental health. He returned to his family a well man and become a productive citizen of the village.

Jesus is not only changing entire villages, but also individual hearts and lives! Today may you find Christ where you need him most, for He isn't only concerned for your whole "village" but for you!

Audra Sowersby
Former Missionary to Africa

> *Thank you, Father, that you care for me and that you
> sought me out and brought me to yourself...*

"He who dwells in the shelter of the Most High will rest in the shadow of the Almighty. I will say of the Lord, 'He is my refuge and my fortress, my God, in whom I trust.'"

PSALM 91:1-2

Psalm 91 has meant so much to me lately. During our term break from the Bible School we traveled to West New Britain. After a ten hour ship ride we arrived to the very friendly village of our Provincial Supervisor, Pastor Aloy. There Keith and I put on a pastors and leaders conference.

It might sound a little boring and uneventful, but let me tell you what it was really like. We were so humbled to be a part of it. The pastors and leaders that came sacrificed so much just to get there. Some of them traveled by foot for three days up and down rugged mountains just to attend the three-day conference. Some of them had to pay half a month's wage ($20) just for the PMV boat fare to get there. Some had to travel by boat, car, and then again by boat. It was a 12-hour journey for them.

Even though conditions were tough for us, we realized that we have so much and they have so little. At night we were housed with Pastor Aloy's family and many other people. We had our own room separated by a sheet. The rest, probably 15 others, were piled everywhere else. As the mosquitoes squealed around our heads, our hands would start to tickle as the ants found their way to our warm skin.

In our lives there will be many little annoyances! They don't hurt you, and you are still protected and under the shadow of His wings.

Keith and Cindy Bickley
FMI Associates to Papua New Guinea

Lord, I thank you for those who serve as missionaries. Call many more! Speak to the hearts of those whom you wish to send...

He came to Jesus at night and said, "Rabbi, we know you are a teacher who has come from God. For no one could perform the miraculous signs you are doing if God were not with him."

JOHN 3:2

My husband David often travels to minister in remote areas where we have a Foursquare church, or where we hope to plant a church. On almost every occasion that the Gospel is preached, people come to Christ. It is rare when no one responds to receive Christ.

One day David and the pastor ministered together in an area where we were about to plant a church. After David preached, he gave an invitation for any that wanted to receive Jesus as their Savior to come forward. He was puzzled that no one came.

However, after nightfall, a group of about 30 people came in the shadows to receive salvation. The pastor explained that in this highly Muslim area, people are cautious about making professions of faith in broad daylight.

A few days later, the Jesus film was shown in that place and more lives were touched. The following Sunday, the first church service was held. There were 81 adults in attendance!

Sarah Adams
Missionary to Uganda

> *Lord, I live in a place where it is easy and acceptable to follow you. I pray for all my brothers and sisters who live in countries where persecution will follow a decision to serve you...*

*"...we also rejoice in our sufferings, because we know
that suffering produces perseverance..."*
ROMANS 5:3

"Suddenly, the pastors began to run away!" exclaimed Foursquare pastor Antonio Aluvera. The socialist government of Mozambique had falsely accused a group of pastors of siding with the opposition group and violating the decree that there should be no prayer meetings. They were captured, tortured, beaten, and kept in the forest for three weeks. Weak, tired, and thin from inadequate food and water, they were released and told to stop meeting for prayer. Pastor Antonio Aluvera was among this group.

When he returned to his village, the church met secretly until it was impossible for them to stay in their homes any longer. Pastor Antonio, his pregnant wife, seven children, and some church members fled into the forest. Other church members were killed because they stayed behind to gather up all their personal belongings.

Pastor Antonio and his wife left their children with relatives and walked from morning into the night to arrive in Malawi. Every night, he returned to Mozambique to rescue his seven children, one at a time. Together they went to Mankhokwe Refugee Camp in Nsanje, Malawi.

In the camp he started to hold worship services under a tree. Before long many were saved and he established a Foursquare Gospel Church; the building, made from mud and grass, held 20 families.

This brother is a wonderful example of someone who has been able to "rejoice in his sufferings." In the face of suffering, Pastor Antonio rejoiced and trusted his God to bring him through the darkest of nights, and He did!

Foursquare World ADVANCE, 1993

*Lord, I thank you for the character that you have worked in
me through the times of suffering in my life. I truly do
rejoice in my sufferings, knowing that you are in control...*

June 23 ——————————————————————— Foursquare 75th. Missions

"No weapon formed against you shall prosper..."
ISAIAH 54:17 (NKJV)

"Mommie Europa" was a Filipina, with white hair and a cheerful smile. Even before her graduation from Bible college, this little woman was ministering.

On one occasion Mommie Europa and several others boarded a boat to go to a small neighboring island. They hadn't been invited; in fact, this island had a reputation of not being favorable towards evangelicals. They had prayed about this trip and asked the Lord specifically to protect them as they made their way through the ocean waters in their small boat. They asked the Lord to go before them and prepare hearts.

They were greeted with hospitality, as the culture demanded, and they were invited into a house to eat. The small group of visitors was seated as the hosts stood nearby. The empty plates were before them on the table and they were about to be served, when Mrs. Europa said, "It is our custom to pray before we eat." With that she bowed her head and began to pray—for the household, the meal, and their time on this island. And she ended by saying, "We pray these things in the name of Jesus."

As she said "in the name of Jesus," the plate before each guest cracked in two. The hosts were alarmed and began to confess. They did not want these evangelicals on their island and had poisoned the food they were going to serve them.

Mrs. Europa explained that the true and living God was the one they served and that because He was more powerful than any other gods, He had protected them. The hosts were afraid and began to repent, asking forgiveness from the Lord and from their guests. That day many people on that little island came to know Jesus.

Eloise Clarno
Former Missionary to the Philippines

> *Lord, I am so grateful to you that no weapon formed against me will be able to prevail, and that you will keep me safe from the evil planned against me...*

—— 174 ——

"The Spirit of the Lord is upon me...to preach the gospel...
to heal the brokenhearted, to preach deliverance...
and recovering of sight to the blind."

LUKE 4:18 (KJV)

*T*he day we arrived in Davao, Mindanao, Philippines we had no evangelistic party, no contact of any kind, nothing to entertain the people with, and we were told we were not needed or wanted. This only sharpened the challenge of evangelism within us. Mindanao had never known evangelism with signs following.

We saw the people sick and sin-weary and longed to see them delivered. Obtaining a building on a busy street to preach in, we put up a large sign that said "Have faith in God" and we began having services. Brother Thompson, Sister Annamae (Hamrick) Cheney and I stood together and sang songs the people had not heard before. The building overflowed with people, and the streets were filled around the building—the Holy Spirit was drawing them. I stepped out and gave a simple message of salvation and deliverance. Jesus saved them by the hundreds, and without even preaching on divine healing, many were healed.

Dr. Evelyn Thompson
Former Missionary to the Philippines

> *Father, give me your heart for the lost. Help me to have*
> *your eyes when I look at them, to see them as you see them*
> *and love them as you do...*

> *"Heal me, O Lord, and I will be healed; save me and I will be saved,* for you are the one I praise."
>
> JEREMIAH 17:14

*D*r. Courtney and I had the privilege of being in Barranquilla, Colombia, with missionaries John and Jean Firth. One Sunday, Dr. Courtney was asked to teach Sunday school. The church was full and at the end of the teaching, John gave an altar call for any to be saved. Many responded. When he asked for any who needed healing or wanted to be baptized in the Holy Spirit, the response was great. I stood in wonder as the people responded to the Lord and were rewarded for their faith.

I had noticed a large man with a white cane. During the altar service he came for prayer and afterwards began walking up and down the aisle swinging his cane. He told about meeting a woman on the bus that morning and asking her where she was going. She told him she was going to the Foursquare church and that, "If you will come with me to my church, my Lord will heal you." He had come and experienced two miracles that morning—his salvation and his healing.

God desires whole people. He loves you and desires that you not only know Him as your Savior, but as your healer. Come to Him today, just as you are and ask him to make you whole!

Vaneda Courtney
Wife of Dr. Howard Courtney, Missions Director, 1944-1950

Father, you are making me into a whole person and I thank you for that...

*"For He will command his angels concerning you
to guard you in all your ways..."*

PSALM 91:11

"As a missionary, are you ever afraid?" is a question that is often
asked of those who minister overseas. The answer for most is
"Yes!" However, the fear is most often immediately followed by a reminder
of the closeness of the Lord.

Riding a motorcycle is something I enjoy, but on the hard dirt
Highlands Highway of Papua New Guinea it became a challenge.

One evening I was returning home from teaching at the Bible school.
As I headed into a sharp corner that was deeply corrugated with recent
rains, I saw a pickup truck coming from the other direction at about 50
miles per hour. The driver was cutting the corner so he would not have to
slow down. He came directly towards me; there was no time to brake, only
to lean into the corner to try to avoid a collision. I soon realized I was
going to hit the truck head-on.

It had only been a few months previously that I had gone to the local
morgue to identify the body of another missionary's son who had been
killed in a head-on collision with a pickup truck. Now, it seemed it was my
turn. As the front grill of the truck hurtled toward me, I prayed, "Jesus,
here I come."

Instead of the sudden crunch and quick blackness I expected, I found
myself leaning, bumping and sliding against the side of the truck. As the
truck sped past me, I flew through the air, landing on my shoulder, spin-
ning like a top. The next thing I knew, I was standing on my feet looking
at the only broken bone I had—my right little finger. I was miraculously
spared certain death. I knew my Lord was with me and apparently had
more for me to do in this life.

Phil Franklin
Former Missionary to Thailand

*Thank you, Lord, for the many ways you preserve my life.
You keep me safe and put your angels all around me...*

"I will present my thank offerings to You. For You have delivered me from death and my feet from stumbling, that I may walk before God in the light of life."

PSALM 56:12-13

"I heard a loud crash this morning at around 5:00 a.m. and I saw that there had been an accident on the motorway." said Pastor Abraham Mantey as we sat on his verandah. "The whole side was off the bus." According to a bystander, six people were dead and more were taken to the hospital.

A family from the Mataheko Foursquare Church requested prayer for their brother, who was one of those injured in the bus accident. When the family had gone to the hospital to see him, they had found him already wrapped in a shroud and ready for the mortuary. But some family members reported seeing movement in the body, and the young man was immediately taken to a room.

During the week, pastors from the church visited the boy in the hospital. He looked more dead than alive. However, by the end of the week, the young man was in church with his brother! The brother stood to tell the story of God's healing power, and then the young man turned to the pastor and quietly asked, "I know it is God who has done this for me. What can I do to thank Him?" The pastor's reply was, "You can give your life to Him."

The young man who had been so very close to death received God's free gift of eternal life.

Greg Fisher
Missionary to Uganda

Lord, so many times you have delivered me from death. I will praise you and thank you today and throughout eternity...

"God did extraordinary miracles..."

ACTS 19:11

C elebrating Holy Week is a very special time in Colombia. We decided that our church services would have a very simple Gospel message with an emphasis on salvation and healing. One of the sisters in the church had a vision of a crowd of people standing outside the church doorway and overflowing into the streets.

It came true! The church was filled to capacity, with standing room only, and there were even people standing outside. During one of the services, 25 people came to know the Lord and over 100 people were baptized in the Holy Spirit. The Lord did some extraordinary miracles that night too!

There was a little girl about eight years old who had a brain tumor that had made her blind and had taken away almost all of her hearing. One of our prayer teams laid their hands on her and prayed. As they prayed, the tumor was immediately dissolved and the little girl could see and hear. Her parents began to rejoice and praise God.

There was so much joy in the room that I find it hard to describe, and the healings didn't stop there—another young girl who had been taking cortisone pills five or six times a day was completely healed of lupus!

God is good!

Dan and Heli Larson
Former Missionaries to Colombia

I praise you, Father, that you are a God of miracles! Work miracles in my life and in the lives of these I bring before you today...

"Then I heard the voice of the Lord saying; 'Whom shall I send?
And who will go for us?' And I said, 'Here am I. Send me!'"

ISAIAH 6:8

As a pastor in Venezuela for over 15 years, I never even mentioned the word missions. Then I was invited to join other pastors for a three-day missions conference. God used that very meeting to touch my heart and speak to me about the importance of praying and preaching about missions.

In 1989 I was invited to attend Lausanne II, the Congress on World Evangelism in Manila. While I was there, the Holy Spirit placed a great burden on my heart for the country of Nicaragua. With tears I prayed, "Lord, if one day you would like me to go to Nicaragua, I am willing."

By God's sovereign design, that day I met Don McGregor, the Foursquare Missions representative. He heard my heart and encouraged me to write to Foursquare Missions International, telling them of my burden. So I did as he suggested.

Just days following my return to Venezuela, I received a call to minister at the Nicaraguan National Convention. When I returned from Nicaragua, my burden was greater. My wife, Alva, and I put up a big map of Nicaragua that month and we and the church interceded for that nation.

One month later, God spoke to us, "Don't just pray for Nicaragua any more. Prepare your suitcases to go live in Nicaragua." Two weeks later, Foursquare Missions International invited us to become missionaries in Nicaragua. For the next 12 years we lived and ministered there.

God touched our hearts. God called us, sent us and remains faithful.

Serafin Contreras
Missionary to Panama and Nicaragua

> *Lord, make my heart willing to go anywhere you want me*
> *to go. Prepare me for the call you have on my life and for*
> *the work that you want me to do...*

"So shall My word be that goes forth from My mouth;
It shall not return to Me void,
But it shall accomplish what I please,
And it shall prosper in the thing for which I sent it."

ISAIAH 55:11 (NKJV)

A Mexican drug trafficker reads a simple piece of paper—it tells him that Jesus loves him—and his life is dramatically changed as he gives his life to Jesus. Eventually his entire family comes to Christ and their lives are changed forever.

A Muslim man in Nigeria, despite dismissing a Christian's argument regarding Mohammed, reads a gospel tract that invites him to pray and receive Christ. He does so. "From that moment, I became a changed man and born-again child of God, a true follower of Christ."

A Malaysian man—in and out of jail for 11 years—starts to use a tract for paper to roll a cigarette. He reads the words, "He can make you the man you should be…" and then comes to Christ. For the past 10 years he has been the director of a Christian drug rehabilitation facility.

These are just a few of the stories of lives changed by Christ through the written word produced by Foursquare Missions Press. However, these individual lives are just beginning points—entire villages, cities and countries have been impacted by believers who are armed with tracts and a heart for the lost.

God's Word is powerful. Written or spoken—God's Word is life changing!

Robert Hunt
Director of Foursquare Missions Press/FMI Communications Coordinator

I praise you, Lord, for your Word is powerful and does
indeed accomplish the purpose for which you sent it. Help
me to be both a sower and a doer of your Word today...

*"I entrust my spirit into your hand. Rescue me, Lord,
for you are a faithful God."*

PSALM 31:5 (NLT)

The American team jolted around in the back of the pickup for hours. No one complained as they sweated and bounced, but you could sense the questions in their minds. Where are we going? Why did we take the roughest route? When are we going to get there? Are we going to get there?

Suddenly the pickup came to a jarring halt and two soldiers appeared at the back of the tarp-covered pickup bed. Inadvertently, we had driven into a military restricted zone and caused a major problem for ourselves. The soldiers stood on the bumper and we bumped along for another hour or so. To aggravate the situation, one of the team members wanted to capture the moment and started taking pictures.

That was the last we saw of the camera, but they let us keep the camera's owner. After arriving at their headquarters we sat in the truck while my friend Shadrack, a national of the country, talked to the authorities. I was struck with a brilliant idea—let's pray!

One hundred miles out in the middle of Africa, in the middle of a military restricted area, things looked a bit hopeless. But not for our Father. Shadrack returned and said, "You won't believe who is the commander of this force—my uncle!"

Glen Mickel
Former Missionary to West Africa

*In the midst of difficulties, Lord, we look to you alone for
our help and deliverance...*

"For we walk by faith and not by sight."
2 CORINTHIANS 5:7 (NKJV)

She had just taken one of the biggest steps of faith in her life and yet her thoughts turned to pizza.

Ilya Carrera, the senior pastor of a Foursquare church in Panama City, often recalls the topic of pizza when faith-demanding circumstances confront her. After giving up a prosperous fourteen-year career as an architect for the U.S. Navy, Ilya took on a small church that was located in an area better known for drug deals and prostitution than for the gospel. "When I left my job, I didn't know how much the church could pay me. I didn't care because God had called me."

One day, without a church salary and in a moment of absolute hunger, Pastor Ilya cried out to God, "Lord, if I was working for Uncle Sam I could buy a pizza. I don't care if I won't eat pizza, but I want to thank you for the pizza by faith!" Twenty minutes later a woman from the church knocked on Ilya's door and surprised her with a much-appreciated pizza. It would become a benchmark in a life lived by faith.

In 1927, Dr. and Mrs. Arthur Edwards became the first Foursquare missionaries to Panama. "Without knowing the country, without speaking the language and without knowing anyone, they came…" Ilya recalled with a sense of awe. "Since then, all Foursquare Panamanians live by faith. We don't see obstacles…we go for it!"

Walking by faith can sometimes be difficult. It is then that we must remember the pizza story—and that our God delivers!

Robert Hunt,
Director of Foursquare Missions Press/FMI Communications Coordinator

Teach me, Lord, to trust you for every need, whether great or small…

Jesus said to her, "I am the resurrection and the life.
He who believes in me will live..."

JOHN 11:23-26

Maria, a Bible school student in Papua New Guinea, received word her mother had died. As she journeyed to her village, she talked to her Heavenly Father. "God, I don't understand, I know that she is with you now, but my mother was young and what about my little sister?"

The Lord said to her, "Maria, I am going to raise your mother from the dead."

Maria responded, "Yes, I know You are coming for Your own."

When she arrived home, the scene was typical: women had covered their bodies with mud and some had cut off the tips of their fingers, letting blood drip on their bodies to show the spirits they were sorry.

Maria told the villagers that she wanted to pray for her mother.

"You are a bit late," they mocked her, but they showed her the hut where her mother lay.

Maria prayed, "God, please show my people they do not need to mourn." Suddenly she realized that she no longer heard wailing. She ran out of the hut to see her mother standing in the middle of the village.

"I have been somewhere so beautiful, with beautiful streets and houses!" she said. "Someone touched me and said, 'That is your house. You may enter, but if you do, you must stay.'"

"I have a three-year-old daughter," she replied, "I need to go and take care of her." And with that, she awoke, to the amazement and great joy of her family and village!

Mason and Virgene Hughes
Former Missionaries to Papua New Guinea

Thank you, Father, for your resurrection power! Help me to
believe you for great things in all the circumstances of my
life...

"The God of peace will soon crush
Satan under your feet."

ROMANS 16:20

In 1971, Haiti was dedicated to Satan by Haitian leaders in defiance to Christianity. In 1991, then President Aristide rededicated the country to Voodooism as its "cultural heritage." The enemy has laid claim to the land of Haiti, but God has other plans.

Earlier this month Jerry and Betty Poppe, FMI missionaries to Haiti, held a medical clinic session in Payan. Both spiritual and medical ministry were offered to those who came with powerful results. In all, 750 people were treated in the clinic and 123 of them accepted Jesus as their Lord and Savior. One of those saved through the clinic was a woman known as a "Rah Rah Queen" and her entire family. As a "queen,' she wore brilliant, outlandish costumes to lead the national parades on Good Friday to celebrate Satan's victory over Jesus. The celebration observed and exalted the dominion of Satanism and Voodooism in Haiti!

After she and her family were saved, she returned home, gathered up all of her bizarre costumes and burned them. This act left no doubt as to the reality of her conversion and her clear-cut decision not to turn back to her old life!

Foursquare Global REPORT, 2000

Lord, may your glorious light shine upon those who are now
in darkness. Thank you, Lord, that one day every knee will
bow and every tongue confess that you alone are Lord!

"Don't be afraid; just believe, and she will be healed."

LUKE 8:50

A woman rushed in just as our ladies Tuesday afternoon prayer meeting was getting underway. Obviously very upset, she told us, "My little neighbor girl has just been seriously burned and needs prayer. They have taken her to the hospital and she will require skin grafts. Please pray."

After the lady calmed down she told us what happened. She had been preparing wax for her floor by heating wax and kerosene together. The mixture caught fire and the flames began to run up the curtain near her stove. She grabbed the flaming mass and carried it to the door. Not realizing that the little girl was playing there, she threw it out into the yard. The burning mixture had covered the little girl, burning her severely on the face, arm and chest. Realizing the urgency of the situation, our ladies immediately began to pray.

The next week this same lady came in with a little girl. She explained this was the girl who had been so severely burned the week before. God had worked a miracle. The girl was completely healed. There had been no skin grafting and where the burns had been, there was beautiful new flesh. Only God could have done such a perfect work.

Irvin and Florence Espeseth
Former Missionaries to Guatemala

I thank you, Lord, for your words of peace. Help me to have faith, and to not be afraid today in every situation I face. I bring before you now these people and situations that need your healing touch...

"... though outwardly we are wasting away, yet inwardly we are being renewed day by day."

2 CORINTHIANS 4:16

"Your son didn't eat anything but rice, bread, and hot tea the whole time he was with us!" exclaimed one pastor's wife after a convention in Santiago, Chile.

Stan was the supervisor of this 3,000 mile long South American country. He traveled extensively nine months of the year, sometimes 10 to 14 days out of the month. One of our four children, third-grader Robby, was being homeschooled. He and I would do intensive studies and then he would be off with his father.

II Corinthians 4:16 says, "though outwardly we are wasting away yet inwardly we are begin renewed." This was Robby. He witnessed the moving of the Holy Spirit in candle-lit, dirt- floored churches. He visited churches in remote islands. Alongside his father, he prayed for people facing critical losses due to a volcano. He worshiped in authentic Andean style music and visited one of the largest copper mines in the world.

Yes, Robby would come back thinner after his trips with his father due to his picky diet, but inwardly he was being shaped and marked with an eternal purpose.

"Don't worry, while he ate little physically, he feasted spiritually." would be my response again and again. "With physical eyes, one can't always see what is happening on the inside."

Molly Doland
Missionary to Spain

Lord, help me to remember today that even though I am wasting away outwardly, and I'm not as young as I used to be, that you are renewing me inwardly. Renew me today and give me eyes to see your renewing power at work in the live of those around me...

*"I will build my church, and the gates of
Hades will not overcome it."*

MATTHEW 16:18

*I*n Sri Lanka tourism and trade are mainstays of their economy. But
tourism has been negatively impacted by civil unrest and there continues to be a mass exodus of professionals and local business people to other
nations.

The ethnic war that began in the mid-1980's continues to bring bloodshed as the opposition political party is still on the warpath, trying to topple the government. Public demonstrations and violence are common, and
the security and political climate of the nation is very volatile.

Recently a militant Hindu group attacked the homes of Foursquare
believers and drove them to shelter in a little village church. Many of our
pastors have been threatened. But all of this is only half of the story.

Foursquare ministers in the north central province conducted a series of
revival meetings in a small village. A Buddhist man who was totally deaf
began to hear for the first time. The following day he brought his twelve-year-old son who could not speak. He was miraculously cured and spoke
clearly. More than 30 people gave their hearts to the Lord.

In the first six months of the year 2001, the national church grew from
515 to 725 house churches. One leader said, "In the midst of the turmoil,
war, bloodshed, economic distress, and political upheaval, the Church is
alive and well."

Eloise Clarno
Former Missionary to Sri Lanka

*Thank you, Lord, that you are building your church in Sri
Lanka and around the world and that the gates of hell will
not overcome it. I pray now for churches and nations that
are on my heart today...*

"Do not be terrified; do not be discouraged, for the Lord your God will be with you wherever you go."

JOSHUA 1:9

*B*eing a missionary is filled with the miraculous! But there are times that being a missionary isn't that fun… especially for the wives! Here is one such occasion:

We were ministering in the area of Bizana (South of Durban) in the Natal area, South Africa. We returned quite late one night from the evening meeting to the mud hut where we were staying which only had two very small, single beds. Terry got into her sleeping bag and felt something crawling in the mattress underneath her sleeping bag! She realized that she was not alone. She jumped out of bed, grabbed her flashlight and looked under her bed, only to discover a whole nest of rats living in the mattress. She immediately jumped into my single bed with me.

As soon as we got settled again and blew out the candles, the rats started jumping onto our bed and running over our sleeping bags! Terry decided that she had had enough, and needless to say, spent the night in our car! I was too exhausted to care and drifted off into much needed sleep.

Even in the "rattiest" of situations, we must trust that God is with us, and that He will give us peace and a way out!

Howard and Terry Manthe
Missionaries to South Africa

> *Lord, deliver me from all kinds of fear. Keep me from being terrified by anything; knowing that you will keep my safe in every situation and give me peace…*

> *"Ten men who had leprosy met him (Jesus)*
> *... and as they went, they were cleansed."*
>
> LUKE 17:12,14

"We had begun a church in our home in Bangalore, India. Each Friday was fasting and prayer day, concluding with a service. One Friday, Geeta came to the service. Her legs were swollen and she was covered with sores. She asked for prayer for a "skin disease." After prayer, Vijaya and I felt we needed to take her to the hospital to have her admitted for treatment. While we waited, we visited others who were patients there.

When the doctor came in, he asked if we knew this woman was a confirmed leper. Vijaya and I went to see Geeta and confronted her. She began to weep and confessed she had leprosy. I asked God for courage for whatever would follow.

Then I asked her to show me her arm; the whole forearm was a sore. After a moment of hesitation, I put the palm of my hand on her sore and we began to pray. Vijaya and Geeta's husband stood with us. Later, Geeta was discharged from the hospital without treatment.

A week later her friend came to tell us that she had been completely healed. A few weeks later Greeta was in church testifying of her healing and giving the glory to God for his unfailing love and faithfulness!

John Gnanaolivu
Founder of Foursquare India

Lord, I thank you that no matter how shameful my condition,
you are always willing to touch me and make me clean...

*"He will cover you with His feathers, and under
His wings you will find refuge..."*

PSALM 91:4

*I*n July of 1998 a tidal wave devastated a 15-kilometer stretch of the north coast of Papua New Guinea. Pastor August is a young man who was pioneering a Foursquare church in the area. His story follows:

"It was a Friday and we had been working in the sun all day harvesting coconuts and cocoa. At about 7:00 p.m. we felt an earthquake and part of our home (made of bush material) collapsed. We went outside and I felt an urging to call the church together to pray. Most of the young men were tired but I sent out the word and went to the house where we were meeting (the house was built on stilts near the beach) and began to play my guitar and sing. People started to gather and as darkness came we were powerfully moved in an intense time of prayer and worship.

"As we finished and began to get ready to go back to our homes we noticed that everything around us looked white. Someone with a flashlight shined it around the area and we discovered that we were surrounded by water and sea foam. As we were praying, the sea had rushed in and covered the entire area. We were standing on an island of refuge in the middle of a disaster. Realizing what had happened, we began looking for people and bringing the injured and dead bodies to where we were. Some church members lost loved ones that night but all of us who were gathered to pray were safe. The next morning we discovered overturned houses, uprooted trees, and destruction all around. God was our refuge that night and we were covered and protected in the shelter of His wings."

George Butron
Missionary to Papua New Guinea

*You are my shelter, Lord. you will keep me safe, even though
all around me is death and destruction. May I dwell in you
forever...*

"I cried unto thee, and thou hast healed me."

PSALM 30:2 (KJV)

As God's people take Him at His word, and boldly confess their faith and ask Him publicly for healings and miracles, God hears their prayers and grants their requests, as former missionaries Edgar and Darlene Coombs testify:

"In August of 1978 a miracle occurred in our Foursquare church in Penonome, Panama. One of the Sunday School boys died on the operating table at one of our local hospitals. His grandmother had taken him there for the removal of a cast from a broken hand. When the doctor saw the hand would remain deformed, he ordered an operation. A second anesthetic was ordered when the first one failed. Suddenly, the attending doctor and nurses realized the child had died from the overdose. The medic went into the waiting room to inform the grandmother of her loss.

"Trembling, she stood to her feet and felt she should pray, but she felt ashamed to pray in front of the people crowding the waiting room. Finally, she just fell to her knees and threw up her hands and cried to God to restore the child's life. She also asked God to heal his deformed hand. Just then the medic returned to tell her that her boy was alive again! She rushed up to him and begged him not to operate on the hand. The doctor then came out and told her to take the boy home because the operation wouldn't be necessary! The boy had been completely healed!"

Edgar and Darlene Coombs
Former Missionaries to Panama

Father, give us the courage to boldly proclaim our faith and to reach out to others and pray for them in every situation. Help us to swallow our pride and to put aside doubts and fear...

"For I am not ashamed of the gospel of Christ:
for it is the power of God unto salvation."
ROMANS 1:16 (KJV)

Mrs. Wang had worshiped at her "god-shelf" for over 80 years. Every morning from her earliest childhood she had approached the red decorated wooden shelf hung on her wall to honor her ancestors. She would place wine, pieces of chicken, oranges, and other valuable mementoes for the "council of the ancestors" to enjoy and to cover any wrath that the spirits may have had toward her. She went through this ritual three times each day, and fervently hoped she had gotten everything right.

A friend invited Mrs. Wang to attend one of the Foursquare churches in Hong Kong that preached about a person named Jesus Christ. As she listened to the preacher share the message of redemption, something happened in her heart. She realized Jesus had died for her sins once for all and that she no longer had to try to appease the wrath of any deity or dead ancestor. She gave her heart to Jesus and began to learn about Him.

On the day that her pastor and church members came to destroy the god-shelf, all kinds of evil manifestations were evidenced. As the service proceeded and the pastor and other church leaders destroyed the wood and ceramic idols with an axe, the room was suddenly illuminated with a bright light, and the peace of God filled the entire room. From that moment until she went to be with Jesus at age 85, "Grandma" Wang became a bright witness of the gospel.

The gospel is truly the "power of God unto salvation."

Dr. Ron and Carole Williams
Former Missionaries to Hong Kong

I thank you, Lord, for the power of the Gospel that breaks
down strongholds and idols in our lives. Destroy these
strongholds in my life and in the lives of others...

> *"For this son of mine was dead and is alive again;*
> *he was lost and is found."*
>
> LUKE 15:24

ou should have seen the crowds of people running onto the soccer field in the city of San Pedro Sula, Honduras. Foursquare Pastor Misael Argenal held a crusade which shook his country. For three nights, 40,000 people were in attendance, and on the fourth night over 65,000 people gathered. Tens of thousands made professions of faith. Thirteen radio stations carried the crusade every night and three television networks broadcast the service live to the entire country.

Among the many dramatic conversions and healings was that of a gang member. Earlier in the year he had tried to murder his mother and had left her to die. After giving his heart to Christ at the crusade, he was interviewed on the platform by Pastor Misael. After some counsel, this young man agreed he needed to ask forgiveness from his mother. He was downcast and convinced she would never forgive him.

The next evening he appeared once again at the crusade. He was full of joy as he related that the lights were on and the door wide open when he got to his mom's home. She was animated in her joy to see him. It seems she was offering forgiveness even before he could ask.

She told him that she had been watching the crusade on television and had given her life to Christ. Immediately after her conversion, she had seen her son being interviewed by the pastor, saying he had given his life to the Lord. As only God could orchestrate it, both mother and son were saved simultaneously, through the same ministry, yet miles away from each other.

She somehow knew that God would give her back her son.

Jim Tolle
Former Missionary to Colombia and Argentina
Missions Director, 1996-1999

> *Thank you, Father, that you forgive your prodigal children.*
> *Bring back to yourself these that I bring before you today...*

> *"But the King replied to Araunah, 'No, I insist on paying you*
> *for it. I will not sacrifice to the Lord my God*
> *burnt offerings that cost me nothing'."*
> ### 2 SAMUEL 24:24

*A*rmenia at the time of my visit had been free from communism for nine years. The country was hard-pressed to keep the infrastructure going. So it was quite a surprise to see a church that owned a former shoe factory in a small city in the country. The building was full on a weeknight and it was a time of incredible worship, even though it was in a different language. The local television news crew was there as well as a few ex-KGB agents who asked a few questions after the service.

When I was alone with the pastor, I asked him about the church and how it functioned in a post-communist society. It was an interesting story of God's great grace and favor on a people willing to give everything they had to Him. When I asked how a struggling people could purchase a building like this and renovate part of it into a church, he shared an incredible story.

The story was a great testimony of God's power at work, but what really struck me and challenged me to the very core of my American brand of Christianity was when the pastor shared about how he had stood before the people and how he had told them of God's love, and how the property could be theirs, and how he had then asked them to bring their wedding bands and rings and present them to the Lord. When they were collected and sold, the money was used to purchase the property.

How long has it been since my offering to God has really cost me?

Glen Mickel
Former Missionary to West Africa

> *Father, help me to not hold back and to give everything to*
> *you. You are my all in all. Help me to live that way and to*
> *sacrifice whatever you ask me to give up for you...*

"Now we know that if the earthly tent we live in is destroyed,
we have a building from God, an eternal house in heaven,
not built by human hands."
2 CORINTHIANS 5:1

"I can't believe tomorrow I'll be home," were the last words my husband spoke before going home to heaven.

En route to the U. S. to "retire" after 34 years of missionary ministry in Latin America, Ed and I stopped in Honduras to attend the church convention. There our missions director, Leland Edwards, asked us, "Would you be willing to return here after a rest in the States? We have no missionary to send and, because these people say you are their 'Mamma' and 'Papa,' I know you can encourage them at this time."

Ed quickly responded, "Yes!" and I agreed.

At the end of our time in the United States, we were in Los Angeles with suitcases packed and ready to leave for the airport early the next day. To us, going to Honduras was "going home." After praying together Ed said, "I can't believe that tomorrow I'll be home." Then we slept.

At 2:00 that morning Ed suffered a massive heart attack and God called him to his heavenly home. I know he had a great welcome and heard Jesus say, "Well done, thou good and faithful servant."

My heart was filled with deep sorrow, but at the same time great rejoicing. Ten days later I did return to minister in Honduras for four years. I went without my husband, but I did not go alone. Jesus was true to His promise, "Lo, I am with you always…"

Vonitta Gurney Boylan
Former Missionary to Latin America

Father, thank you that I do have a home in heaven, and
one day I will be there with you, to remain for all eternity.
What a comfort to my heart to know you are waiting for
me there...

"I pray also that the eyes of your heart may be enlightened in order that you may know the hope to which he has called you, the riches of his glorious inheritance in the saints..."

EPHESIANS 1:18

A young lady showed up at our Sunday evening in service in Belize and sat in the front row stoically taking in everything. Regardless of what was happening in the service, her facial expression remained the same—a blank stare. Even as I delivered the message that night I could not help but wonder what kind of life this young girl must be living. She could not have been more than 16 years old, but there was a cold, hard, callous spirit emanating from her. That evening as I asked those who wanted to meet Jesus to look up and make eye contact with me, my eyes slowly made their way to her side of the room. Several people made commitments that evening but this young woman's decision to accept the Lord surprised me so much that it was difficult to concentrate as I led them through prayer.

The Bible speaks of scales falling from Saul's eyes when he met Jesus. In a similar fashion, it was evident that hardness and bitterness fell from this young girl's countenance as she received the Lord. Following the service, I learned that she was the girlfriend of the Crips gang leader I had been working with in recent months!

Her conversion is a tangible reminder of what we all know—that God can open the eyes of the most callused heart and heal the pain of the most wounded spirit. No matter whom the Holy Spirit might bring to mind, know that he or she is not too far-gone for the Lord to reach them. Bring them to Him in prayer, asking Him to open the eyes of their heart that they might see the hope of a changed life.

Jimi Calhoun
Former Missionary to Belize

Lord, help me not to judge by what I see. Nothing is impossible for you, and I ask you to change the hearts of these people...

> *"And my God will meet all your needs according to his glorious riches in Christ Jesus."*
>
> PHILIPPIANS 4:19

Lilia was the only Christian in her tribal family. Her people were animists who worshipped the trees, wooden sticks, and other items of nature. Lilia, however, had received Jesus as her Savior, and God had called her to Bible college.

During one school vacation, Lilia returned home. She shared about Jesus and many were saved and healed.

When it was time to go back to school, Lilia did not have enough fare to get all the way back to college. She reasoned, "Well, if God wants me to return to Bible college, He will provide somehow." She decided to get on the bus and go as far as her money would allow and then see what God would do.

As long as the bus was moving, the tropical breeze circulated and the heat was tolerable. However, the bus had a flat tire and things began to heat up considerably. Lilia looked in her purse for something to use as a fan. All she had were a few tracts. She soon began sharing her "fans."

"Here is something to use as a fan."

"Would you like this to fan yourself?"

Some wanted to know how much they would cost. "Oh, they are free. They tell the story of God's love and about Jesus who died for our sins." Many took the "fans" for free, but some insisted on paying her for them. Before the bus was ready to travel again, Lilia had enough money for her fare all the way back to the college.

Eloise Clarno
Former Missionary to Sri Lanka

> *Thank you, Lord, for the ingenious and faith-building ways you choose to meet my needs! Help me to continue to trust you for provision of every need...*

"...Daughter, your faith has healed you. Go in peace"
LUKE 8:48

*J*uanita, a sister from our church, called me one Sunday afternoon and asked me to come to her home and pray for her, as she was going to the hospital the next morning for surgery. The doctors had told her she had a large tumor in her stomach. We began to pray and all of a sudden she let out a little cry. I asked what was the matter and she said that it moved. She said it felt like she was pregnant and the baby had dropped into place. The next morning, just before noon, one of her sons called and said, "Pastor, I think you had better come to the hospital and hear this for yourself!"

I went and was told by the doctor that he had never seen anything like this in all his life. They had opened her up and found a highly cancerous 22-pound tumor in her stomach cavity. It had thousands of roots going in every direction. "The amazing thing," said the doctor, "is that every root had been cut and all we did was reach in and take it out. Where the roots had been cut, every one of them looked like something cauterized them and they were all dead".

The doctors sewed her up, and sent her home where she lived another 17 years, never to face that sickness again! What a mighty God we serve!

Dean Truett
Former Missionary to Honduras

Lord, you are the Great Physician. You touch our bodies and we receive the healing we need. I pray for those who need your healing touch and your peace today...

"...The Lord sets prisoners free..."
PSALM 146:7

*I*n the city named 'The Peace' resides a man called "Bear." Bear owes his nickname to the inmates of a prison in La Paz, Mexico, who knew him as the toughest, most brutal inmate the prison walls had ever kept from society.

Today, he walks in and out of those same walls as both a free and a changed man. Bear, whose real name is Roberto, came to know the reality of Jesus Christ through the prison ministry of Foursquare Missionary Jeff Whiston. Once he was saved, he used his "kingpin" status to lead dozens of fellow inmates to the Lord. Since 1987, over 1,000 inmates have come to Christ. In fact, Pastor Whiston's large church in La Paz was planted as a result of many conversions among inmates and their families.

Since his release from prison, Bear faithfully returns each Saturday to continue his growing ministry within the prison. He is a respected member of Jeff's church and it is no coincidence that he leads the security team at one of the new churches in another city.

Foursquare World ADVANCE, 1998

Father, I thank you that even though some things seem impossible, with you nothing is impossible. You can save the most resistent, hardened heart and bring the worst sinner to salvation...

"...be strong in the Lord and in the power of his might."
EPHESIANS 6:10

One evening I was asked to speak in a church in the greater Sao Paulo area. I took our 13-year-old son Danny with me. The praise and worship was rich.

Opening to my text, Ephesians 6, I began preaching about the authority we have in spiritual warfare. At the end of the service, an usher who had been stationed at the door throughout the entire service asked if he could share a brief testimony. He went on to tell us that three armed men had ascended the steps of the church during my message, with plans to shoot the man preaching and rob the nearly 300 people of all their possessions.

Having heard the message on authority, he said to the men, "In the name of Jesus, you're not coming in here!" With that, the men turned and left without further incident.

As Danny and I were starting home, I asked him if he heard and understood what the usher had just said. He had. I then asked him what we should do, thinking he would say, "Wow! Let's praise the Lord!" Instead, he said, "Wow! Let's go to McDonalds and celebrate."

Dale Downs
Former Missionary to Brazil

> *Father, I ask you to show me the spiritual authority you*
> *have given me in Christ, and that I would live victoriously*
> *through the power of your mighty indwelling Spirit...*

"He is your praise; he is your God, who performed for you those great and awesome wonders you saw with your own eyes."
DEUTERONOMY 10:21

When I was in high school, my friends and I would throw rocks at the Foursquare Church in San Cristobal, Venezuela. One time a rock struck the face of the assistant pastor while he was speaking, nearly causing the loss of an eye. In those days, evangelical believers were the objects of much scorn and mocking, and we considered it great fun.

On a Sunday evening shortly after that incident, I exited a movie theater into a heavy downpour. The only shelter was the Foursquare Church. The service had already ended, but a family in the sanctuary loaned me a rain jacket. The next morning when I returned the jacket, the family invited me to attend the service that night. On June 14, 1963, at the age of 16, I accepted Jesus Christ.

Missionaries Edgar and Darlene Coombs were my first pastors. They influenced my life in the most marvelous way. Their love and godly example taught me about God's love and acceptance.

Never did I imagine that twenty-seven years later I would be pastoring that same church which I had stoned, and that from there, I would be appointed as a Foursquare missionary.

I went from throwing stones at the church to throwing arrows of the Gospel throughout Central America. What a great wonder He performed! Praise the Lord.

Serafin Contreras
Missionary to Panama and Nicaragua

Lord, you have turned my life around! Let me never forget where I was when you rescued me from sin, and the miracles you have done in my life to bring me where I am today...

"How awesome is the Lord Most High,
the great King over all the earth!"
PSALM 47:2

*D*uring the holiday from school, two of the students from Nigerian Bible College went to Dahomey to visit some of their people. They conducted street meetings, did personal evangelism, and spoke in churches. They encountered an old man who had been sick for some time. He was a pagan and had his juju (charm) in a small gourd, which he carefully hung around his neck. He believed this juju was keeping him alive.

The students witnessed to him and explained the way of salvation and divine healing. They prayed with him and he accepted the Lord into his heart. While they were praying for his healing, he removed the juju from his neck and broke it. Instantly the Lord healed him of his sickness.

The enemy's power is so very small compared to the POWER of our Savior. Jesus saves, delivers and gives us life everlasting. What an awe-inspiring God we serve!

Audra Sowersby
Former Missionary to Africa

> *Lord, I thank you that your power is greater than all the*
> *power of the enemy. Help me to trust in your great power to*
> *deliver, save, and heal...*

"... and it came to pass, when the people heard the sound of the trumpet, and the people shouted with a great shout, that the wall fell down flat ... and they took the city."

JOSHUA 6:20 (KJV)

I asked God to "heal our sin-sick city." On March 31, members of our church set out at 2 a.m. to drive around the city, much like the Israelites did when they marched around Jericho. Three thousand people circled the city each day for six days, and then seven times on the final day. We prayed for evil to be destroyed and for the nation to be healed. Around the same time, I also rented a helicopter and anointed the city with oil.

As a result of answered prayers and the fruit from yearly crusades, the attendance of the church's five services has reached nearly 25,000. The church has some 1,200 home groups that meet weekly for spiritual teaching and discipleship. Overall, there are 3,000 leaders who make up the ministry team of La Cosecha.

Over the past several years, 28 new churches have been planted from our mother congregation. We have sent missionaries to El Salvador, Guatemala, Nicaragua, and Atlanta, Georgia, and we plan to send many more. By the end of the decade we envision 200 new Foursquare churches in Honduras and other countries in Latin America.

Misael Argenal
Pastor in Honduras

Thank you, Father for the fruitfulness of the church in Honduras. Give me and my pastor and our congregation the faith, boldness, and passion to take strong action in our spiritual warfare and in our efforts to win our city for Christ...

*"Trust in the Lord with all your heart and lean not
on your own understanding; in all your ways acknowledge him,
and he will make your paths straight."*
PROVERBS 3:5-6

We wanted to begin a church in Mexicali, the capital of Baja. We soon rented an old theater building for fifty dollars a month. The neighborhood the theater was in was very poor and overflowing with children.

Soon after we began having meetings, over one hundred children were attending! However, the building proved to be dangerous and beyond repair, so we prayed for a better building and location. A friend owned a building he would give us free of charge, but he wasn't sure if it could be used because drug addicts continually broke in and destroyed everything in the place. I said we would try.

We fixed up the building and locked it securely. When I returned a week later, my first impulse was to run—the building was a mess once again—but I said, "Praise the Lord, this is really where we belong."

We repaired the building again and a married couple moved in to make it secure. Before long, this church grew to become one of the strongest in that area.

We "belong" where God's will takes us. Sometimes the enemy will try to discourage us from that place, but remember God's power far outweighs the enemy's schemes. Trust God and He will lead you.

Ludwig Manthei
Former Missionary to Mexico

*Lord, I do trust in your leading. Help me to know where
you want me to go today, and keep me from giving in to
any discouragement...*

"You must accept whatever situation the Lord has put you in, and continue on as you were when God first called you."

1 CORINTHIANS 7:17

*W*hy is it when you are hoping everything will go well, everything seems to fall apart?

Foursquare President Dr. Rolf K. McPherson came to visit us at our convention. It was an important occasion—the missionary had resigned as chairman of the National Board and a Korean had been installed. Now the co-pastor with whom we had started a church assumed full responsibility for that church. Those were happy months.

We hosted Dr. McPherson during his time in Korea. As we were on our way to the convention in the city of Taejon, the muffler and tail pipe of the mission van we were driving fell off. Dr. McPherson took this in stride.

Once in Taejon, we had the responsibility of shuttling our guest from the convention site to his hotel. Wouldn't you know it, the electrical system in the van shorted out, and our headlights would not work for the twenty minute ride between the hotel and the convention. My heart was in my throat as we drove slowly down the dark road from Taejon to the neighboring community. At least the roar of our muffler-less van alerted the people on the road that we were coming!

There is no answer to our question—we really don't know why things seem to "fall apart." But we must learn to continue on in all situations knowing God is in control…learning to be flexible, keeping our sense of humor and most importantly trusting our God!

Ron and Charlotte Meyers
Former Missionaries to Korea

Lord, thank you for being in control of every situation. I ask you to keep me from the need to control my own life. Help me to surrender each day to you…

*"Your right hand, O Lord, was majestic in power.
Your right hand, O Lord, shattered the enemy."*

EXODUS 15:6

While my husband, Elmer, and I, along with our children Jim and Joan and a Nicaraguan pastor by the name of Elmo, were ministering in a village, I overheard two men saying they were going to kill the men and take Joan and me with them.

I did not say anything, but during the service kept Joan close to me and purposefully stood in front of these men. When they moved, we moved. After the service we began the seven mile walk to our car.

Some of the people accompanied us for a short while and then returned to the village. When I stopped to get some dirt out of my shoes, Jim told me to hurry on; there were several men with machetes following us. We reached the car and returned to Managua.

About a month later when we returned to the village, we were astonished when a man gifted us with a beautifully carved cup. The man told us that when we had visited the last time, he and several other men had planned to kill us. They followed us on the trail, and when the Christians returned to the village, they knew this was their chance. They were almost upon us when a large curtain descended and they couldn't see us. When the curtain left, we were far ahead. They ran to try again, but the curtain came down again. When they saw us again, we were in the car.

The man explained, "As we walked back to the village we began talking among ourselves. What did the missionary's God have that we didn't have? We decided to go to the home of the Christians to ask them."

As a result, these men accepted Jesus as their Savior. Our enemy had become our brother.

Marjorie McCammon
Former Missionary to Latin America

*Thank you, Lord, that you frustrate the enemy's plans!
Continue to protect us and show us the schemes of Satan...*

> *"But just as you excel in everything...see that you*
> *also excel in this grace of giving."*
>
> 2 CORINTHIANS 8:7

One great influence on us in the eight years we spent in Chile was the UFW (United Foursquare Women, now known as FWI).

All the missionaries had the wonderful opportunity of "shopping" at the Alabaster House before going overseas. It cost nothing, because everything we "bought" had been paid for and donated by the women in Foursquare churches throughout the United States. We took linens, small household appliances, personal items, and all kinds of ministry aids. We were very blessed

As we recounted the story of the investment that UFW had made in us, we began to see it produce a desire in the women of Chile to invest in the ministries of their own nation. Instead of looking elsewhere when there was a need, the Chilean ladies' groups began to catch the vision of God as their Provider and that He might want to use them to bless others.

At this same time, there was a young pastor and his family who lived in southern Chile and walked five hours from their home to the outstations where he preached. As these women became aware of the pastor's ministry, they caught a vision to provide a vehicle for him. Through various projects, they raised the needed money in a very short time. At our annual convention, they presented a Suzuki van to the pastor and his family.

Thank you, Foursquare women around the world, for your giving has inspired others to do the same—to give!

Glen Pummel
Former Missionary to Chile

> *Lord, use me today to give to others, especially to advance*
> *your kingdom around the world...*

"I will declare your name ... in the presence of the congregation I will sing your praises."

HEBREWS 2:12

*I*n the warm climate of Papua New Guinea, our church meets under a tent awning without walls. During a recent Saturday night youth service, a young man came in through the side of the church. He was holding a large knife up as if he were about to attack one of our young people. Chris, a 16-year-old boy, walked straight over to the man, put his arms around him and hugged him! Then, in the midst of all the confusion, he began to minister the love of Jesus to this man.

To our amazement, the attacker burst into tears and dropped his knife. Chris led him to a seat in the church. The man was shirtless, so one of our young men took his off and put it on the weeping man. At the end of our meeting, the would-be attacker came forward, tears running down his face, and gave his life to Jesus Christ.

Later, I reminded the youth that we had dedicated this land to the Lord before we ever started using it. No wonder this man could not harm us. With prayer, praise, and pots of oil we had walked the land, anointing it and declaring that the name of Jesus is powerful!

Bill Page
Missionary Pastor in Papua New Guinea

> *O Lord, your name is so powerful. I know that no weapon formed against me will prosper, and that you will protect your children who call upon your name...*

*"By day the Lord went ahead of them in a pillar of cloud
to guide them on their way and by night in a pillar of fire
to give them light, so that they could travel by day or night."*

EXODUS 13:21

The FARC is Colombia's most powerful and violent guerilla group. While we were pastoring in Villavicenico, the nation's constitution was being rewritten there, and the FARC had not been invited into the process. In their anger they targeted Villavicenico, and their tactic was to block the only road that connected us with Bogota and dynamite the power towers that brought our electricity. This repeatedly plunged us into darkness and left us isolated.

As Kathy was expecting our first child, we wrestled with safety issues and finally decided to fly to Bogota a month before her due date. Then the FARC began bombing landing strips in cities throughout Colombia. If they were to do that in Villavicencio, we would be completely isolated, with inadequate medical help in case of complications. We knew we need-ed to return to Bogota.

The topic for my last sermon in Villavicencio was on the way God guided Israel with a cloud by day and a pillar of fire by night. The day we left for the bus station was a beautiful blue-sky day, except for one puffy, white cloud—right over the only road to Bogota. God is faithful to lead his people. Even when it seems there is no way…He always makes a way!

Dennis and Kathy Pendergast
Missionaries to Mexico

*Lord, I thank you for your guidance in my life. You have
shown me the way so many times when I did not know
which way to turn. I ask you to always show me the right
paths…*

"Therefore, as God's chosen people... clothe yourselves with compassion, kindness, humility, gentleness and patience."

COLOSSIANS 3:12

It was quite an event when the Hughes family moved from our native hut into the timber house with tap water caught in a galvanized tank! We even had a full bathroom, so there were no more long walks down the path. Several hundred New Guineans surrounded the house daily to see all the strange things this white family did.

One day a new face appeared. Mason talked with Fake and discovered he had walked several mountain ranges to see this "white family." Mason told him if he wanted to spend the night with some of the workers, he would give him a ride tomorrow when he went to town.

Fake was ready early, excited to ride in a vehicle for the first time. As they neared Fake's path, Mason looked in the mirror to see Fake standing and walking off the back of the truck. At 10 miles an hour, Mason could stop quickly. Fake was stunned; he did not know he could not jump from a moving vehicle.

Mason wiped his wounds and tied his white handkerchief around Fake's head. Fake refused to go to the town for medical help and started up his mountain path.

On his way back home that afternoon, Mason stopped in a village for a scheduled service. There were more people than usual at this service under the bamboo. As he checked out the faces, he saw his white handkerchief. Fake had told his village about this kind white man. They wanted to see him for themselves.

That day Fake's village heard about Jesus for the first time and they all accepted Jesus as their Savior.

Mason and Virgene Hughes
Former Missionaries to Papua New Guinea

Thank you, Father, that kind words and acts of compassion cross cultural barriers. Help me to preach the gospel today, not just with words but with acts of compassion...

*"Each one should use whatever gift he
has received to serve others..."*

1 PETER 4:10

A medical and evangelism team from the Church On The Way in Van Nuys, California, traveled to Roung Kho, Cambodia, to minister to the impoverished people of Cambodia. Each day the team had to close the gate to the makeshift medical clinic at around 11 a.m. because the tent that served as a waiting room was already full with more than 500 people. While the people waited for medical treatment, the evangelism team ministered the Gospel to them though worship, drama, puppets, literature, and words of hope and encouragement.

Rev. Phil Star, who led the team, reports that, "More than 3,000 men, women and children made decisions for Jesus in the waiting room and another 1,500 came to Christ through ministry opportunities at the gate, where we were praying for people and ministering to the people we had to turn away."

God loves to bring deliverance, healing and wholeness to a hopeless world. He uses the gifts of His people, people like you and me, who are willing to serve Him and others to see this blessed task accomplished!

Global REPORT, 2000

*Help me today, Lord, to use the skills and gifts you have
given me to serve others and to bring glory to you...*

"...choose for yourselves this day whom you will serve..."
JOSHUA 24:15

Every new missionary faces the challenge of learning the local language, but often God uses this challenge to reach people for Him.

Baboo was our teacher who taught us Malaysian. Although from a Catholic family, he was quite involved in Hinduism. In his home was a shelf filled with idols.

Over the week as we talked with them, Baboo and his wife confessed faith in Jesus Christ. As they began to read the Bible and attend church regularly, they grew tremendously, but did not remove the idol altar from their home. We encouraged Baboo to "learn to listen to his heart and do what God says."

Baboo and his wife moved to the other side of Penang Island, and we didn't hear from him for several months until he called to ask if we could come to dedicate his new house to the Lord. Michael hesitated, knowing he could not do that with an idol altar in the house, but decided to go anyhow, trusting God for wisdom.

When Michael arrived, he asked about the idol altar. Baboo said he had remembered him telling him to "listen to his heart and obey," and that his heart did not want the idols in their home, so they were gone!

What a blessing to see Baboo and his family walk through each room of their home, dedicating it to the Lord while quoting Joshua 24:15.

Michael and Jannie Stubbs
Missionaries to Malaysia

> *Lord, this day I want to serve you! I pray that my entire family would serve you. Remove any idolatrous thoughts from our hearts...*

"*The harvest is plentiful...*"
LUKE 10:2

After the morning service, a new convert said he had arranged for some of his friends to be at his house in the barrio that afternoon to hear the Gospel. Another young man, Don, said some of his university friends were at the beach and were waiting to hear about the Lord too. Somehow it was decided that I would first go to the barrio and then to the beach.

Sunday afternoons in the barrio can be festive and this day was no exception. Some were drinking tuba (coconut wine); there was shouting and laughter, along with the noise of many children, dogs and pigs. The little house was very hot and crowded with people. As soon as I sat down, a young man began questioning me about "religion." He was quite agnostic. The Lord gave me answers and patience. A drunken woman wandered in and out of the house, talking very loudly. I continued to bring the conversation back to the need of a new birth and the promise of a new life. Finally, after an hour and a half, I asked who would like to be born again. The first to respond was the young agnostic. Five prayed to receive Jesus as Savior.

When I finally arrived at the beach, Don and the students were sitting under a coconut tree, enjoying the sea breeze and having a wonderful discussion about the Lord. All six of them received Jesus!

It was a wonderful, fruitful afternoon and my feeling was "I was made for this."

Sharon Nicholson
Former Missionary to the Philippines

Lord, thank you that I function best as I do your will. Open my eyes to the ministry opportunities all around me, and let me be one of the workers in your harvest field...

"You show that you are a letter from Christ...written not with ink but with the Spirit of the living God, not on tablets of stone but on tablets of human hearts."

2 CORINTHIANS 3:3

Sometimes on the mission field or in other ministry situations the Lord will teach us a deeper meaning to some of our favorite Scriptures. In my case, it was 1 Peter 3:15, which has always been a favorite scripture of mine: "...and if you are asked about your Christian hope, always be ready to explain it."(NLT) In my limited thinking, I reasoned that this meant I should be able to put in words what I believe. I thought I should be able to explain it and debate it and convince people through my pursuasive arguments. On the mission field, though, I realized that the real power was in living it rather than explaining it.

For example, while traveling to the Middle East, I realized that Christians living there were often unable to put what they believe into words, for to do so could cost them their lives. As I observed my brothers and sisters who live where it is against the law to preach the Gospel, I saw the clarity of the Good News through their living. Words could never explain the love and sacrifice I saw lived out in the daily routine. Their Christianity was not hidden, it was respected. Why? Because the original purpose of God in man's lives was real to them – they lived the reality. They were living books, read and known by all men.

Glen Mickel
Former Missionary to West Africa

Help me, Lord, to use fewer words and more deeds to show you to those around me...

> *"By this all men will know that you are my disciples,*
> *if you love one another."*
>
> JOHN 13:35

*H*uern lived in the jungle outside the village of AnLong Veng with his four children. His wife had died of malaria and now he was sick and unable to work. Every day his children came into the village to beg for their survival.

The local medical clinic had sent the man away, telling him they could no longer help him and that he would die soon. He had no close relatives and no one wanted the children. We arranged for Huern and his children to board at the orphanage temporarily.

When I saw the man, I realized why there was doubt that he could even make the trip to the orphanage. He was six feet tall and weighed about 70 pounds. His pain was not just physical; he ached because of the past and the way he had to raise his children. Now, seeing the orphanage where his children would be taken care of when he died, he cried for joy.

Pastor Daniel and I prayed with him to receive Jesus into his heart. He accepted Jesus, thankful for both his salvation and the security of knowing his children would be sheltered. A few weeks later we prayed together for the last time. The next morning he died.

The last weeks of his life Huern had been surrounded by people that showed him love. He lived in a safe place and was released from concern about his children. Huern's children will be raised by people who love them and they will know Jesus.

Don Matteson
Missions Teams Specialist, Cambodia

Lord, may I show your redemptive love to everyone I come
in contact with today...

"Then will the eyes of the blind be opened..."
ISAIAH 35:5

Our team paddled in dugout wooden canoes to reach the many villages hidden in the dense foliage along the tributaries of the Amazon River. In village after village we would worship, preach, and then pray for the sick. There was an amazing anointing for healing. Deaf ears, bad backs, heart problems, toothaches and tumors were healed, to list just a few of the instantaneous miracles.

When word got out among the villages that the Americans were coming, and that they brought healing from God, we were inundated with offers to come. One lady had a special request and I was told to go alone with my interpreter to pray for her. I learned she was blind in one eye. When I arrived to her home, it was obvious that her left eye was completely swollen shut and infected. After laying hands on her, we noticed a progressive improvement until finally after about 45 minutes of prayer her eye was completely open and normal. We tested her eyesight, which was perfect.

Our rejoicing was short-lived, however, when she told us that it was her right eye that was blind, not the left one! Could we pray for the other eye? After regrouping our faith, we prayed for her right eye until it too was totally healed.

Needless to say, it was a miracle I will never forget!

Robert Hunt
Director of Foursquare Missions Press/FMI Communications Coordinator

Lord, may we contend in faith to see people completely healed of their afflictions for your glory!

> *"So what shall I do? I will pray with my spirit,*
> *but I will also pray with my mind..."*
>
> 1 CORINTHIANS 14:15

*C*hile was under a dictatorship when we lived there. We lived through blackouts, 10:00 p.m. curfews, demonstrations, random military roadblocks (complete with machine guns!), tear gas at the public pool, bombs in the mall, military personnel swarming the house near us, and days when American citizens needed to stay home.

During the transition to democracy we lived in the capital city of Santiago. As a couple, we would quietly slip out of the house early in the morning and have prayer walks around our lower middle class neighborhood. Among other things, we prayed for the people in the homes we were passing by, believing for their salvation.

A new president was elected, and Chileans were joyous and celebrative. While listening to the news, we realized the president lived along one of our prayer routes. The next morning we took that route that led by the house of our now famous neighbor. Military stood guard, easily marking his house. I must admit there was a bit more of an edge to our prayers.

Many times when we pray we have no idea for whom it is that we could be praying. Stan and I had no idea we were praying for the president of Chile—but God knew!

Molly Doland
Missionary to Spain

> *Thank you, Father, that you lead me as I pray and even*
> *answer prayers in ways I could not even imagine. I lift before*
> *you now the things you have placed on my heart today...*

"Commit your way to the Lord; trust in him..."
PSALM 37:5

During our first six months in the Philippines, we faced one of the greatest trials of our entire ministry. As we prepared to move from Manila to Odiongan, a town with no electricity, running water, or telephones—tests confirmed that our one-year-old son had tuberculosis. Our family doctor suspected our older son also had the disease. Because Odiongan had only limited medical facilities, the doctor advised us not to move our children there.

Of course, we shed many tears and spent much time in prayer. Should we go where we felt God was calling us? Should we follow the doctor's advice? Should we return to the United States? The Lord spoke to our hearts and assured us that, if we were willing to go where He wanted us to go, He would take care of our children. We chose to go to Odiongan.

We were told our boys would need medication for 12 to 18 months and that their lungs would always have scar tissue. Nine months later, when we took our sons for check-ups, neither showed any trace of tuberculosis. The report came back, "Completely healed!" When our doctor saw what had happened, he received Jesus as his Savior.

Today one of our sons is a pilot and routinely passes the top-level medical exams. There is no trace of scar tissue. What an amazing God we serve! We truly can trust Him!

Gary Loop
Former Missionary to the Philippines

Thank you, Father, that as I commit my ways to you and trust in you, you will take care of me...

> *"You are the God who performs miracles; you display*
> *your power among the peoples."*
> PSALM 77:14

*I*n the Lahu Village of Ja Chu Shi, an hour and a half walk from the nearest roads, a miracle has taken place. There was a two-year-old boy with a bulge in his right eye. His parents were told by the medical doctors that there was no hope for him to ever use that eye, and the witch doctors were also unsuccessful in healing him. They tried all sorts of methods and rituals, all to no avail. I was filled with compassion the first time I saw him.

The villagers had never heard of Jesus and did not know of the power of the Gospel, so I decided to challenge the father. I said to him, "If my God can heal his eye will you accept Him, Jesus, as your personal Savior and Lord?" He accepted the challenge; we laid hands on the child and prayed for him. Then we removed the strings and tokens that he was wearing, which were given to him by the witch doctors.

When we returned on February 15, the eye was completely healed. The boy could see with it, and he was acting like a normal two year old—running around, laughing and jumping, happy. Now the father wants the whole family to believe in Jesus. The rest of the village saw the miracle, and now they also are ready to believe in Jesus. Praise the Lord!

Timothy Tang
Foursquare Pastor, Singapore

> *I thank you, Lord Jesus, for your miraculous power. Display*
> *your power in my life today and in these situations I bring*
> *before you now...*

"For the kingdom of God is not a matter of talk but of power."

1 CORINTHIANS 4:20

The following comes from e-mail from Jerry and Betty when they were serving as missionaries in Haiti in 1999:

"God is moving in Haiti! There is a hunger for the truth of God. During recent healing meetings, many have come to know the Lord through the ministry of deliverance and healing.

"The church is full of people; there's not even standing room outside of the church. Recently a mute child was healed and is now able to speak. Another lady was healed of her elephantiasis. Many demon-possessed people (who were loudly telling the pastors and leaders, "Don't look at me!") were delivered and set free. The church has three services on Sunday and every day through the week there is something happening there.

"Praise the Lord! The Kingdom of God is at hand!"

Jerry and Betty Poppe
Former Missionaries to Haiti

Thank you, Lord, that the kingdom of God is not a matter of talk but of power. When your reign comes upon people, lives are changed as people are healed and set free. May your kingdom come and your will be done in these people and situations that I bring before you today...

"...for your Father knows what you need before you ask him."
MATTHEW 6:8

Throughout the years, mission teams have ministered in nearly every country where we have a Foursquare church. And their ministries have been many and varied. In fact, when anyone signs up for a ministry team and prepares to go, they never know how they might minister.

In August 2000, a team of 39 youth arrived in Santo Domingo to help evangelize the youth of our city. Our hopes were high, and everything was planned. Then Darla came down with dengue fever. She had suffered with a high fever for four days when I came home sick with salmonella poisoning.

On Sunday morning, as the visiting team conducted the special children's program at a nearby church, the missionaries weren't there to help—we had both checked into the hospital. Thankfully, this team was well trained and knew exactly what to do. Their ministry never missed a beat. Children's programs in the park grew. The coffee house ministry in the evenings continued for the rest of the week.

After three days, I was released from the hospital. A precious Dominican prayer warrior stayed in the hospital with Darla that third night, and the next day the team members walked the halls praying for the sick and interceding for Darla. Her white blood cell count jumped up dramatically that night, and she was released to go home the next day.

During those days, 300 people accepted Jesus as their Savior. That team ministered to all of us in an extraordinary way that week. God knew exactly who to send!

Charlie Finocchiaro
Missionary to the Dominican Republic

Thank you, Father, that you know what we need even before we ask you, and you have everything under control. Help me to walk in that understanding, full of your peace and looking to you in all things...

> *"...I will deliver you, and you will honor me."*
> PSALM 50:15

"Here comes the devil!" the children cried, referring to their demonized father as he returned home each night to the mud hut they called home. His days were spent wandering aimlessly around the Transkei hillside, clothed in nothing but a blanket. While he was asleep one night, he was awakened with the words of a hymn playing over and over in his mind. He immediately got up, found the hymn, and even though he was both illiterate and uneducated, he miraculously began to read the words of the song. That night, the Holy Spirit touched him and he received Christ and was delivered of the demons that possessed him. From that day on, he honored the Lord with his life.

This man is now is the owner of two small stores and he also pastors two Foursquare churches in a rural area of the Eastern Cape province of South Africa. Although this man, Pastor John Goni, is still unable to write his name, he can read the Bible and a hymnal. His children also attend our private Christian school in Willowvale. Truly our God is a God of miracles!

Howard and Terry Manthe
Missionaries to South Africa

Lord, you have given us every ability and talent we possess. May we in turn give them back to you in service, bringing honor to you...

"The Lord will protect him and preserve his life..."
PSALM 41:2

"Mom! Gabe's been bitten by a snake."

Matthew was breathless with this heart-stopping news of his twin's calamity. We had been in Nigeria a year, living on the rural campus of L.I.F.E. Bible College just outside Lagos. The college students had warned our sons about going barefoot, but Matt and Gabe were 10 and rambunctious.

We examined the fang marks; the skin had been pierced only slightly. A visit to the town doctor wasn't helpful. He didn't know the snakes in those parts and didn't have snake serum anyway.

We kept the snake in the freezer that night and prayed fervently, waiting until the next day to go to a church attended by many missionaries. We took the freezer baggy, knowing that one of the missionaries was a "snake expert." He peered at the snake over his nose-perched glasses and then looked up at us.

"Yes, this is a highly poisonous snake," he replied. "But this is a baby snake and your son's toe was too big. This snake has its poisonous fangs at the back of its throat rather than in the front teeth. Had the snake been bigger or your son's toe smaller, you would have had a different ending to this story."

Kathy Kieselhorst
Former Missionary to Nigeria, now serving with her husband, Bill, in South Africa

Lord, I exalt you today for your mighty power, your ability to protect and watch over me...

"In my distress I called to the Lord; I cried to my God for help.
From his temple he heard my voice;
my cry came before him, into his ears."

PSALM 18:6

Taking our children with us to the mission field means an added commitment from them as well as from us. Our children were a blessing to us as we served overseas. At the same time, we faced the same challenges other parents face, such as when Juliana, our fourth child, nearly died.

We were in Papua New Guinea when Juliana became sick. Her fever soared; she fainted, and became convulsive. Our response, along with intensive prayer, was to bathe her in cool water to try to get the fever down. As we worked with her, she stopped breathing and turned blue.

We sent for Angelita Lagasca, a missionary from the Philippines who was working with us, to come and join us in prayer. As we interceded for Juliana, we tried artificial respiration and mouth-to-mouth resuscitation, but nothing helped. We began examining our hearts. "Lord, if this is a test of our commitment to you calling us here, then know we will not give up. We are committed to the work you have given us to do."

The Lord answered, "This is not my doing!" Then we knew this was an attack from the enemy. With fervor we demanded, "Satan and death, we bind you in the name of Jesus! Take your hands off our daughter!"

Juliana started breathing; her color came back. She opened her eyes and began to cry. We put her in bed, rejoicing over the power of God over the enemy.

Phil and Diane Franklin
Former Missionaries to Papua New Guinea

Lord, I will call out to you. Rescue me in my troubles; come
and deliver me from the evil one...

"And we know that in all things God works for the good of those who love him, who have been called according to his purpose."

ROMANS 8:28

Piro Poga, affectionately known as Pipo, has been with us from the opening of the Stephen Center in 1994. He worked as our general maintenance man. He was driving our van when he was involved in a head-on collision with a truck, leaving him in critical condition with multiple fractures and trauma. The doctors said they had done everything they could to help him, but he was in shock and had lost a considerable amount of blood from the open wound in his leg. It appeared to us that he would not survive.

Pipo was never a particularly religious person and had often been a concern to us. He had suffered financial losses during the crisis in Albania in 1997 and had not fully recovered emotionally. Mistrust and cynicism had become a part of him and we knew he needed healing in these areas.

Now to survive physically, he needed emergency surgery and blood transfusions. We were able to secure a Greek visa for him and his wife, Gani, and they was transported to Thessalonica, Greece, for several surgeries. In the end, his life was spared, but his left leg had been removed. Throughout this ordeal, Pipo was sure God was at work in keeping him alive and he gave Jesus the glory.

The transformation in Pipo can only be called miraculous. He is a new man and gives God all the praise. He knows he owes his life to Him.

Chris and Laura Dakas
Missionary to Albania

> *Father, help us to see the events of our lives through your eyes and to trust you to bring something good out of even the worst circumstances...*

"Where is your faith?"

LUKE 8:25

As soon as I stepped into the small room, I was aware of a strong spiritual presence. Pastor Nathaniel and I had driven to the village of Wasa Afransie and stopped at a particular house to, as he put it, "pray for a certain sister."

We arrived at Christina Ntore's house to discover her lying on the floor. One of her legs was swollen about twice the normal size and the foot and toes had turned a dark black color, and were beginning to open from the pressure of the swelling. I was shocked. It looked like gangrene. Many relatives and friends filled the room; they came to see what we would do. Sweat was pouring off my face and ran into my eyes.

Pastor Nathaniel and I began to pray, and after many hours of worship and prayer we felt a spiritual bondage break. Then Pastor Nathaniel insisted that the girl travel to his home. I couldn't believe what he was saying! She was not in any condition to travel, but she returned with us. Two days later, Christina's leg was looking even worse. Huge pockets of fluid appeared on the surface. Every time I questioned Nathaniel, he would simply smile and say, "Oh, she will be healed!"

I must confess I wasn't so sure. On the third day, though, the swelling went down and after two more days she was walking! Within one week Christina's leg was normal and she was completely healed!

Greg Fisher
Missionary to Uganda

Father, give me faith to believe for miracles. I confess that I sometimes lack faith and have a hard time trusting you. Open my eyes to see your power at work in the lives of people around me...

"For I consider that the sufferings of this present time are not worthy to be compared with the glory which shall be revealed in us."

ROMANS 8:18 (NKJV)

lmer and I had been through a severe storm in a small boat to get to an island off the shore of Chile where we went only once a year to minister. In addition to the regular service, we dedicated babies, and had a memorial service for those who had died since we were last there. It had been a long day.

When the service ended about 11:00 p.m., we were bone tired and still had to walk about a mile to the home where we would spend the night. Just as we were about to leave, some Christians from the other side of the island arrived. They were excited, "Pastor, we had to work in the potato fields before walking many hours to get here. Can't you tell us just a little more about Jesus?" Elmer looked at them and said, "Why, yes, we were just getting ready for the next service. Come right in."

That service ended about 2:30 a.m. But they were so happy. At the conclusion of the service, we saw a sight that will remain with us the rest of our lives. We noticed that some of their feet were already cut from walking, and some people had old tires cut and wrapped around their feet. They hadn't said a word about their tired bodies or hurting feet, but went off to return home, singing, "Where He Leads Me, I Will Follow." They had not complained; they were just happy to hear about Jesus once more.

Marjorie McCammon
Former Missionary to Latin America

Father, help me to endure sufferings with great joy as I follow you today. Thank you for the glorious inheritance that awaits me in Christ Jesus, and help me to share it with others...

"Even a fool seems wise if he doesn't open his mouth."
PROVERBS 29:11

During the height of the civil uprising in 1997-1998, we had very little food coming into the country. I decided to bring in a load of supplies from Greece.

After loading our van I started my return to Tirana. When I reached the border I was confronted by a young Albanian customs agent. He was adamant that I should pay tax for these supplies even after I identified myself as the director of the Stephen Center, a non-profit organization with tax-exempt status.

At a point of frustration and after discussions with other customs agents, I turned to the young man and said in Albanian, "You are acting like a child and I am embarrassed for you." In my frustration, and because "child" (chuni) and "dog" (cheni) are similar sounding words in Albanian, I mistakenly called him "a little dog" and said I was ashamed to be speaking to him. He became furious and informed me that now I would not be allowed to enter with the supplies under any conditions!

I left my van and took a taxi to Korce to bring Pastor Cimi back with me. By God's grace, he was related to the young customs agent. After much discussion and sincere apologies on my part, he let us pass without paying the tax.

The above Proverb weighs heavy on my heart whenever I am about to speak in anger. Although I still make mistakes, I am working to keep in mind the wisdom of the Bible.

Chris Dakas
Missionary to Albania

Father, help me to keep a tight reign on my tongue today and everyday. Let me use it to praise you and encourage others. Keep me from doing evil and causing pain to you and others by the things I say...

> *"The strong right arm of the Lord is raised in triumph. The strong right arm of the Lord has done glorious things!"*
>
> PSALM 118:16 (NLT)

*A*rlene was brought to the Foursquare church in Novaliches, Philippines, on a Sunday morning by her friend Angie. Arlene needed the Lord to bring freedom to her life—she had been tormented by many demons. She seemed fine in the beginning of the church service, but when the worship began she started screaming. The demons wanted to bring attention to themselves and disturb the service. The pastor requested the deacons and elders to bring her to the parsonage. While the guest minister spoke to the congregation, the pastor ministered to Arlene. He rebuked the demons in the name of our Lord Jesus.

Prayer lasted from 8:00 a.m. to 3:00 p.m., and one by one the demons left as the pastor and others prayed. But two of the demons were very stubborn until finally the Holy Spirit gave wisdom to the pastor to ask the parents of Arlene if they had idols in their house. The parents said, "Yes, we have several." The pastor requested that they send for those idols.

The idols represented lust, greed, hate anger, immorality and pride. When every idol was rebuked, cast out and bound in the name of Jesus Christ, Arlene was totally delivered and set free. The idols were broken to pieces and burned in the name of Jesus. That day Arlene was delivered and her family came to know Jesus as their personal Savior.

Once again, the Lord is triumphant! And once again we were reminded that we serve a loving and powerful savior who does glorious things!

Derly Suan
Foursquare Philippines

Thank you, Lord, that you are triumphant in my life and in the lives of others. I give glory to you now as I look for victory in these situations...

"And pray in the Spirit on all occasions with all kinds of prayers and requests. With this in mind, be alert and always keep on praying for all the saints."

EPHESIANS 6:18

Some years ago while we were missionaries in Okinawa, a pastor wrote us from America saying that a new lady convert in his church was awakened by the Lord to pray for the safety of Jack Francey in Okinawa. She asked her pastor if he knew someone by that name and he told her that he was a Foursquare missionary there.

I knew why God had awakened her that night—I was going around the village by car, announcing our upcoming tent meeting with a loudspeaker, when suddenly a mentally crazed woman came to the car and began throwing huge rocks, hitting the windows and windshield.

Miraculously, nothing was broken and I was safe. I believe it was because a lady back in the USA was obedient and prayed for me, a missionary whom she had never met before!

Jack Francey
Former Missionary to Japan

Father, help me to be sensitive to the leading of your Spirit, and to pray and obey even when I don't completely understand the whole picture...help me to remember the power of prayer, and to simply walk in obedience, praying and doing my part and trusting you to use it for your glory...

"Believe in the Lord Jesus, and you will be saved—
you and your household."

ACTS 16:31

"Jesus' tomb is empty; Mohammed's is not. Jesus rose from the dead; Mohammed is still buried in Mecca!"

These were the words of the evangelist who had come to my town. I had gone simply to hear the music; as a Muslim seminary student, I was not allowed more. But as I listened to the words, the Holy Spirit convicted me of my sin. I wanted to respond, but was afraid of what my brother would do. The next day, when the altar call was given, I went forward to receive Christ as my Savior. Jesus did what Mohammed could never do; He gave me peace in my heart.

As with most Muslim families, when one member becomes a Christian, the family excommunicates that one. My letter to my parents, telling them of my conversion, was not answered. My brothers, charging me with changing from the religion of our forefathers, told me we could no longer live together. Without family finances, I had to drop out of school.

After a year I returned to visit my parents. They were happy to see me, though unhappy about my faith. For four days, I tried to explain the reason for my belief in Jesus Christ. My father listened; my mother was angry. They tried to change my mind. I continued to pray about our relationship and their salvation.

I thank God that my grandfather accepted a Bible and began reading it. One of my brothers who originally expelled me from home received Christ. One by one they are beginning to discover the One whose tomb is empty and is alive even today!

Pastor G. Mposa
Foursquare Pastor in Malawi

> *Lord, I pray for those in the Muslim world. May your Holy*
> *Spirit speak to their hearts about Jesus Christ and His*
> *power to take away their sins...*

"Is any one of you sick? He should call the elders of the church to pray over him and anoint him with oil in the name of the Lord. And the prayer offered in faith will make the sick person well; the Lord will raise him up."

JAMES 5:14-15

My husband, Ed, felt strongly about anointing the sick with oil as we prayed for them. So that is what we did as we began the ministry in Honduras.

The Foursquare work in Tegucigalpa, Honduras, started with a two-week evangelistic campaign led by Claude Updike. Hundreds were saved and healed and we witnessed signs and wonders, so much so that some of the local doctors became concerned about what "remedies" we were using.

As Ed and I continued the work, finally moving into a rented mission hall, some of the doctors came to talk with us. "Do you have a medical license?" "What are you rubbing on their head?" "How do you explain all these happenings?" It was all so new to these men; they had never seen anything like it.

After Ed patiently explained the Biblical teaching about this, they asked him not to continue using oil. But of course he could still pray for people, as there was religious liberty in their country. Ed happily complied but said, "With oil or without oil, Jesus heals."

Through the years we were able to once again use oil in praying for the sick. And the Lord continued to bless and multiply the believers in that country.

Vonitta Gurney Boylan
Former Missionary to Latin America

Lord, I thank you for the many promises you have given to me regarding healing. Today I bring to you those who need your healing touch today...

*"O Lord, you will keep us safe
and protect us from such people forever."*

PSALM 12:7

The civil war in Sri Lanka has pitted the Sri Lankan armed forces against the terrorists. The jungle is often the battlefield.

In the eastern part of this nation there are many Foursquare churches in cities, villages and even jungle areas. One such jungle church is pastored by two young women. When they first arrived to pastor this church, it was in a safe zone. Over the years, the war came closer until the army camp was on one side of the church with the rebel camp on the other. Often the battle literally raged over them.

Because of the danger, their district supervisor advised them to leave that area. Their response was, "No. God has called us here and He will protect us." However, at the suggestion of the local police, they wore a "uniform" which identified them as clergy.

One night the sleeping pastors were awakened to laughter and loud pounding on their door. Scurrying to dress, they put on their clerical garb before opening the door. A small group of soldiers stood there, obviously bent on having a good time. Suddenly their attitude changed. One man exclaimed, "Sisters, be careful!" and warned them that rebels were wandering in the jungle. With that, they left.

That night several people were killed or wounded in the surrounding area.

Eloise Clarno
Former Missionary to Sri Lanka

*Thank you Lord, for your protection in my life, and in the
lives of all those who serve you...*

"The one who calls you is faithful and he will do it."
1 THESSALONIANS 5:24

Shortly after being saved, I realized my heart was drawn towards overseas ministry. Ours was an independent church and we had no mission board. I was a single mom with a 15-year old son, and things did not look very encouraging. But God had put this calling on my heart.

My pastor suggested we contact Arthur Edwards, who was a Foursquare missionary in Panama. The warm response came back—they would be glad to have us come.

Harold and I left Charlotte by train for New Orleans where we would take a United Fruit Company ship to Panama. The New Orleans dock workers went on strike, and the delay was not only frustrating, but potentially very expensive. We checked into a hotel and waited. On the weekend, I called the Foursquare Church in New Orleans which was being pastored by Rev. and Mrs. Paul White. Rev. White came and picked us up and to took us to the service. He and his wife seemed pleased to have us play the piano and accordion; we were able to support them at a difficult, struggling time. They insisted we check out of the hotel and stay with them. God allowed us to bless each other. And the small congregation responded by bringing in food for us all.

The strike finally ended and God was about to perform another miracle. On our ship was the man in charge of customs in Panama. We became acquainted with him and, upon arrival in Panama, we showed our papers with his signature and entered duty free. Our God is faithful!

Mary Barkley
Former Missionary to Panama

Lord, you will help me accomplish the tasks you have given me to do. Help me to lean upon you and walk in your will...

"Now may our Lord Jesus Christ . . . comfort your hearts . ."
2 THESSALONIANS 2:16-17 (NKJV)

My husband Edgar was killed in a terrible auto accident in Zambia while I was visiting in the US. After the accident, my daughter Vonnie and I returned to settle our affairs and bring back the things I wanted to keep.

The hardest part of all of that was his office. Everything was as he had left it—the calendar had all his appointments for the weeks ahead, and on his desk was the work he had started to do that day. As we were clearing things out, I came upon an index card with a scripture. The verse was from 2 Thessalonians 2:16-17: "Now may our Lord Jesus Christ Himself, and our God and Father, who has loved us and given us everlasting consolation and good hope by grace, comfort your hearts and establish you in every good word and work."

I found this verse written and placed in several places throughout the house. He was memorizing it! But I knew it was from God to us, his family. God surely had our comfort and help in His mind. And those verses continue to minister to us.

Darlene Coombs
Former Missionary to Zambia

> *Lord, thank you that you comfort me when I am struggling to overcome grief. Help me to receive your comfort and to extend it to others who are also suffering...*

> *"He will bring you a message through which you and all your household will be saved."*
>
> ACTS 11:14

We planted the Kampala Foursquare Church in our two-car garage. That first Sunday was an awkward experience. Dave Adams led worship and I preached the sermon. Margaret, Sarah and Rebeka Adams were the "crowd." The second Sunday was a bit better. We had 10 visitors and they all got saved. Among them was a young man named Luben.

Almost as soon as Luben got saved he began to ask us to come to his home village and share the Good News. After about a month, Dave, Margaret and I made the three-hour trip to Buwimba. Luben gathered his entire family of 10 to 12 people and we sat down together in the largest room in the house. Luben began by sharing how he had found Jesus Christ as his Savior and Lord and told his family he wanted them to have the same Good News. Margaret, David and I shared testimonies, a gospel message, and an invitation to receive Christ. The first person to respond was Luben's father and following him was the entire family.

As we took time to pray with each person, we could sense the presence of God's Holy Spirit. It was a precious time as the entire family began to experience the joy of salvation. After our prayer time, Luben's father wished to make a statement on behalf of the entire family. He told us that in 1955 he had heard a man on the radio preaching about Jesus saving people, but the preacher never explained how to be saved. He had been waiting 45 years for someone to explain to him the way of salvation.

Greg Fisher
Missionary to Uganda

> *Lord, it is amazing that some people wait so long to hear about you. Let me be an answer to someone's prayer today, someone who wants to know how to find you...*

"Therefore go and make disciples of all nations..."
MATTHEW 28:19

*H*ave you ever wondered if the seeds you have planted will produce fruit? Missionaries often wonder what becomes of those who were saved under their ministry.

Imagine my wonderment when we visited Oizumi, Japan, and discovered that many of those who were children in the pioneering years were now strong Christian adults. Mr. Ohtani was now a professor in a Japanese university. Bashful Mr. Myuoshi became a famous television sports announcer. Our interpreter, Mr. Kajiki, is in Christian ministry and his classmate is now Emperor of Japan. Another young man was an evangelist. It was amazing! And oh the joy that we felt when we saw for ourselves what God had done!

I wonder about others too, like the elderly priest I met in a Buddhist Temple. He told me he wanted to find true peace before he died. I told him he could never find peace until he found Jesus. I gave him some gospel literature and told him the plan of salvation. I wonder if he ever found that peace.

We may or may not get the chance to know what happens in the lives of those to whom we've witnessed or ministered. The one thing we do know is that each of us must walk in obedience to God's word that says, "GO! Go and tell them…"

Billie Charles Francey
Former Missionary to Asia

Lord, I pray that I would touch someone today for you. You can change a life forever; may I be obedient to speak to those whom you have already prepared to hear…

*"Praise be to God, who has not rejected my
prayer or withheld his love..."*

PSALM 66:20

*A*lberto was a regional sales executive for a major pharmaceutical company in Cali, Colombia. He and his family attended one of our churches. His wife contracted cancer; the situation looked hopeless because her liver was failing and she was losing weight rapidly. Her doctor told her that even if she was healthy, there was only a one in 100 chance that surgery could completely remove the large cancerous mass in her chest. She pleaded with the doctor to operate because she was so confident that God could do a miracle if he would only operate.

It just so "happened" that the doctor's father, who lived in New York City, had been diagnosed with brain cancer. The doctor, admiring this woman's faith, asked if she would pray for his father. She took the doctor's hand, and with her husband, they prayed for God to heal the doctor's elderly father. The next day the doctor reported that his father's brain tumor completely disappeared at precisely the moment they had prayed in Bogotá! Later, after Alberto's wife prayed over the hands of every member of her surgical team, she was operated on for five hours and every trace of cancer was removed.

Coincidence? I don't think so—we serve an awesome God!

Lee Schnabel
Former Missionary to Guatemala and Panama

> *Thank you, Father, for hearing our prayers and moving in power even when the situation is beyond our control or involves people who are thousands of miles away. I bring before you now these people and situations...*

"Rise and go; your faith has made you well."

LUKE 17:19

In the 1960s, tuberculosis was very widespread in the Philippines. And while there was treatment for it, few were completely healed. Melba Fornal, one of our believers and church members, was not feeling well and had a large swelling on her neck. She went to the hospital for an examination and was diagnosed as having tuberculosis. The treatment was rest and daily injections at the hospital.

Melba lived outside of the city and would have to walk five miles each day to get to the hospital. While we were pondering what to do, her father said, "We will trust the Lord." After praying together, Melba and her father went home.

God honored their faith. The disease did not progress. She grew stronger and in the years ahead married and bore several children.

Have faith in God… He can do the impossible!

Jack and Aline Richey
Former Missionaries to the Philippines

> *Father, give me faith to trust you in all circumstances, even those that seem impossible...*

"They will tell of the power of your awesome works, and I will proclaim your great deeds."

PSALM 145:6

I was visiting two young pastors and they asked me to visit a school for the deaf and blind. I was reluctant to go to the school because the two young pastors had told the staff that their pastor would come and pray for the children and all the children would be healed. These two young people were so excited, and they thought I would be very happy too. Instead, I thought, "There goes my afternoon nap! And—no pressure—but all must get healed!"

When I got there, I realized that this deaf and blind institute was also a Buddhist temple. When I got inside, their workers met me and said, "Well, our boss said you were coming…do your thing." And my two young people, standing next to me, were saying, "Pastor, go for it! Go for it!" One of them said, "I'll check the blind," and the other said, "I'll check the deaf, and bring them up for testimonies." They were so expectant that something would happen.

By faith, I proclaimed the Good News of Jesus Christ and asked the children if they would like to give their lives to Jesus and receive prayer for healing. Every single child raised their hand; every single child received prayer; and—much to my surprise—every single child was healed!

Blind eyes were opened and the deaf could hear. The one who had been translating for me said, "No, miracles do not happen!" But there were about five or six parents of these children who had come to visit the kids, and they came up and said, "Miracles do happen—we know our children and God healed them!"

Leslie Keegel
National Leader in Sri Lanka

Thank you, Lord, that you open the ears of the deaf and give sight to the blind. Give me faith for miracles in the lives of the people I bring before you now...

"Then the angel showed me the river of the water of life, as clear as crystal, flowing from the throne of God and of the Lamb..."
REVELATION 22:1

*E*ighty-three people were baptized in the muddy river, and it took four pastors quite a while to finish this important ceremony. Actually, it was definitely more than just a ceremony. As I struggled to put a young man down into the quick-moving water, it seemed that he was struggling to stay out of the water. Each one acted the same way. As if they were afraid of the water.

The pastor must have realized what I was thinking. This river, he said, is a river of death to these people. It floods over its bank during the rainy season and many people, young and old, are swept away and lost in the river. Yet eighty-three people this day obeyed Christ's words and were baptized. This was not just a ceremony or even a step of obedience. This was a leap of faith. Faith that God would bring them out of this river of death, and not just as a new person but as one who had won a victory over the river.

Life's difficulties seem to be God's opportunities to do something new and fresh, strong and lasting, in the lives of His children. Struggles can cause us to walk deeper in our faith or to choose the safer and less adventurous path.

Glen Mickel
Former Missionary to West Africa

I thank you, Father, that you rescue us from the river of death and place us on the banks of the river of life...Help me to persevere through whatever hardships and fears that I might face today, knowing that you are with me...

"Prepare the way for the Lord, make straight paths for Him."
MARK 1:3

In May 1981, Foursquare believers from Benin and Nigeria held several crusades. The night before the crusades began, the Lord appeared in a dream to a commissar, a man of great influence in the city. In his dream the commissar saw four men come and sit in his room.

One of the four spoke to him in the dream, saying, "These are my men, they are coming to talk to you about God. You are to listen to them; you are to help them." The man woke up and recognized the significance of the dream. He sensed that the one who spoke in the dream was the Lord Jesus Christ.

As he pondered this dream the next morning, there came a knock on the door. When he opened the door, he found three Foursquare church members who told him, "We have come to talk to you about God and want to share the message of Jesus Christ with you."

"Come in," said the man, and that morning he accepted Jesus Christ. He helped them get the permit needed for the open-air meeting, the first permit to preach outside in the Republic of Benin since 1972, when Communists took over the government.

Without this permit, the crusade would have been stopped the first night, and the eight hundred decisions which were made for Christ would not have happened. When the Lord wants to move, He always prepares the way! What a miracle!

Audra Sowersby
Former Missionary to Nigeria

Lord, prepare the way before me today as I go forth to do your will. Guide me to those people to whom you have already been speaking and give me the right words to touch their hearts for you...

"Well done, good and faithful servant! You have been faithful with a few things; I will put you in charge of many things."

MATTHEW 25:23

The average African family has two parents and seven children. Poverty is so great in the rural areas that parents must choose which one of their children gets to go to school. Books, pencils and uniforms are required, and are paid for entirely by the family.

Shadrach was from a large family and lived in rural Kenya. Despite his family's poverty, he made it all the way through high school.

God had gifted Shadrach with a sharp mind. Early in his education, he talked his parents into buying him two pencils instead of one. He used one for his schoolwork and sold the other to the richest kid in school who lost or forgot his pencil. Of course, there must be a price increase! With the extra money from the sale, he bought more pencils.

This was the beginning of a successful business that not only put Shadrach through school but also demonstrated a godly principle. If we use what God has given us, we will be blessed. If we squander away our gifts and talents, we will be brought to poverty.

Glen Mickel
Former Missionary to West Africa

*Lord, help me to discover the gifts and talents you have
given me, and use them for your kingdom and your glory.*

> *"...I am the one who looks after you and cares for you..."*
> HOSEA 14:8 (NLT)

*M*issionary kids (MK's) find themselves in a variety of countries and many schools during their growing-up years. Our daughter Jenica is an example of a typical MK.

Jenica was born in 1988 and had grown up in Finland where she loved her school. She was also very close to her grandparents and her friends at church. When we felt God leading us to move to Malaysia, we understood that there would be many tears. So we prayed, asking the Lord, "What can we do to help Jenica not dread the first day in her new school?"

The International School that Jenica was going to attend was in a beautiful setting along a sandy tropical shoreline. As we approached the compound that day, Jenica was shaking like a leaf. She was new; she knew no one. We prayed, "Lord, help Jenica."

Just then a pack of five girls ran toward them shouting, "Jenica, Jenica, Jenica!"

These girls knew Jenica was coming and had anticipated her arrival. Needless to say, Jenica warmed up to the girls quickly and eventually made very good friends. God knew that Jenica needed the warm welcome and extra care. We were blessed to see how God had even prepared a little welcoming episode in advance for our daughter.

Michael and Jannie Stubbs
Missionaries to Malaysia

> *Lord, I pray for our Foursquare missionary children. Help them to make those adjustments to new schools, new homes, new friends, and new cultures...*

"I have given you authority to...overcome all the power of the enemy; nothing will harm you."

LUKE 10:19

*C*hildren's ministry around the world has borne much fruit. Often children have very little variety in their lives, so when someone shows concern for them specifically and takes times to be with them, they are open to the love of Jesus. This was true in Panama.

Another woman minister and I traveled to the Darien province to conduct children's meetings. To get there we traveled for several hours on dirt roads and crossed streams where the bridge had been washed out. But the reception the children gave us more than compensated for the trip.

That night we stayed in the "motel," a building that offered little privacy. It also was a place of questionable reputation. Throughout the night we could hear people come and go. But it was the only place to stay!

About 1:00 a.m., shortly after I had dozed off, I felt the door of my room open. I sensed a presence in my room. My heart started to pound and I was frozen in my bed. I could not move or talk. The forces of Satan had entered the room. He wasn't happy that we had entered his territory.

I began to call out to God in my mind, praying in the Spirit. My heart continued to pound, but as I continued to pray, the presence began to slowly withdraw from the room. God is powerful!

Bonita Schwartz Sanchez
Missionary to Panama

> *Lord, I thank you for protecting me, especially as I move*
> *into territory that Satan has called his own. Let me move*
> *forward under your guidance and in your authority...*

> *"...He gave them power and authority to drive out*
> *all demons and to cure diseases..."*
>
> LUKE 9:1

*W*e rode a jeep for several hours, took a pump boat to a small island, and walked several kilometers to a small hut where a woman named Venida had been restrained for 17 years. She was a violent mentally deranged young woman whom no one could help.

We were introduced to this demon-possessed woman who spoke incoherently in her own dialect for years and had to be held down by several adults when not tied to her bed or to a tree. We knew we could do nothing; only God could help this woman.

We prayed for guidance, rebuked demons, and claimed deliverance and salvation for this tormented woman. Gradually she calmed down. When spoken to, the demons spoke through her in perfect English, a language she had never heard. After several hours of praying and waiting on the Lord, we saw a great improvement in Venida. She was calm; no one was holding her and she wanted to eat.

Sharon was sitting next to her, reading Scripture. Suddenly, Venida swung her fist and hit Sharon on the jaw. The demons were still tormenting her and did not like to hear God's Word. By the end of the day, we witnessed a transformation that only God could bring. Venida was talking and acting normally. Her family was ecstatic. We thanked the Lord for His power and mercy.

A pastor visited the home weekly after that and shared the Word with Venida, her family, and the neighbors. The miracle of deliverance remained.

Don and Sharon Nicholson
Former Missionaries to the Philippines

> *Lord, I am thankful that you have given us power to drive*
> *out demons. Help me to understand and act upon the*
> *authority I have in you...*

"The one who calls you is faithful..."
1 THESSALONIANS 5:24

My life is in boxes once more.
  After nine years of being away
We're going back to Africa, the continent of colors
God still has a plan for our lives –
A plan that takes us away from our children
Away from our grandchildren
Away from our dogs and cats
Away from our home in tree-lined Oregon

All these always must lead somewhere—
At least that's what I tell myself, after all it's His plan—not mine especially
If it were my plan, I'd stay put. I'd enjoy the fruits of my labors.
My kids are grown. I have grandchildren to take to the movies.
I have holidays to cook for—all the loved ones who would come and share
The warm feelings of the season.
Why isn't that enough? What's missing in all of that?

It must be the call, that elusive word.
It must be God's will, that ultimate mystery.
It must be gifting, that unique code of being.
It must be the desire of my own heart that God still grants me
Even when I forget it's mine
He's faithful and I'm reminded only again
By each box I pack.

Kathy Kieselhort
Former Missionary to Nigeria, now serving with her husband, Bill, in
South Africa

> *Lord, thank you for the harvest of souls that is reaped*
> *through the many sacrifices made by our missionaries...*
> *Bless them today as I lift them in prayer...*

"Those who are with us are more than those who are with them...
'O Lord, open his eyes so he may see.'
Then the Lord opened the servant's eyes."

2 KINGS 6:16-17

After arriving at a small church among the Central Bontoc tribe, another fellow minister and I were unloading equipment from our truck when several men from the barrio came along. All of them had been drinking, and one of the men was bragging he would live forever. To prove him wrong, another man stabbed him in the back.

The next day a group of young people came running down the road, chased by a man with a bolo [machete]. That night, during the service, drunken men prevented people from responding to receive Christ.

By the next day, I was discouraged and wanted to go home. In addition to the "craziness," I sensed the presence of demonic spirits. Many of the people of the Mountain Province worshipped and sacrificed to pagan spirits.

After fasting and praying, I sensed the Lord telling me that those who were with us were more than those who were with the enemy. As I went to preach that night, I asked the Lord to allow me to see the people with His eyes.

Immediately, I felt an intense love for them. That night we had no problems or disruptions. In fact, some of those who had prevented others from receiving Jesus the night before were the first to come to the altar to accept Christ.

Gary and Johnell Loop
Former Missionaries to the Philippines

Open my eyes, Lord, and show me your power today. Let me
see people the way that you see them...

"If you believe, you will receive whatever you ask for in prayer."
MATTHEW 21:22

*I*n one of our Foursquare churches in Sri Lanka, the Fernando family's 10-year-old daughter was diagnosed with brain cancer. The only suggestion the doctors offered—that of an operation—provided no guarantee. The church began to earnestly pray for the girl and her parents.

When the day came for the operation, the child was admitted to the hospital, but the operation was delayed. During the time of delay, the parents prayed and decided to take the child home in faith that the Lord had healed her. The young girl, paralyzed on one side of her body from her head down, was carried into the church during the Sunday service. Hands were laid on her as everyone joined together in fervent prayer. They began to praise God for her healing.

Miraculously, within a few days the young girl had completely regained movement of her body. God had answered prayer. She now testifies to the healing she received from Jesus and is back in school and church!

Jim Tolle
Former Missionary to Colombia and Argentina
Missions Director, 1996-1999

> *Thank you, Father, for the power of prayer. Give me faith to exercise that power and to keep my eyes on you in every situation, believing for divine healing and miracles in all the circumstances of life...*

"O Lord, you will keep us safe and protect us ..."
PSALM 12:7

*W*e had heard the machine guns and the cries of the victims throughout the night as war happened all around us in the barrio. Our constant silent prayer was for His protection upon us. Suddenly, there came a knock at the front door. Our eyes locked and our hearts swelled within us. That which we feared the most, I thought, had come upon us. Our girls were safe in the back room. Jerry and I looked at each other, in silence. We knew what each of us would have to do. We had talked about it many times.

Again, we heard the knock at the front door. Jerry started toward the front door of that missionary house where we had welcomed and cared for so many. Then, suddenly, we heard a whisper: "Jerry! Jerry!" I stopped and listened. It couldn't be the enemy, I thought. They wouldn't call our name. Who could it be? Jerry opened the door. There stood two very disheveled but very relieved missionary colleagues!

Once again, our missionary house had become a place of refuge. We learned that those two colleagues had been kidnapped, robbed of all their possessions, then driven to an open field where their captors intended to kill them. Then, they were suddenly forced back into the vehicle and driven back to the spot from which they had been kidnapped, and they were left along the road to be shot by the enemy. No one was to be out and about that hour of the night and, if spotted, they would be shot on sight.

The prayers of the saints back home, however, took over. Those missionary colleagues became invisible and, in the dark of that fierce night, they somehow found their way to the Foursquare missionary's house, where they knew they would be safe for the night.

Jennie King
Former Missionary to Nicaragua

> *Thank you, Lord, that you watch over and protect those who call on your name. Watch over the missionaries and loved ones that I bring before you now...*

"For in the day of trouble he will keep me safe in his dwelling..."
PSALM 27:5

Linda and I attended an evening service in Belem, Brazil. After the service we were fellowshipping with about 25 other pastors and leaders. As we were noisily talking and rejoicing in the Lord, we were interrupted by intruders. Three men with handguns rushed into the office where we had been talking.

At first everyone thought it was a joke by some of the young men of the church. Then the men began threatening everyone and demanding the offering from the evening. When Pastor Jose told them the money had already been taken to the bank, they threatened to kill him. So the pastor opened the vault to show it was empty. They then robbed each person, taking their watches and personal jewelry. They still did not believe that there was no cash. One thief put his gun between the pastor's eyes and said, "You have one last chance. Tell me where the money is or I will kill you."

Pastor Jose kept very cool and replied, "Why kill me? There is no money." Miraculously, the robber turned and left the office. Three weeks later we read in the newspaper that the police had located the gang of thieves, the same men we had encountered at the church. A gun battle had ensued which left all three men dead. The article also indicated that these same men had murdered victims on at least three other occasions while committing robberies. Only then did we realize how dangerous our situation had been and what a miracle God had done by keeping us safe!

Jack Gustafson
Former Missionary to Brazil

I praise you and thank you, Father, that you keep me safe in the day of trouble...

"No one is like you, O Lord; you are great,
and your name is mighty in power."
JEREMIAH 10:6

*P*racha Dang, a member of the Serm Sook Church in northern Thailand, cares for the church property and is a member of the church council. A former Army veteran who served in the Korean War, he now lives on his government pension.

For many years before his conversion, Pracha had been plagued by extremely poor health, including tuberculosis. He received Christ as Savior when Foursquare pastor Art Chutong went to his home, prayed with him, and led him to the Lord.

When Pracha came to the church worship service, one of his physical problems was healed instantly. A month later he was hospitalized for tuberculosis, but Pastor Chutong visited him and prayed for him. The next day he was released from the hospital with a clean bill of health—he was completely healed of tuberculosis!

A short time later, God had another surprise for Pracha and his wife—a new son, born 18 years after the birth of their last child! They named their son David.

However, David began having problems with his eyes recently. His eyesight became dimmer and dimmer until he couldn't see anything. He came to a Friday night prayer meeting and the church prayed for him. His healing began. By Sunday he was completely healed and his eyesight remains perfect. If anyone questions if God heals today, have him call Thailand and speak to Pracha Dang!

Phil Franklin
Former Missionary to Thailand

I praise you Lord, for your name is great and you are
mighty in power. Nothing is beyond your ability, and I bring
these matters before you today...

> *"Therefore, if anyone is in Christ, he is a new*
> *creation; the old has gone, the new has come."*
> 2 CORINTHIANS 5:17

We were asked to return to minister in the city of Bucaramanga, where we had been so severely persecuted some years before. The people had experienced a change of heart, and our home was soon flooded with medical students, business owners, priests, and people of every walk in life—people who wanted to know about Jesus. A nun from the elite girl's school was healed of cancer and began telling her students. They were saved, and when their parents began to investigate, they too received Jesus.

A young medical student asked us to speak at a celebration of Pentecost at his school. Evangelicals were to give messages on "God is Love." I could not believe what I saw. There were no idols in the chapel. The priests and nuns held Bibles and chanted, "Jesus is alive, He lives in me." A young priest—in a checked sport shirt—led us in singing "There Is Power In The Blood." A beautiful young nun stood, tears streaming down her face, as she praised God in her heavenly language. When the students had opportunity to ask questions, God gave us wisdom to answer them.

Those who had once spit at us and paraded against us came and hugged me and said, "Thank you for coming. We love and appreciate you." Over the years we prayed many times for these people and saw God restore marriages, bless businesses, and bring many of their friends to Jesus. God is so good!

Virginia Martin
Former Missionary to Bolivia and Colombia

> *Lord, I pray that my community would experience a change*
> *of heart also, and that your Holy Spirit would draw hearts*
> *to you and that many would be saved...*

"...The blind receive sight, the lame walk..."
LUKE 7:22

*W*hen my husband John went to Sydney, Australia, to attend a pastors' conference, he had planned to have time to see a little of this country where he had never been. God had a better plan.

Rudy and Pam Peleis had graciously opened their home for John to stay with them. Rudy had been in a wheel chair for seven years, after a work accident in which he was hit with an iron bar and his spine was broken. He was in much pain and had considered suicide more than once.

John wondered why God had placed him in this home. As he prayed, the Lord gave John a vision of Rudy's healing. Rudy had been prayed over by many people and therefore had a bit of doubt when John told him about his vision.

On the third evening of the conference, Pastor Jim Hayford preached from Acts 3:1-10, and the Lord quickened the message to Rudy's heart. After the message, Pastor Hayford invited several other pastors to join him and gave an invitation for any who were sick to come forward. Rudy came.

John took Rudy by his hands and said, "Brother Rudolph, in the name of Jesus Christ rise up!" Rudy tried to stand; he wanted to stand up and praise the Lord. Suddenly his legs began to come alive; they supported his weight. Shouts of praise and clapping filled the air. Rudy felt a strong sensation flood his legs and feet. He was now standing without help. God had healed him.

Within three months, Rudy had discarded his crutches as he gained strength and was completely healed.

Vijaya Gnanaolivu
Co-founder of Foursquare India

> *Lord, no matter how great our injuries, you can heal us. Today I pray for those I know with chronic illnesses and depression...*

"And if he finds it, I tell you the truth, he is happier about that one sheep than about the ninety-nine that did not wander off."

MATTHEW 18:13

It had been a long day of ministering, stretching from early morning to evening. The tropical heat had taken its toll on our energy, but there was one more service. We were meeting in the public plaza where a large crowd had gathered.

The people stood, listening respectfully for the entire service. We had prayed for the anointing of the Holy Spirit and we were not disappointed. When I finished the message and gave the invitation, several responded.

As we left the area, a few people joined us as we walked toward our vehicles. The conversations centered on the response of those who came to Christ. Someone in the group said, "Tonight, one hundred forty-six people gave their hearts to Jesus."

I was aware of a young man following close on my heels listening to the report. I will never forget the tug I felt on my sleeve as I heard him say, "I want to be number one hundred forty-seven."

It was the most rewarding moment of the day as once again the value of one single soul pierced my heart.

Allan Hamilton
Former Missionary to the Philippines

> *Lord, even though you created the universe, you are aware of each individual life. Thank you so much that I matter to you...*

"Do you show contempt for the riches of His kindness, tolerance and patience, not realizing that God's kindness leads you toward repentance?"

ROMANS 2:4

*J*eff was a young man who was a leader of a gang of rascals (criminals) who terrorized people in Papua New Guinea by robbing cars and trucks. They usually operated as a team but early one morning, Jeff set out by himself to rob a car.

As he waited on a deserted stretch of road, he saw a Land Cruiser. He stepped into the road and stopped the car, telling the driver to throw out his wallet. The driver reached down, but instead of pulling out a wallet he produced a semi-automatic pistol and started firing at Jeff. The first two bullets shattered the car windshield. The driver then knocked out the loose glass and plastic, rested his hand on the steering wheel, and took careful aim between Jeff's eyes.

Jeff stood frozen on the spot, waiting to die, and watched in what seemed to be slow motion as the man squeezed off the next shot. The gun bucked and fire leapt from the muzzle, but Jeff saw a hand raised in front of his face and it stopped the bullet. Just as quickly, the hand disappeared the driver accelerated, almost running Jeff over as he sped away.

Jeff went back to his village, wondering what had happened to him. Realizing that God had intervened, he searched for the Bible he had received in school and started to read. When he happened upon Romans 2:4 he was stunned by the question that was being asked, "Do you despise the riches of His goodness, forbearance and longsuffering, not knowing that the goodness of God leads you to repentance?" Several months later Jeff gave his life to the Lord and today continues to serve the Lord!

George Butron
Missionary to Papua New Guinea

> *Lord, help me to never take your goodness and mercy for granted. May my heart always remain soft toward you and the work you want to do in me...*

> *"You will keep him in perfect peace,*
> *whose mind is stayed on you..."*
>
> ISAIAH 26:3 (NKJV)

As new missionaries in the Dominican Republic, we searched in vain for a house to rent. We felt God's peace despite the inadequacy of all the houses we had seen. We knew the Lord would direct us. We were surprised to find just how perfect God's plan really was!

After two exhausting weeks of house hunting, we drove up to a lovely house on a tree-lined street. As soon as we saw the house, we knew it was for us. It was green (Charlie's favorite color) and there was a rose bush in the front (I like roses). It was behind an elementary school, so it would be quiet at night. There was a big streetlight next to the driveway for security.

When we were allowed to see the rest of the house, it was even better. There was an office, a living room large enough for Sunday services, and a lovely mango tree in the backyard.

Having lived here five years, we understand even more that there could not have been a better place for us. It has been the perfect home—it is just a six-block walk from the place where visiting teams stay each summer and our new church facility is nearby. On several occasions we have ministered in the elementary school near our home, and as a result have been invited to share in other public schools.

God does take care of the little things, and the big ones too—we can rest in His peace!

Darla Finocchiaro
Missionary to the Dominican Republic

> *Father, give me your peace today as I give you the details*
> *of my life...*

*"Pure and lasting religion in the sight of God our Father
means that we must care for orphans..."*

JAMES 1:27 (NLT)

Shortly after my husband, Henry, our three sons and I arrived in Quito, Ecuador, to serve as Foursquare missionaries, an elderly man came to our home in search of someone who would be willing to take over his ministry in the Quito Penitentiary. When Henry went to the prison to investigate, he took a group of young people with him, and they met the director. His response was not very encouraging: "You evangelicals are all alike; you all want to preach to us, but no one wants to help us!"

During Henry's tour of the prison, he found 54 children living in the maximum security section, including a 12-year-old girl living on the men's side with over 300 hardened criminals. These children were there because the relative who cared for them was in prison. They went out during the day to beg and steal from the market places and then at night they slept on the cold concrete floor under their relative's cot.

That night while leaving a barrio church where he had preached, Henry found two boys living under the church building. It was as if the Lord spoke to him, "You just preached a wonderful sermon on how I meet all your needs. Tell Me, how do I meet the needs of these two boys?"

We decided we had to do something, so we started a home for children. Over the next two months a series of miracles confirmed God's hand in this. It was as if the puzzle pieces fell into place and the Houses of Happiness Orphanage was born.

To date more than 1,000 children have become part of this ministry. Graduates include pastors, lawyers, doctors, teachers and other professionals who are serving Jesus.

Dorothy Davis
Former Missionary to Ecuador

Father, break my heart with the things that break your heart. Give me your love for orphans, the homeless, disadvantaged, poor, and those in difficult circumstances...

"Do not despise these small beginnings,
for the Lord rejoices to see the work begin..."
ZECHARIAH 4:10 (NLT)

*H*ouses of Happiness Orphanage just outside Quito, Ecuador, began with an old tumble down shack which we rented for $7.50 a month. After we had cleaned up after the cows and chickens that had lived there, repaired the roof and built plywood beds, we took 36 children who were living with relatives in the prison and moved them into this new "home."

For one year they cooked over an open fire. The children went to bed early on Saturday night so their clothes could be washed and mended for another week. Only one of the 36 children had a pair of shoes, but at least they had hot meals and a warm blanket, things they did not have in prison.

This ministry came to the attention of the wife of the President of Ecuador and my husband, Henry, was made administrator over her social work in the country. One day she said to Henry, "You will not let us pay you, so we have decided to honor you in a way you cannot refuse." The President decorated Henry with a medal of honor and gave him the title deed of 50 acres of beautiful land in a valley on the outskirts of Quito. It is on this very same land that the Houses of Happiness Orphanage was eventually built.

Today it houses many orphans who need to be loved and cared for. Praise be to God, who provides even the fertile ground to plant the seeds for the kingdom!

Dorothy Davis
Former Missionary to Ecuador

Father, help me not to despise small beginnings in my life or
in the lives of others... give me faith to see things through
your eyes, help me to see the potential and to have faith in
you to provide every need...

*"Again he prayed, and the heavens gave rain,
and the earth produced its crops."*

JAMES 5:18

omas Castro, a young villager from Boca Chica, worked on a large ocean ship. When he was saved, Tomas felt the Lord wanted him to go to the other islands to spread the Good News. And he didn't want to just go sometime, he wanted to go now!

We encouraged him to wait until he had some training and we invited him to our home for Bible study and prayer. He drank in every word, and pressed to go with the Gospel. As we prayed, the Lord said, "Turn him over to the Holy Spirit." So we did.

God began using Tomas to lead people to salvation. He prayed for the sick and they were healed. Many were baptized in the Holy Spirit.

Tomas led our first missionary team to the island of Isla Fuente. After a two-day boat trip, they arrived to find the people discouraged as it had not rained on their island and their crops were failing.

While he was preaching, Tomas said, "Tonight it will rain; not too much or too little, but just enough to save your crops." One young girl on the team was upset. "You are so crazy! You have just ruined our chances of ever coming back and planting a church here."

"Go to bed and don't worry," Tomas said.

That night rain began to fall.

Today there is a strong flourishing church on Isla Fuerte.

Virginia Martin
Former Missionary to Colombia and Bolivia

Lord, I thank you that you are in control even of the weather! Have mercy on our land, Lord, may we receive your favor...

"Lead me to the rock that is higher than I."

PSALM 61:2

A mountain stream flows through the mission property at Hageri, in the Eastern Highlands of Papua New Guinea. On hot tropical days, the Bible school students and missionaries would often take a swim in this stream. When the water was high, due to the rains upstream, you could not see the huge rock in the middle of the stream.

Usually the top of the rock was hidden just a few inches under the water. You had to know where the rock was in order to swim to it. But once there, a person could stand on top of it with just their feet hidden under the water. No matter how swift the water was, we could always know that, if we could get to the rock, we would be safe. It was strong and immovable.

Since those days, when I read Psalm 61:2, "Lead me to the rock that is higher that I," I think of that rock and how it is like our Lord.

Larry and JoAnn Six
Former Missionaries to Papua New Guinea

Thank you, Lord, that you are like that immovable rock, and that I can stand on you today. Whatever the fast-moving rapids of life brings my way, I know you will be there to hold me up and keep me above the water...

> *"Jesus said, 'I am the resurrection and the life.*
> *He who believes in Me, though he may die, he shall live.'"*
>
> JOHN 11:25 (NKJV)

One morning we received a telephone call telling us that Mr. Mui, who was an elder in the Tai Kok Tsui Foursquare Church in Kowloon, Hong Kong, had experienced a severe heart attack and had died at the hospital. Jumping in a taxi with a fellow minister, I felt we were about to witness the resurrection of the dead. At first, I tried to excuse the feeling, but en route, the conviction grew stronger.

Fifteen minutes later when we arrived at the hospital, we found Mr. Mui sitting up in bed, eating his lunch. The family and the doctor's charts confirmed that Mr. Mui had originally been dead for more than two minutes.

Several weeks later, on the evening before Easter, there was a "Celebration Service" at the Mui family residence. Mr. Mui testified that God had sent him back to warn his family of their spiritual condition. Eight hours later, as the Foursquare church was holding its Easter Sunrise Service, Mr. Mui suddenly died in his easy chair at home.

That morning, one of our sons asked, "Dad, why would someone have to die on Resurrection Sunday?" The answer was obvious: "Because of Resurrection Sunday, death for the believer only becomes a doorway into an even fuller life."

Dr. Ron and Carole Williams
Former Missionaries to Hong Kong

> *Father, thank you for the dispensation of grace in Mr. Mui's*
> *life and in mine. Thank you that he was able to get his life*
> *in order and warn his family; help me to get my life in order*
> *and to warn my family and friends of the importance of*
> *embracing Christ and the life He offers...*

> *"This is what the Lord Almighty says: All this may seem*
> *impossible to you now ... But do you think this is*
> *impossible for me, the Lord Almighty?"*
>
> ZECHARIAH 8:6 (NLT)

"*G*et your own lawyer. I will sign whatever you want."

These words were music to our ears. We had come to Puerto Rico to serve the Lord by establishing the third Foursquare Church and the Bible school. After much prayer, we knew the Lord had placed it on our hearts to open a place for drug addicts. But there was a big problem (so we thought!). Dr. Acosta, the owner of the building we wanted to buy for our drug rehab home, had been offered one hundred and fifty thousand dollars from a group that wanted it for a bar and night club. We could only offer him $75,000 with the stipulation that we would have to rent it for the first year for $150.00 a month. He laughed when he heard the offer we made him. I told him why we wanted it. As we left the office I handed him my card and told him we had claimed it for God and to call me.

A few days later his secretary called to say the doctor wished to speak with me. Our miracle came. He said he had talked it over with his wife and she said that as a child she had attended church there when it had been a Lutheran mission. She wanted God to have the property.

I then told him our first year's rent would be used as the down payment with no interest penalties on the remaining balance. After a moment he shook his head and said, "Get your own lawyer. I will sign what ever you want." We shook hands and I left.

Jim and Mary Tucknes
Former Missionaries to Puerto Rico

> *Thank you, Lord, that you open doors that no man can*
> *close and do things that seem impossible to us...move in*
> *miracle power in these requests I bring before you now...*

*"She opens her arms to the poor and extends
her hands to the needy"*

PROVERBS 31:20

*B*elow is a letter sent to Kurt Fuller, FMI Youth Missions Coordinator. May we too be like Caitlin, who truly represents the outstretched arms of Christ to a hurting and needy world!

Dear Foursquare Youth Outreach,

I just wanted to let you know that God really does bless those who give faithfully.

When I came to camp this summer, I found out just how far $8 could go. God really spoke to me and I decided to help. I got a sticker and began saving the money I earned from babysitting.

Once I started giving, I began to receive more and more jobs. I believe God was blessing me for sowing into His kingdom. Since July 16, I have earned $200 babysitting. It is enclosed in this envelope and I hope it can be used to bring many people to Christ.

Caitlin Cundy, 13
Charlotte, North Carolina

Father, I want to be like Caitlin, giving to you with a joyful heart and a pure faith that you will meet my needs and even prosper me so that I might sow even more into advancing your kingdom and being a blessing to others....

"So what shall I do? I will pray with my spirit,
but I will also pray with my mind."

1 CORINTHIANS 14:15

Our prayers really do matter. When we pray, things truly do happen, even if we never see the answer to prayer or hear about the results:

Albert was the head rascal (criminal) on Barola Pass near Kainantu, a highland town in Papua New Guinea. Much criminal activity, including highway robbery, rape, terrorism and murder took place in that pass. The missionaries sent requests home for the churches to pray specifically for this area. Unknowingly, Albert was one of those being lifted up before the throne of God.

Albert began to feel conviction for his sin and came to the Kainantu Foursquare Church for "relief." He soon accepted Christ as his Savior and began to bring some of the other young criminals to the church. One man was under deep conviction, but refused a strong plea to give his life to the Lord. The following week, he was shot and killed.

Soon after the killing, Albert began a Bible study for the rascals at his home. The house where these men had designed weapons and planned attacks is now a church where former criminals are being discipled as followers of Christ—God answers prayer!

Foursquare World ADVANCE, 1995

Lord, I thank you that when I pray, you really do change
things! Show me what to pray, that I might be led of your
Spirit even as I intercede...

"As the heavens are higher than the earth, so are my ways higher than your ways and my thoughts than your thoughts."

ISAIAH 55:9

A nineteen-year-old girl came to the medical clinic with serious congestion and fever. There was no air movement in the base of her lungs. She was given immediate treatment and then stayed the night in the local village, as it was a four day walk back to her home. The next day, however, she returned to the clinic for further treatment. The interpreter for the medical team spoke with her about the care, love and forgiveness of Jesus Christ. She received the Savior into her heart.

The interpreter also shared about receiving the baptism with the Holy Spirit. The girl prayed and began speaking in tongues. She then reached up and took the Hindu symbol off her forehead and threw it to the side. According to the medical team, the peace in that setting was incredible. The young girl asked if she could remain with them for a while and they agreed. The team even gave her a new name, "Grace." A few hours later, however, Grace quietly and very peacefully stopped breathing and went to be with Jesus.

In the meantime, Grace's family had heard the Gospel and asked Jesus into their hearts. The gift of "Grace" in Nepal had become very obvious!

Foursquare World ADVANCE, 1995

Lord, your thoughts are above my comprehension. You are in control in every situation, and your plans are perfect...

> *"The angel of the Lord encamps around*
> *those who fear him, and he delivers them."*
>
> PSALM 34:7

When one of the Lescano sons came to Christ, he immediately became concerned about the salvation of the rest of his family. He begged my husband, Al, and I to visit his small town and tell his family about the Lord. He told us none of them were Christians and that throughout his family there was an excessive drinking problem.

The day we went, Al asked me to present the Good News. God was merciful, and the father and mother were among those who accepted Jesus as their Savior. However, we did not know until later what was happening just outside this house.

One of the Lescano sons and his friend had been hunting and drinking. When they returned home, I was preaching. As they looked through the window, the son told his friend he didn't like what I was saying. His friend asked, "Why don't you shoot her?" With that in mind, he picked up his gun and aimed it at me. For "some reason" the trigger wouldn't pull.

In the years that followed, God's Word bore much fruit in this family. The parents, their nine sons and daughters, and their families all received Jesus as their Savior.

Mollie Chaves
Former Missionary to the Philippines

> *Father, you protect me even when I am unaware that I am*
> *in danger. Keep me safe today from trouble of every kind...*

"As your words are taught, they give light…"
PSALM 119:130 (NLT)

*H*ow the correspondence course from the Foursquare Church got into the hands of the high school student no one knew. But when he came to Lesson Five, he had to make a decision if he would receive Jesus as his Savior. He decided to do that, filled out the form, and returned it with his request for the next lesson.

Some weeks later, a pastor in that area visited his home and talked with him about his decision. He was sincere, and knew exactly what he had decided. When his mother heard this message, she also accepted the Lord. The young man told the pastor he would gather his friends if the pastor would return and begin a Bible study with them. The pastor promised and in the weeks that followed several more received Christ.

This teenager is one of more than 5,000 people throughout this island nation who regularly study the Scripture through this correspondence course from the Foursquare Gospel Church in Sri Lanka. Lesson Five calls them to make a decision about receiving Jesus. Hundreds each year make this same decision, many of which have a Hindu or Buddhist background.

God's Word is powerful! It calls us to salvation, comforts us, teaches us, and brings light to the dark paths in our lives.

Eloise Clarno
Former Missionary to Sri Lanka

Lord, may your words go forth in the darkness of this world and bring light. May your word shine upon my life and bring me to repentance of any areas of darkness there…

"O Lord my God, I cried unto thee,
and thou hast healed..."

PSALM 30:2 (KJV)

"Revival on the Air" was a church broadcast that the Thompsons did in Davao City, Philippines. In 1962 it had already been on the air for seven years. God used this "mighty voice" to reach many, and the story below is just an example of the many wonderful things God did through the radio ministry:

A mother stood by her door with a baby in her arms, ready to take it to the hospital, when a voice from the "Revival on the Air" broadcast in Davao City asked, "Are you in trouble? Are you sick? Is your child sick? (and, as if the voice also saw into the home) Mother, with sick baby in your arms, Jesus loves you and the child. Be saved and as we pray, Jesus will heal your child." The woman stopped. "Yes Lord, I believe; heal my child."

And Jesus did heal that very instant. The mother brought her well child to the church, gave her testimony, and the entire large family received the Lord and became members of the church.

Dr. Evelyn Thompson
Former Missionary to the Philippines

Lord, thank you that through your healing touch many have
come to know you. I pray that as I hear your voice and
obey, people would be healed and turn to you for their salva-
tion...

"Let the little children come to me, and do not hinder them, for the kingdom of heaven belongs to such as these."
MATTHEW 19:14

*M*issionaries often work with children, and it doesn't take long to realize that they are precious to the Lord and have a special place in our Father's heart.

As our preschool class took a break for cookies and a drink, it started to rain. And it rained hard. The children began fussing about the rain, and I stopped them by telling them, "We need the rain. Without the rain there would be no flour and sugar and the other things which we need to have cookies to eat."

One little boy piped up, "I saw a cookie tree once." All the children started making fun of him, telling him that couldn't be true. One little boy asked him, "Why didn't you pick one?"

The original storyteller turned to the boy with disgust. "They weren't ripe yet, ya dummy!"

It has been such a blessing to visit churches where my husband and I ministered. These children are now all grown-up serving as leaders and pastors. What an amazing thing God has done!

Darlene Coombs
Former Missionary to Venezuela, Panama and Zambia

> *Lord, you have made children so special and unique! Thank you for each one of the children you have put in my life. I bring them to you in prayer today and ask for your special blessing on each one of them...*

"...this gospel is bearing fruit and growing..."
COLOSSIANS 1:6

*W*hen the Francey family went to Okinawa as missionaries, we rented a building in the city of Nishihara, and began passing out fliers announcing the meetings. One elderly woman took one of these papers home to her son.

The son wrote to us, saying he was a very bad sinner. He had jumped on the Bible to destroy it. Could our God, Jesus Christ, forgive him? We were glad to have a "Yes" answer. This man, Tokeshi, came to the meetings and was saved. He asked God to deliver him from drinking sake (rice wine) and God did! His mother couldn't stop thanking us for what we had done. We reminded her it was Jesus who did it.

Tokeshi had a serious heart condition, and he asked for prayer and God healed him. Then, he needed a job. Again we prayed, and God gave him a government job where he worked for years.

Some years later our family was invited to visit and minister in Japan and Okinawa. We visited the church we had pioneered in Nishihara. Tokeshi greeted us by pulling out of his pocket the worn flier his mother had given him years before. He was still serving the Lord.

Billie Charles Francey
Former Missionary to Asia

> *Lord, I am in amazement at the way you change hearts and lives all around the world, not just here in my little corner...*

"All the believers were together and had everything in common."

ACTS 2:44

The cultures of Africa are as varied as the number of tribes in each country. My wife and I had not been in our home in East Africa very long until we began to notice that things were disappearing. Through a process of elimination and some deductive reasoning I arrived at the conclusion that it was one of our church leaders that was walking off with things like a hoe and a machete.

One thing I remember my father teaching me was that if you borrowed anything you always returned it, so I confronted my brother about the missing items. He didn't say he had taken them, he just asked me if I was ready for them. Without getting hostile, I said, "Yes, I could have used the hoe yesterday morning when it was cool."

The next morning it was leaning back up against the house as if nothing was wrong. I couldn't let this go so I asked him why he had taken my hoe. He said he hadn't taken our hoe. After a brief explanation from him, I realized that his idea of ownership was closer to the Bible's then mine. If I own something it is available for everyone to use and all that is required is that we be good stewards of it so more people can use it.

Glen Mickel
Former Missionary to West Africa

Father, help me to be a good steward of what you have given me. Help me to lend freely and give generously so that others might be blessed and you might be glorified...

"Occupy till I come....It will be good for that servant whom the master finds doing so when he returns."

LUKE 19:13...LUKE 12:43 (KJV)

*W*e were beginning to look like our passport pictures, so we decided it was time to go home. We left the heat and humidity of the Philippines, stopped in Singapore and Malaysia, took a 36-hour train ride in India and dodged cows and garbage in Nepal before we arrived in Los Angeles. There we double-locked the doors as the city was girding up for possible riots. We were back in the good old USA.

Reverse culture shock set in. We had forgotten the privileges of America—hot water from the tap, safe drinking water, dishwashers, orderly traffic, clean streets, and fast service at the post office and the bank. And the choices! Soup or salad? What kind of salad dressing? Baked potato or French fries? Whole milk, 2%, or non-fat? Choose from 25 kinds of cereal, and wear 55% cotton and 45% polyester or 100% polyester or 100% cotton or any number of other combinations. There is no end to it.

After a three-month trip sharing in churches about what the Lord is doing in Asia and encouraging participation in the mission mandate that Jesus gave to all of us, we retired from Foursquare Missions. But we were not retired from serving the Lord; there is unfinished business.

Our first seven years of "retirement" have meant three trips to Nepal and three to the Philippines, 11 months in Malawi, three months in Singapore and Cambodia, and a planned trip to Romania.

Missionaries don't retire; they just keep going and going and going.

Don and Sharon Nicholson
Former Missionaries to the Philippines

> *Lord, you are never finished with us, and you never discard us. I thank you that you have a purpose for me at each stage of my life; I ask that you would reveal to me the plans you have for me right now...*

"My frame was not hidden from you... your eyes saw my unformed body. All the days ordained for me were written in your book before one of them came to be."

PSALM 139:15-16

*I*n 1952 I was born in Sri Lanka in a village called Nedimala. When my mother was about to give birth to me, she fell. I was born deformed—my legs were blue and lifeless below the knee, my chest was bloated, and my head was oversized. I was unable to walk and talk for quite a few years. My mom and grandmother did not know what was wrong with me, but they prayed. Finally after many years of prayer, the Lord healed some of the problems with my body. I was able to walk and talk, but there were still constant problems with my stomach. The Lord continued to heal me and little by little my chest started going back to normal size.

When I was 12 I wanted to commit suicide. I didn't have a good family background. My father drank a lot and did not treat our family well. I also had a very poor self-image because of what had happened during the early years of my life. It was then the Lord appeared to me in a dream on two consecutive nights. He was hanging on the cross and His blood was pouring down his body. His eyes were pools of love. He said, "If you give Me your life I will touch you and change your life completely. I will give you hope, I will use you in your country and around the world and you will do great things for Me. I will make you a prophet to the nations."

I didn't understand all these things, but the voice was compelling and was spoken with such love that I gave my life to Jesus—I opened my heart and surrendered my life to Him.

Leslie Keegel
National Leader, Sri Lanka

Thank you, Father, that you heal both the body and the soul. Make me an agent of your healing touch today. Touch people through me as I pray and minister to others today...

"Therefore God exalted him to the highest place...that at the name of Jesus every knee should bow, in heaven and on earth and under the earth, and every tongue confess that Jesus Christ is Lord..."

PHILIPPIANS 2:9-11

A local witch doctor attended the women's meeting so that she could disrupt it. She arrived in her usual attire—beaded goatskin amulets hung around her ankles, wrists, and across her chest and encircling her waist. Her white turban and incantation stick set her apart and marked her status.

We began to pray in Jesus' name, binding the demons that bound the witch doctor and interceding for her salvation. The women began singing praises to the Lord and testifying of His work in their lives. The witch doctor crouched over her stick as demons tried to disrupt the ministry of the Holy Spirit.

When the women laid hands on a lady who was ill, the witch doctor tried to match and block these prayers. But as the women prayed, the presence of the Lord was too strong for the witch doctor. I invited those who had needs to step into the center of the circle, and the witch doctor crawled forward on her knees. I explained the plan of salvation and the need for her to lay aside her craft to follow Jesus. When I asked if she wanted to accept Christ into her heart, the witch doctor nodded her head and handed me her incantation stick. She removed all her amulets, charms, turban and even washed her face before uttering a prayer of repentance, asking the Lord Jesus to be her Savior.

An awestruck joy spread across the woman's face. After the meeting, the women gathered outside to encircle the pile of amulets, clothes and stick, and the former witch doctor herself lit the match to burn the paraphernalia and mementos of her past.

Terry Manthe
Missionary to South Africa

> *Jesus, thank you that we have authority over all the power of the enemy! May captives be set free as we intercede...*

"and you will be my witnesses...to the ends of the earth."

ACTS 1:8

*B*eautiful savannah stretched out before us as we traveled deep into the bush of Africa. Plains turned to gullies with rocks the size of small houses. The trusty four wheel drive truck crawled up and over every obstacle with obvious delight. Coming out of an area of dense trees, we stopped to avoid a herd of elephants. We were far from civilization, and everywhere we looked we saw animals.

After traveling most of the day, we came to a village and we began to look forward to some chai and samosas. As we approached the outskirts of the village, we noticed people began to run from our vehicle, the adults hiding in their huts and the children running into the maize fields.

One brave young man finally came out of hiding and we discovered the problem we had caused. These people had heard of white-skinned people but had never seen any, and the children had never seen a vehicle. They actually thought our vehicle was an animal that you could see inside and it had eaten some people and was digesting them (which was why they turned white).

Because of these events we had their complete attention as we began to witness to them about Jesus and His love for them. That day, the Gospel came to that remote place.

Glen Mickel
Former Missionary to West Africa

> *Lord, show me how to partner with you in bringing your good news to people who have never heard about you. I will pray; I will give so others can go; I will even go myself if you tell me where you would like me to go...*

> *"How good and pleasant it is when brothers
> live together in unity!"*
>
> PSALM 133:1

*J*eová was a convicted bank robber. He was known as a hardened criminal. While he was serving his time in prison, the Foursquare women's group visited him and he gave his life to the Lord. After his release on probation, he began attending the Foursquare Church.

As he sat in church one day, he could hardly believe his eyes. Walking into the sanctuary was Judge Paulo Jussara, the judge who had been over his probation process. Judge Jussara was known for his tough decisions. Some thought he was excessively harsh with all criminals with whom he dealt, as he had been with Jeová. The sentiments between Jeová and Judge Jussara were resentment, mistrust and bitterness.

But now they were meeting not as judge and criminal, but as two pardoned sinners before the throne of God. Brother Jussara spoke with Brother Jeová. As they talked they both rejoiced that just as Jeová had given his heart to the Lord, so too Judge Jussara had recently met the Lord in a Foursquare church in a neighboring city.

Jonathan Hall
Missionary to Brazil

> *Lord, forgive me for any feelings of bitterness or unforgiveness that I harbor in my heart. I give all such feelings to you, and I forgive all who have wronged me, just as you forgave all my sins in Christ Jesus...*

"Since you have heard all about him and have learned the truth
that is in Jesus, throw off your old evil nature and your former way
of life...you are a new person, created in God's likeness!"

EPHESIANS 4:21,22,24 (NLT)

Twenty people crowded onto the bamboo veranda of the tiny one-room house as neighborhood prostitutes and drug addicts watched curiously. Soon, the sounds of praise and worship of God filled the air, attracting some of them. One woman who came was the wife of Norman, an opium dealer. Norman noticed that his wife began changing after she started attending the group. He was so intrigued by the changes he saw in his wife that he began to listen to the preaching from a hiding place behind a bamboo wall. For many weeks, he listened to the message behind the wall, until one day he came forward and asked for prayer for protection from the violence permeating the slum. Soon thereafter, Norman accepted Jesus Christ as his Lord and Savior.

FMI Missionary Greg Fisher reports Norman is now a changed man. His face radiates the love and grace of the Lord. When the original cell group pastor left the area, Norman quietly began to take up the responsibility—bringing people to cell group, gathering them together for the walk to church each Sunday and bringing others to Christ. Last week the full depth of Norman's conversion became evident in a new sign posted on the front door of his small house. It reads, "No Opium Here. I am now a Christian."

Norman, the onetime opium seller, now serves a new and better Master.

Foursquare Global REPORT, 1999

Lord, I want to see the kind of changes in my life that will
cause the unbelievers around me to draw near to you!
Please show me those areas in my life that need to be sur-
rendered to you...

"God, who has called you...is faithful."

1 CORINTHIANS 1:9

"Newly arrived in Madrid, Spain, I took a get-acquainted walk by myself through our neighborhood stores and shops. We had four children, ages two through twelve. I was horrified at the prices for simple things like pants and shirts, let alone shoes! My knees felt weak and I wanted to sit alongside the curb and cry.

"Lord, we will never make it here, not due to the ministry assignment or to our not being accepted, but financially! Does the missions board know how expensive it is, even with our cost-of-living adjustment? Do they realize we have four children?" I whined right there in the street.

In a reassuring and quiet voice, I heard His Spirit speak to me, "The board did not send you. I did." A flood of peace poured over me. That was in 1990 and though it was sometimes tough financially, we never went hungry and the children always had shoes and clothes to wear.

More importantly, I learned my life is in the Lord's hands. We knew and were very grateful that the board and missions director had sent us to Spain. However, we also knew that the great Sender was behind that decision. He would remain faithful. What a safe place to be in.

Molly Doland
Missionary to Spain

Thank you, Lord, that there is no safer place to be in than in the center of your will. I answer your call today, and though I at times feel inadequate and unworthy, I know that you will be faithful to help me to do the things you are calling me to do...

"'If you can?' said Jesus. 'Everything is possible
for him who believes.'"

MARK 9:23

On one trip to the village of Nakento, in the Dutania Valley of Papua New Guinea, we had to leave the Jeep at the river and walk to the village because the heavy rains had swollen the river.

When we arrived, the Christians met us, exclaiming that one of the mothers of the village had died. Before her death, she had told her son that she was going to put a curse on him. Then after she died, when her son tried to leave the gravesite, he felt hands around his neck, choking him.

My response was simple and direct, "Let's pray!"

We did pray, and then I sent someone to go get the son. The people were hesitant to go to the grave, thinking that he would be choked to death when he tried to leave. "No, we have prayed," I responded.

To their surprise, they were able to lead the son away from the grave, and he had no choking feeling. We gathered around and prayed a prayer of deliverance. After everyone's eyes were opened, the son was standing there with a great big smile. That day he received Jesus as his Savior, and many came to Christ because of this miracle.

Christ is an awesome miracle worker. In every situation, nothing is impossible for Him!

Mason and Virgene Hughes
Former Missionaries to Papua New Guinea

Thank you, Lord, that nothing is impossible for you. Give
me faith to believe and to trust you in these situations that I
bring before you today...

"But I have raised you up for this very purpose,
that I might show you my power and that my name
might be proclaimed in all the earth."

EXODUS 9:16

O n the final night of an outdoor crusade in the western district of
Kenya, the Holy Spirit moved in a profound and unusual way. When
the invitation was given to receive Christ, the response was so large that
sufficient counselors and pastors couldn't be found to pray with everyone.

As we prayed, God began to move through them with words of wisdom
concerning demonic bondages that He was breaking. People began remov-
ing their witchcraft charms. A pastor collected all the charms, placed them
in pile on the platform, soaked the pile with gasoline, and set it on fire. As
the charms burned, people began calling out that they were being healed.

All the activity attracted more and more people seeking deliverance and
salvation, and the crowd of six hundred began to swell. Another pastor
climbed on the platform and exhorted the people to expect God's healing
power, which caused another wave of healing. By then the crowd refused to
disburse. The exhausted crusade team continued to minister until finally a
huge driving rainstorm forced the crowd back into their homes.

The name of Jesus is so very powerful. It breaks bondages, heals bodies
and souls, and brings life to people who were once dead. Praise His Name!

Greg Fisher
Missionary to Uganda

> *Thank you, Lord, for the power that is in your name. Help*
> *me to walk in that power today and to proclaim your name*
> *and testify to your goodness in every situation and at every*
> *opportunity...*

"Watch out that no one deceives you."
MATTHEW 24:4

At the end of the road out of Panama City toward Colombia is a small town called Chepo. One evening the Foursquare church there gathered for their Christmas program. The children were costumed, the recitations were ready, and the visiting missionaries, Arthur and Leland Edwards, were the guests.

As the evening progressed, the missionaries asked to take pictures of the program. The people were both delighted and intrigued. However, the flash unit would not work. Flash bulbs for cameras were new to many of the people and it was hard to explain why there was a delay. Finally, the missionaries were able to plug their flash bulbs into the light socket that hung from the ceiling. Everyone was poised. As they turned the switch at the socket, there was a terrible flash. The lights had blown out and the people began running into the night. Mothers with babies in their arms jumped through open windows. Everyone left the church through whatever means of escape was available. Only the pastor and the two missionaries remained. Only after it was evident that the church was intact and there was no damage did the people return.

Some time before our visit, an enemy of the church had predicted that lightning would strike the church and destroy it—the people were convinced the bulb was the lightning and they were doomed.

The enemy of our souls tries to do the same thing in our lives—he tries to trick believers into believing that an uncontrolled bolt of lightning is about to hit their lives when in reality it is a flash of light controlled by God.

Dr. Leland Edwards
Former Missionary to Panama
Missions Director, 1965-1988

Lord, I thank you that no curse against me will prevail. I have peace, knowing that you watch over me at all times...

*"The Lord is my helper; I will not be afraid.
What can man do to me?"*

HEBREWS 13:6

*I*n 1967, the Nigerian-Biafra Civil War was raging. Military check points on the roads were every 20 miles. The few whites remaining in the country were all "suspect" of being agents of the enemy. Conditions were deplorable.

I was returning home from some church business in the "up country" some 60 miles from our Jungle Mission Compound when I came to one of the checkpoints. No soldiers were present, but I did notice some soldiers gathered together with some other soldiers at the upcoming barricade some 200 yards away. I coasted the car down to where they were and stopped. Hurriedly, a soldier opened my door and jerked me out. His companion jammed a rifle into my gut and demanded, "WHY HAVE YOU RUN THE BLOCKADE?" I explained I was only trying to make it easier for them. They never heard a word I said. "GET OVER AGAINST THAT WALL!" one said. Both men had their rifles now and I heard the click of the bolts as they chambered shells into the magazine. "I'VE KILLED WHITE MEN BEFORE AND I'M GOING TO KILL YOU!"

Standing against the wall they continued to harangue and harass me for several minutes. In the meantime, a jeep full of soldiers pulled up. It was time to change the guard. The officer in charge demanded they release me. I thanked him as I left to make my way home to the compound with only three more checkpoints remaining to go through.

Jim Kitchell
Former Missionary to Nigeria

*Lord, what can man do to me? You are the one who holds
my life in your hands. I will not be afraid...*

> *"Therefore put on the full armor of God, so that when the day of evil comes, you may be able to stand..."*
>
> EPHESIANS 6:13

We were stopped dead in our tracks in the middle of our small-town market by a delivery truck that wasn't moving until he had completely unloaded his goods. While cars coming from either direction were noisily protesting his affront to traffic flow, the kids and I sat in our own car watching the ocean of shoppers roll past in their brilliant Nigerian colors.

Suddenly I sensed the market crowd shift in its own flow of traffic to make way for some procession. Just ahead came four local priests of a cult society known in our town. Each man was wrapped in a white toga-type robe and each had a staff that was intricately carved, indicating various levels of power. Their heads were shaven and around their necks were medicine pouches filled with magic potions. They walked barefoot; their posture was bold and exuded the power they knew they had.

I stared at them as they came right at our car. I wanted to exhibit some kind of "power posture" so they would sense I was a priest of the Most High God. I naively hoped that they would know my Power Source was greater than theirs. It didn't happen. They brushed our car as they went their way.

I was left to ponder my own notion of how spiritual encounters take place. But one thing had been confirmed in my life: the forces of evil are not brushed aside by just any trivial stance I may take as a Christian. It is warfare of the grandest scale. But God guarantees victory to the Christian who is fully prepared for battle.

Kathy Kieselhorst
Former Missionary to Nigeria, now serving with her husband, Bill, in South Africa

> *Lord, help me boldly face the battle against the enemy. Give me your wisdom as I stand where you have called me...*

"...Unless you become like a child..."
MATTHEW 18:3

*H*aving the faith as a child means believing God to do the impossible. In the beginning days of our church in Ecuador, the faith of the new converts was awesome.

Petita and her children lived behind a humble dwelling in a hut, located in the middle of a muddy area. It was all she could afford from the income she had from washing and delivering clothes.

The owner of the hut, however, raised the rent and she could not afford the new rate and began looking for another home. She wanted to live near the church and so she began looking at the "shacks" near her present home. She could not afford any of them, and she came to us asking for prayer. As we prayed, the Lord impressed on me to tell her to stop looking for the worst house, but to find the best one. In her simple child-like faith, she began to look.

The new group of apartments nearby was made of cement, with a faucet on every porch unit instead of one faucet in the patio for everyone to use. When she spoke to the owner, the rent was far beyond what she could pay.

"Well, how much can you pay?" the owner asked.

She told him she was a Christian and attended the church up the road. "I wouldn't lie to you; I can pay that amount every month without fail, but no more." The owner rented the apartment to her at her rate.

"I looked for the best and the Lord gave it to me!" she rejoiced.

Art and Marian Gadberry
Former Missionaries to Ecuador

> *Lord, give me the faith like a child to believe that you can do anything...*

"...My elect shall long enjoy the work of their hands."
ISAIAH 65:22 (NKJV)

The city of Maesai is in northern Thailand, near the Myanmar border. After Philip Ahone, the Foursquare national leader in Myanmar, and I ministered in the Maesai church, Philip discovered he was restricted by his passport from crossing back into Myanmar. Philip wondered if there were any Burmese in that area to whom we could minister that evening. He discovered there was a gem factory nearby that employed Burmese laborers.

When he arrived at the factory, Philip discovered that a factory foreman was a brother of a friend of his. This man had been praying for three weeks that God would send someone to help him start a Sunday evening service among the workers. Philip encouraged him to gather the workers together and told him that he and an American missionary would return to speak to them.

That evening approximately 75 people came to the service. After our worship time and a simple message, we gave an invitation to any who wanted to respond to the Gospel. What started as a trickle of people turned into the whole assembly coming forward to either accept Jesus as their Savior or to recommit themselves to the Lord.

Some great fruit was produced that night—two who came forward that night now assist in the Tachilek church, another is in Bible school in Yangon, Myanmar, and a fourth is pastoring in the village of Monlin. Wow! God once again proves that he has a great plan that produces great fruit and great enjoyment for those who serve Him!

Phil and Diane Franklin
Former Missionaries to Thailand

Lord, I pray that as I do your work, there would be lasting fruit and that you would be glorified...

"Jesus told his disciples a parable to show them that they should always pray and not give up."

LUKE 18:1

*V*icente, with his wife Lidia and six small children, pastored one of our barrio churches in San Salvador. They were very poor and he was often unable to secure a job, so Lidia took a job working for us in our home in order to be able to feed their children. After we retired in 1980, Lidia kept in touch with us through correspondence. About two years later she wrote to us asking for prayer and counsel. She said that Vicente had left her and the children and was living with another woman.

We told her that we would agree with her in prayer for God to convict him of his sins and to help him to repent and return to his family. We also told her that she must not become discouraged if her prayers were not answered right away, because it sometimes takes a long time to make a person willing to do God's will, and God does not force His will upon people.

Each year she would write that her husband had still not returned but she was still praying. One Christmas, she wrote that he had returned and asked for forgiveness, and that they were now attending the Central Foursquare Church in San Salvador. God is faithful!

Charles and Nelwyn Gosling
Former Missionaries to El Salvador

Lord, there are so many prayers that I gave up on because the answer did not come immediately. Give me a heart to persevere in prayer and not quit until I have an answer from you...

"Pray also for me, that whenever I open my mouth, words may be given me so that I will fearlessly make known the mystery of the gospel...Pray that I may declare it fearlessly, as I should."

EPHESIANS 6:19-20

Myanmar is a country under martial law ruled by a military government. In 1964, all missionaries were expelled. Buddhism is promoted and there are restrictions on public meetings; some pastors have even been jailed.

One Wednesday evening, Philip Ahone, our national leader in Myanmar, was visited by four strange men. "You are summoned by the government!" they barked at him.

Knowing that this meant arrest, Philip asked for a reason. Their reply was, "You have no right to ask!" Blindfolded, they led him away to jail.

"Please allow me to bring my Bible," said Philip. "I am a pastor."

"You are not a pastor, you are a prisoner!" they replied.

"I am a Christian and would like to take my Bible with me."

"No Bible may come into the jail."

"If you do not allow me to take in this Bible, all the curses in it will fall on you!"

Philip was taken—with his Bible—to a stuffy, congested jail occupied by 400 inmates. At 5:00 a.m. the next morning, the prisoners were aroused and commanded to worship the picture of a Buddhist temple. He refused, as did a few others. When asked why, they gave a clear Christian testimony. That evening he preached to the prisoners, beginning with "I have good news for you…" Seventy people knelt, confessed their sins and received Jesus as Savior.

His boldness was answered by the authorities placing him in solitary confinement in an eight foot by ten foot cement cell.

Continued on next page…

Gary Cooper
Former Missionary to Hong Kong

Lord, so many are suffering for your sake. I pray that you would strengthen them and that they might be set free...

"He has delivered us from such a deadly peril, and he will deliver us. On him we have set our hope that he will continue to deliver us..."

2 CORINTHIANS 1:10

Continued from previous page...

After one week in solitary confinement, Philip's entire body began to ache, shaking and trembling with weakness. The sergeant who had charge over him took pity, explaining that his illness was the result of poisoned water. Secretly, fresh water was smuggled into the cell for Philip to drink.

There was little improvement over the following week. He was taken outside to receive some sun and fresh air. As he walked by the cell next to his, Philip called to the other prisoner, "How long have you been in your cell?" There was no answer. Another of the prisoners answered for the silent one, "Twenty-two years."

Out of his suffering, Philip began to weep, "How long, Lord? I am nothing. Please help!" Two weeks later, the cell was opened and a hood was placed over Philip's face.

Philip was taken to a place where a paper was shoved in front of him and he was ordered to sign it. To his amazement, it was a declaration that he would not sue the government! He quickly signed it, and he was released and placed in a car which took him home.

Not only is Philip Ahone's testimony a miraculous example of God's protection of His servants, but it is typical of what many of our pastors and Foursquare believers are experiencing in several areas across Asia.

Gary Cooper
Former Missionary to Hong Kong

> *Lord, the captives are set free thanks to you. You help all those who call upon your name. I continue to pray for my brothers and sisters behind bars today...*

"Heal me, O Lord, and I will be healed..."
JEREMIAH 17:14

For all of his life Richard Bennin had been plagued with sickle-cell anemia syndrome. The disease is a genetic disorder of the blood that causes the body to produce deformed red blood cells. The cells are bent in the shape of a sickle and therefore do not carry oxygen to the body efficiently. The disease causes otherwise healthy looking individuals to experience severe pain in the joints, and have sudden onsets of illness.

Recently during his devotional times, Richard earnestly prayed to the Lord, asking for healing from the disease. He said nothing to the other people living in his house, but waited patiently to receive healing. During a recent visit to the clinic on another matter, he asked the doctor to test him again for the sickle-cell trait. The test was performed, and several days later the results confirmed what Richard already knew by faith: There was no evidence of sickle-cell anemia! This indeed was a mighty miracle.

Greg Fisher
Missionary to Uganda

Thank you Lord, for the health you have given me. Heal me in those places where I need your touch...heal my friends and loved ones as I lift them before you now...

> *"The steps of a good man are ordered by the Lord,*
> *and He delights in his way."*
>
> PSALM 37:23 (NKJV)

*I*t is the very special divine appointments that come our way as we travel that affirm to us the truth of Psalm 37:23, that a good man's steps are ordered of the Lord.

For example, once when we were walking down the streets of Stockholm, Sweden, we met a young man from Norway who was selling post cards to finance a trip to work with disadvantaged children in Africa. As we stopped and talked with him about how he could really be a help to the children of Africa, the Holy Spirit moved on that young man's heart and he openly accepted Jesus Christ right there on the street. He prayed with all his heart, and was receptive to what God was doing in his life at that very moment.

On another occasion, as Carol walked by a restaurant in Baguio City, Philippines, she struck up a conversation with a beautiful young lady and she invited Carol to lunch. The conversation quickly turned to God's love and plan for their lives. As the Holy Spirit caused her heart to open, she responded to God's love, and joined hands with Carol and offered to let Jesus be her Lord.

There are so many stories we could tell about God's divine appointments. Be on the lookout for appointments that God has for you to minister his love and grace to the people that He not only loves but also died to redeem.

Fred and Carol Dawson
Former Missionaries to Hong Kong and Singapore

Lord, come and order my steps today. Give me divine
appointments; lead me and guide me so that I might come
across those to whom you would have me minister. Give me
the right words and the right actions in every situation...

"...greater is He that is in you, than he that is in the world."
1 JOHN 4:4 (KJV)

*W*hile brother Vinton Johnson, missionary to Panama, was away for two weeks doing itinerary work in the other regions of Darien, Mrs. Johnson was left alone in the Choco Indian camp.

One of the Indians and his wife came to her and suggested that they stay with her at night because they were afraid that some danger might befall her.

"Before I was saved," the man explained, "I did many things to try and kill Brother Johnson. I tried to set a fire under the house, but it would not burn. I paid money to the witch doctor to have him destroy Brother Johnson, and I even tried to poison him. Now Brother Johnson is away, and I'm afraid that others who have not found Christ as their Savior and Lord will try to harm you. Please let us spend the night here with you."

But Sister Johnson said no. She explained to the troubled Indian couple, "Since Christ has come into my heart, and into yours as well, Satan has no power over us. He that is within us is greater than he that is in the world."

Foursquare World ADVANCE, 1965

> *Father, help me to remember today that He who indwells me is greater than he who is in the world. Thank you for your protection, and that you are going before me and guarding over me in ways I don't even recognize. Teach me to walk in Christ's victory over Satan and give me bold confidence in every situation...*

"For my thoughts are not your thoughts, neither are your ways my ways," declares the Lord. "As the heavens are higher than the earth, so are my ways higher than your ways and my thoughts than your thoughts."

ISAIAH 55:8-9

When our team left the village, we had inaugurated the newest Foursquare church in Ghana. Their first service had 46 adults and over 40 children. Unfortunately, we were not able to conduct a water baptism because of the dry season that we were in the midst of. There was no water, and the people expected no significant rain for at least two months. Thankfully, God intervened!

The very first night that we were in the village there was a downpour. As a result, an elderly woman came to the door early the next morning to have the holy man pray for her severe headaches. She had determined that I was the holy man because the much-needed rain had come with me. The amazing thing is that we had downpours every night I was in the village.

One night it rained so hard and for so long that we could not conduct the service. I was disappointed and quite honestly wasn't sure what demon or curse to bind! It wasn't until the last night in the village that Pastor Nathaniel informed me of the talk in the village center—that I must truly be a man of God with a message to be heard because it had rained every night that I had been there.

I saw the rain and the canceled service as a failure, but the people saw it as a sign from God!

Manny Hernandez
Former Missionary to Benin

> *Father, help me to trust in your ways and to recognize that my thoughts and my ways of looking at things are not always the best way. Give me faith to trust you to work even in ways that are not immediately apparent...*

> *"Blessed are you when they revile and persecute you, and say all kinds of evil against you falsely for My sake. Rejoice and be exceedingly glad, for great is your reward in heaven..."*
> MATTHEW 5:11-12 (NKJV)

Not long ago three government agents visited Pastor Takesure, who pastors in Nyamapanda on the Mozambique border. The agents demanded to see his party membership card. He, of course, did not have one, so he was forcibly taken into Kotwa township for "re-education," along with a number of others from the area.

Upon arrival the captives were ordered to chant pro-government slogans. All of them agreed to do it except Takesure who declared his loyalty to the Lord Jesus Christ. He then proceeded to chant his own pro-Jesus slogans. This made the CIO agents furious and they began hitting him with large sticks. All the while the others were witnessing this and continuing with the pro-government slogans. The angrier the CIO agents became, the more Takesure cried his allegiance to Christ.

After a number of hours, seeing they were getting nowhere, they said they would only allow Takesure to go if he paid $100 ZIM (about 30 US cents) for a government membership card. Takesure paid the money and then declared to them all, "You have taken my money but you will never have my heart—it belongs to the Lord Jesus Christ and one day you too will have to confess that He is Lord."

Alan and Anneke Frank
Missionaries to Zimbabwe

> *Lord, give me boldness to testify for you and to live for you no matter what the circumstances are around me...*

"Therefore I tell you, whatever you ask for in prayer,
believe that you have received it, and it will be yours."

MARK 11:24

The Agape Foursquare Church in Croatia was praying for a woman in their congregation whose husband was being wrongfully held in an Italian jail. Not only were they praying for his release, they were also praying for his salvation.

One night a powerful beam of light flooded the jail cell and the man was knocked to the floor. An audible voice spoke to him about Jesus Christ. He asked the Lord to have mercy upon him and to come save him. Immediately the man was baptized in the Holy Spirit.

The man could not afford a lawyer, so he prayed, "Holy Spirit, please be my attorney." When he was brought before the court, he began his defense with his testimony. By the end, the judge was in tears and ordered his release from prison!

FMI Communiqué, 1994

> *Lord, I thank you for the powerful answers that you send*
> *when I pray to you. Give me more faith to trust in your*
> *goodness and your power to act...*

> *"Our mouths were filled with laughter, our tongues*
> *with songs of joy. Then it was said among the nations,*
> *'The Lord has done great things for them.'"*
>
> PSALM 126:2

Two things happened soon after I arrived on the mission field that make me chuckle now.

The Tolle family had warmly welcomed me, as had the hot Nicaraguan weather, and as I prepared to go to bed, they warned me not to open the window's wooden covering. There was no glass or screen in the window and it was unsafe to sleep with that window open.

In the hot air, I tossed and turned until I finally got up and opened the wooden covers. In bed again, I slept deeply until I sensed something was wrong. A dark figure moved carefully through the open window towards me. Thinking I could push the intruder back out the window, I jumped up. He fled back the way he came.

Soon lights flashed on the street and there was a call, "La Senorita! La Senorita!" I looked out to see the crowd holding up my intimate underwear and waiting for me to come to claim it. With all the dignity I could muster, I reclaimed my possessions and the police took the thief to jail.

On another occasion, when I was learning the language, I was impressed that many English words have a similar form in Spanish. One day as I was talking with a group of young people, I began telling them about an embarrassing situation. "Yo estaba tan embarazada" I said. This received a puzzled and quiet reception.

Later one of the youth approached me and whispered, "Hermana, in our language 'embarazada' means "expecting a child." So much for words that have the same meaning in both languages!

Dorothy Buck
Former Missionary to Latin America

> *Lord, thank you for all the times you have brought joy into*
> *my life and filled my mouth with laughter. You are so good...*

"The Lord is my rock, my fortress and my deliverer..."
PSALM 18:2

"Most missionaries experience at one time or another that feeling of being alone and a long way from home. Add illness to that, and it can be very difficult. That is what happened to me.

One minute I felt as if I was in a furnace, burning up with fever. Then it seemed someone had put me into a freezer and I shook violently. I had trouble keeping my thoughts logical; I was becoming delusional. Then Satan began speaking to me.

The devil told me what a bad missionary I was. He brought up every sin I had ever committed and made me question how I could even think about remaining on the mission field. I should leave and go home. I knew Satan is "the accuser of the brethren" and a liar and destroyer, but I couldn't get him out of my mind. I felt as if I was going crazy; I could get no relief.

Finally, in my soul, I was able to cry out to Jesus. Almost simultaneously a deafening, booming, crashing thunderclap pierced my consciousness. My mind was clear. I realized God had not abandoned me; in fact, He had beforehand prepared a huge thunderhead over our house to be used at a time of His choosing.

The next day, although weak, I traveled 45 miles for a national meeting. I was healed!

Diane Franklin
Former Missionary to Thailand

Thank you Lord! Your voice breaks through and causes Satan to flee before us. You truly are our deliverer, our fortress, and our rock...

*"The reason the Son of God appeared
was to destroy the devil's work."*

1 JOHN 3:8

The strength and clarity of the message made the voice that spoke seem almost audible: "If you continue to serve Jesus Christ, you will die this year!" Looking around, this pastor of nearly 300 believers in a small village in Myanmar saw no one. Fear immediately gripped his heart and he sought help from an elder pastor/friend from the neighboring village. One week later, that elder died of a stroke. The entire village became so frightened that no one, not even the pastor, would dare enter the door of the church.

Hearing this, Foursquare national leader Philip Ahone was deeply troubled. He boldly arranged for a service to be held in the village and invited everyone to come. No one showed up—but he had an idea.

Visiting the oldest persons in the village, he challenged them, "You're so old that you are going to die anyway! What have you got to lose? Accept Jesus openly so that you can go to heaven when you die!" The invitation was accepted and the first service was held with the eldest folk in the village as participants.

During the meeting, it was learned that someone had brought a man who had been blind for twelve years. When Philip prayed for the man, sight was instantly restored. The man jumped and ran throughout the entire village shouting with joy. Fear was broken and the village recognized that the power of Jesus Christ was greater than any demonic force that had spoken earlier.

Gary Cooper
Former Missionary to Hong Kong

*Lord, I thank you that you do have greater power than
Satan, and I need not fear anything that he can do to me...*

"Go up and take possession of the land I have given you..."

DEUTERONOMY 9:23

*M*y husband Al is from the Philippines and, although we lived there for a while, we never thought we'd go back. However, as we were preparing to leave our home in Dallas and go to LIFE Bible College in Los Angeles, we were surprised when our pastor said, "Who knows... there is a big spiritual need in the Philippines, the Lord might send you back!"

In the weeks ahead at Angelus Temple in Los Angeles, God gave Al a vision. He saw a map of the Philippines in solid gold. The Lord reminded him that, as the 49ers had come to California and staked their claims for gold, he was to claim the Philippines for God.

When Al told me about his vision, the Lord witnessed to me that God was going to send us to the Philippines. From that point forward, we could hardly wait.

In 1955, we were appointed as missionaries to the Philippines. Dr. Herman Mitzner counseled us, "I know you want to see many victories, but you must always remember, before you can have a victory, you must have a battle." The Spirit then reminded us that when David conquered Goliath, he had said, "The battle is the Lord's."

We knew that we had staked our claim, and that God had said "go and take possession," and that ultimately the battle belonged to Him. We left for the Philippines with confidence that victory was before us!

Mollie Chaves
Former Missionary to the Philippines

> *Lord, I thank you that you go before me in every battle, and as long as I am following you, you will make your cause victorious...*

"May your ways be known throughout the earth,
your saving power among people everywhere."
PSALM 67:2 (NLT)

One Sunday I was visiting Bob and Kathy Brack, our Foursquare missionaries in Malawi, on the site of a new church building in Blantyre when I noticed a visitor in the crowd, a young Chinese man who I found out later was working in Malawi as a physician's assistant.

"What an unusual sight!" I thought. "Two Americans in southern Africa praying with a young Chinese man to receive Jesus Christ as Savior and Lord!"

The young man carried with him a brand new Chinese Bible, and he carefully searched the scriptures as we preached the Gospel. He had heard of Christianity since coming to Africa and wanted to know more about the Gospel. At the conclusion of the morning's message, I asked for those who wished to be set free from the bondage of sin and shame to come forward for prayer. As Bob and I prayed and ministered to this young man, the saving power of Jesus Christ came into his life. In time, this young man will go back to his home in China and he will carry with him the message of Jesus Christ's saving power.

Greg Fisher
Missionary to Uganda

Lord, I marvel at how you bring people from all over to
hear the gospel. May your word continue to spread into
every corner of the earth...

> *"He said to the paralyzed man, 'I tell you, get up,*
> *take your mat and go home.'"*

LUKE 5:24

I was preaching an open-air revival in the city of Tela, Honduras, where each night we would pray for the sick. I would have the people who needed healing come forward and place their hands on the part of their bodies that was sick, and I would pray for them. After one such prayer, I noticed a skeletal-looking man arguing with one of the ushers—he wanted to come up onto the platform and give his testimony. They finally let him come up and he testified to what God had done.

After the service, while taking down the equipment, a taxi driver came up and asked about the man. I told him that he had gone home. "How did he do that?" he asked. I told him that he had taken his chair and walked off.

"That's not possible!" the driver exclaimed. "That man has been totally paralyzed from his neck down for the last seven years! I brought him last night and left him setting in his chair at the back of the crowd. After the service, I came back and got him and took him home. I brought him back tonight and left him in the same place. Now where is he?"

After much discussion, we convinced him to go to the man's home and see for himself. He did—he saw with his own eyes and believed.

Dean Truett
Former Missionary to Honduras

> *Lord, I ask you to help me to believe the impossible – that*
> *you can heal any disease, illness or injury, no matter how*
> *severe...*

"Preach the Word; be prepared in season and out of season..."

2 TIMOTHY 4:2

*W*aves of violence have taken many more lives in Papua New Guinea over the years than the recent waves of water. Fights between warring tribes, often lasting for years, are fueled by revenge killings. Despite dangerous circumstances such as these, a pioneer pastor obeyed the call of the Lord and set off for a neighboring village. Suddenly he was stopped by several men with guns.

As they marched him off into the bush he realized they were from an enemy village and that they would probably kill him. Instead, they took him to a house packed with people and told him, "Pastor, we don't really want to hurt you, but you have been ministering to our enemies. We have people here who need the Word, so you must preach to our people!"

The pastor thought it over, looked at the people, then at the guns still pointed at him, and he began to preach! When it was all over, the pastor rejoiced at how God had protected him and used him in a powerful way that day!

Bill Page
Missionary Pastor in Papua New Guinea

Thank you, Lord, for your protection and sovereignty...help me to be ready to share your Word in season and out of season, taking advantage of every opportunity you give me...

"I have given you authority to trample on snakes and scorpions and to overcome all the power of the enemy; nothing will harm you."

LUKE 10:19

One time Jack and Paul Anderson were on one side of the Great Swamp in Bolivia when their horses ran away from them. They knelt down and prayed and said, "All right, Lord, we are going to cross in your name." For three miles they waded through water up to their arm-pits, but not a single alligator or crocodile touched them.

Every morning I wept buckets of tears because of the mercy of God in that country. They had fevers but God kept them alive. If David Livingstone ever did a pioneer work—or Judson or Paton for that matter—they have never lived under more dangerous conditions than those under which the Andersons lived.

For eight years the Andersons have made their sandals by tanning the leather themselves. They have worn these sandals and have never been bitten by a poisonous snake! That is a miracle as they kill the snakes every day. It is possible to find them anytime and anywhere, and they kill them as though it were a common occurrence. It is possible to find them in the bed, in the kitchen, on the food, in the living room. Everywhere you walk you are liable to step on a snake. But they have never been bitten. God has protected them, praise His Name!

Harold Chalfant
Referring to Jack and Paul Anderson in Bolivia

Thank you, Lord, for your protecting power in the lives of our missionaries and in my life...

"He performs wonders that cannot be fathomed..."
JOB 9:10

*W*hile doing missionary work in Finland, we felt a strong leading to travel to Estonia, which was still under Soviet control. We were prompted by the Lord to go, even though we knew that it was only possible if we had a letter of invitation from someone within Estonia, which we did not have. Nonetheless, we felt that we were to go to the Estonian embassy to apply for visas. After ringing the bell for some time, we were informed that the office was closed but we could come in anyway. Once inside, I informed them that we were there to get visas to Estonia. We were told that we needed an invitation from someone within Estonia, and then we were told to have a seat.

They asked us, "For how long do you want the visas?" We told them we would like to have the visa for one year. They responded firmly that they did not give visas for longer than two weeks. They left us to sit alone, and I felt as though we had come to a dead end. However, after a few minutes, a tall, blond young man entered the room. He said, "Give me your passports and I will give you the visas." Fifteen minutes later this young man returned. With a smile he gave us our passports with one year, multiple entry visas attached.

Over the next several years, we came to know everyone who worked at the Embassy of Estonia in Helsinki. I often asked about the blond man who had worked there, only to be told that no one of that description had ever been an employee...it seems like a God thing to me!

Michael Stubbs
Missionary to Malaysia

> *Lord, you truly do perform wonders! Thank you for the way you go before me and do that which is impossible so that your word might go forth...*

"Then your light will break forth like the dawn,
and your healing will quickly appear."

ISAIAH 58:8

While living in Uganda, a Hindu woman attended a Foursquare Bible study and learned about Jesus and his miraculous healing power. Some time later she gave birth to a baby boy who soon quit breathing and turned blue. Distressed, the mother carried him to a medical facility, where she discovered an operating room full of doctors. They examined the baby and told the mother he was already dead and that nothing could be done.

The woman, however, did not give up. She fell to her knees and began to call on the name of Jesus. The child started to breathe again, but before the day was over, he stopped breathing two more times. The last time he stopped breathing, his small body turned completely black and he appeared to be dead. Again, the mother called out to God in the name of Jesus and her son came back to life. Today, that child is alive and completely well and normal.

That experience resulted in more than one changed life. Not only did the mother receive Christ as her Savior and Lord, but now her Hindu husband is attending church with her and is testifying that Jesus Christ is the only True and Living God.

Greg Fisher
Missionary to Uganda

> *Lord, help me to have faith in those "impossible" situations,*
> *that I might see your miraculous power at work in my life*
> *and the lives of those around me...*

> *"...I am with you always, to the very end of the age."*
> MATTHEW 28:20

"*Porque El vive no temo el mañana…*"
Even today when I hear this song (*Because He Lives*, but I can only sing it in Spanish!), I am reminded of a very special service. I am taken back to the place where we all long to be—in His presence:

Bombs and the sounds of machine guns went off all around us outside, but the women somehow felt safe and secure inside La Iglesia Central de la Iglesia Cuadrangular in Managua, Nicaragua. Our voices bellowed out the words to Bill Gaither's song, *Because He Lives*, and that made all the difference.

Those words brought peace to our souls and encouragement to our hearts. In that moment of togetherness, offering praise and worship to the Lord through our voices, we were able to set aside the noises of the war and the cries of pain as we soaked in His presence. With tears flowing down our faces and our hands lifted upward, someone gasped and softly spoke: "Look! A dove!"

We all opened our eyes, and, yes, there it was! A dove had entered the building and was touching every corner of that man-made sanctuary as it flew so freely in our midst. Paz! Paz! Peace! Peace! We knew the Prince of Peace had just blessed us with His presence!

Whether it is in the midst of a war or a storm or during a precious peaceful moment, God always finds a way to show us that He is right beside us and will never leave us!

Jennie King
Former Missionary to Nicaragua

> *Father, I ask that you would visit me with your presence and give me your peace this day...*

> *"Before they call I will answer;*
> *while they are still speaking I will hear."*
>
> ISAIAH 65:24

The narrow roads on the island of Tablas, in the central Philippines, wind around the mountains and over some stretches of steep terrain. One of the steepest grades is just before entering the small village of Guinbirayan.

Pastor Familara and I, along with a group of believers, climbed into our Jeep for the trip to minister in Guinbirayan. As we began the descent into the village, we realized the brakes were not holding. It was a wild ride! We prayed as we gathered speed down the mountain road. God graciously kept the Jeep on the road and we safely reached the bottom of the mountain.

We investigated and found that the brake fluid was gone. We had no brake fluid with us and there was no place to buy any. Again we prayed, and before long a bus arrived in the village. One of our group asked the driver where we needed to go to find some brake fluid. The driver looked at him with wonderment as he said, "I don't usually carry it with me, but this morning I brought along some brake fluid!"

God knew exactly what we needed before we had a clue!

Jack and Aline Richey
Former Missionaries to the Philippines

> *Thank you, Father, that even before I call on you, you have provided the answer. Thank you for being there for me; help me to bring glory to you today...*

> *"For the word of God is full of living power.*
> *It is sharper than the sharpest knife, cutting deep*
> *into our innermost thoughts and desires."*
>
> HEBREWS 4:12 (NLT)

In the city of Maceió in northeastern Brazil, we were at the radio station being interviewed regarding an event the following day when we discovered another Foursquare brother who was being interviewed there as well. The brother had recorded a CD after having been completely healed of throat cancer! The CD was a testimony to God's greatness.

In the city of Castanhal, the Amazon region of Pará, there was a farmer named Tonhâo who was known throughout that region as one of the meanest men around. Most people avoided being around Tonhâo, as his moods were usually pretty nasty. Recently, though, I visited the home of Pastor Waldir Batista and met a gentleman who enjoyed playing with Pastor Batista's children. This kind and gentle man was Tonhâo. He told his amazing story of how God completely changed his life and prospered his farms after he gave his life to the Lord.

Yes, the Word of God is like a sharp, two-edged sword. It cuts deep to take away our sin and we are never the same!

Jonathan Hall
Missionary to Brazil

> *Thank you, Lord, that you not only heal the sick but you also convict of sins and completely change people as they give their lives to you. Do your work in the people I bring before you now...*

"He sent forth His Word and healed them..."
PSALM 107:20

Keith Carey, a young man from California, wanted to spend some time in a rural community of predominantly illiterate Xhosa people in the Eastern Cape province of South Africa. He wanted to share the Gospel but didn't know the language. We gave him the Bible on cassette in the Xhosa language and then took him along with a Foursquare pastor to the home of an unsaved blind woman and her family, who would host him for two weeks.

Every day, Keith would play the Bible on cassette to his host family and then go out on horseback with the pastor, who could hardly speak English, to play the precious cassettes at other homes in the community. When we went to pick Keith up at the end of his stay, we began to pray as is customary upon entering someone's house. During this time of prayer, the blind woman started to manifest demons and was miraculously set free—she received salvation and partial eyesight! The word of God is powerful, and had penetrated her heart and prepared the way for her salvation and healing!

Howard and Terry Manthe
Missionaries to South Africa

Lord, I thank you for your powerful word! Hearing your word brings deliverance, salvation, and healing. You are truly the Lord of Lords...

"For we were all baptized by one Spirit into one body—
whether Jews or Greeks, slave or free—
and we were all given the one Spirit to drink."

I CORINTHIANS 12:13

The zinc roof reflected only some of the torrid sun of Ghana; the rest of the heat hung heavy around us as we stood in this lean-to and worshiped. That same low roof deflected back the saintly noise of our worship: the African drums, the beaded calabash used as a percussion instrument, our fervent voices and the original "ten-stringed" instrument—the syncopated clapping of my African brothers and sisters. They sang in Twe, their national language.

As I stood there, the heat, the drums, the clapping and their voices felt like waves swirling around me; waves going up to the zinc roof and then bouncing back to engulf me. I was awestruck with the intensity of the moment. How could I actively participate in this worship time?

Suddenly I began singing in my prayer language. I sang quietly at first, but I gradually increased the volume as I sensed my place in this wave of worship. Eventually I threw my hands up and sang with abandon. I was harmonizing and blending.

As this continued, I was caught up in the understanding of that one Spirit, as in 1 Corinthians. We were "all given the one Spirit to drink!"

Kathy Kieselhorst
Former Missionary to Nigeria, now serving with her husband, Bill, in South Africa

Lord, I thank you that one day in heaven I will meet all my brothers and sisters. Though time and distance separate us now, one day we will all gather together...

> *". . . none will miscarry or be barren in your land."*
>
> EXODUS 23:26

When Vijaya and I were visiting our children in California, we heard of a friend's daughter who had been married for ten years and had not been able to have children. The couple had worked with three different specialists and each had said the same thing: Colleen could not have children.

They were very discouraged. Their intense desire to have children was taking its toll on Colleen's health. She felt she was failing her husband. This couple struggled to understand the ways of the Lord.

Vijaya and I went to their home to pray with them and several friends. As we knelt together, we read Exodus 23:25-33, and explained that God will keep His promises if we will do what He tells us. I asked them about their belief in Jesus and whether they were regular tithers. Then I asked Colleen to begin the prayer time. She prayed with tears, pleading in her heart. All present prayed one by one and when it came my turn, I just thanked the Lord for hearing these prayers.

Shortly after this we returned to India. After six months we received a letter from Colleen to say she was expecting their first child. She had not taken any medication nor had the prescribed surgery. God had honored their prayers.

Within a few months a beautiful baby was born. God's little miracle had arrived!

John Gnanaolivu
Founder of Foursquare India

> *Lord, I pray for those who long for children but are barren;*
> *I pray that each one of them would know your will for*
> *them. I ask for your healing power to go forth...*

*"But may the Lord forgive
your servant for this one thing..."*
2 KINGS 5:18

Shand grew up in a devout Hindu home in Ipoh, Malaysia. As a young girl, her father would send Shand and her sister to a church on Sundays so he could have some peace and quiet in the home. After they both gave their hearts to Jesus, the father felt he had made a terrible mistake and set out to reconvert his daughters.

Every year there is a special time when Hindus go to the temple, burn incense, and recite prayers of dedication. Shand's father insisted that Shand must go. Being only 12, she could not refuse. Instead, she fasted and prayed and told the Lord, "Father, please don't count this against me. I must submit to my father, but please know that in my heart I will only be worshipping and praying to you. Lord Jesus, as I go into this temple, please cover and protect me and allow me to stay true to you."

She later read the story of Naaman the Syrian Commander who was cured of leprosy (2 Kings 5:1-14). As he was returning to serve the king of Syria, Naaman asked the prophet an interesting question, "Yet in this one thing may the Lord pardon your servant: when my master goes into the temple of Rimmon to worship there and he leans on my hand and I bow down…may the Lord please pardon your servant in this thing." Elijah's answer was "Go in peace" meaning that God would not hold this against him. Shand knew she had found God's grace.

Today she is married to a pastor and together they serve in a Foursquare church in Singapore.

George Butron
Missionary to Papua New Guinea

> *Lord, there are so many ways my life falls short of your glory! I ask your forgiveness, Lord, as I confess my sin in the following areas...*

*"Praise the Lord, O my soul, and forget not all his benefits—
who forgives all your sins and heals all your diseases,
who redeems your life from the pit and crowns you with love
and compassion, who satisfies your desires with good things
so that your youth is renewed like the eagle's."*

PSALM 103:2-5

Twelve-year-old Alfredo was not an orphan, but God brought him to live at the Houses of Happiness (a Foursquare orphanage). He had undergone heart surgery and had been given only three months to live. He was initially placed in the rehabilitation center next door to Houses of Happiness, and often the children could hear him crying hysterically. Then we were asked if Alfredo could come to live at the orphanage.

One day as I was handing out clothes to a group of preschoolers, Alfredo began his hysterical crying. I placed my hand on his chest and it felt like a basketball trying to get out. I called the toddlers together, "Let's pray for Alfredo."

It took us about two weeks to realize Alfredo wasn't crying anymore and not taking his usual long naps. He was out with the other 12-year-olds, pushing the wheelbarrows and helping with the construction.

After six months Alfredo went back to live with his family and we did not hear about him for about four years. One day as Henry and I were stopped at a signal light, Alfredo's father spotted us and came running across the street to the car. Amid horns blasting on all sides, he said, "I just have to tell you that Alfredo is still well and all of our family have become Christians!"

Dorothy Davis
Former Missionary to Ecuador

> *Praise the Lord today for all His benefits. Thank Him that
> He is the God who heals you and that He is the God who
> changes lives like those of Alfredo and his family. Bring
> before Him the needs that are on your heart today...*

"O Lord God Almighty, who is like you? You are mighty, O Lord, and your faithfulness surrounds you."

PSALM 89:8

When our son Scott was 10 years old, he came home from school complaining of pain in his lower back. It turned out he had fallen down a flight of stairs at school. When Carole examined him, she discovered he was still bleeding.

Scott was rushed to the hospital where it was determined one of his kidneys had been severely injured and the second kidney was dangerously swollen. Five days later the hemorrhaging stopped and the doctors determined that, Scott would be unable to participate in any active sports or strenuous activity until we returned to the U. S. where further surgery would be necessary.

About a year later when we returned home, the doctors suggested Scott wait until after Christmas before entering the hospital for exploratory surgery. In January Scott was being prepped for surgery. The surgeon, a born-again Christian, had already examined the series of x-rays that had been taken over the months and just an hour before. He felt led to take one further x-ray. That final x-ray confirmed that between 6:00 and 6:30 that morning God had given Scott two brand-new kidneys. Today Scott is married, has a family and is a healthy pastor.

As we began to share this testimony when we traveled to minister in churches, we discovered that both at the time of Scott's fall and at the time of his miracle, more than 50 Foursquare churches had sovereignly been praying for our family—for reasons they did not know. We can trust God to have it all under control!

Dr. Ron and Carole Williams
Former Missionaries to Hong Kong

Thank you, Lord, that you are in control, and that you are completely trustworthy...

> *"You will hear of wars and rumors of wars...and this
> Gospel of the Kingdom will be preached in the whole world
> as a testimony to all the nations, and then the end will come."*
>
> MATTHEW 24:6,14

As missionaries Greg Fisher and David Adams made their way up the steep and curvy mountain road in Burundi, the rumors of war became all too real. Soldiers lined the road, the sound of automatic gunfire ricocheted through the hills, and our courageous missionaries scrambled out of harm's way to change a flat tire in a record time. But even the threat of imminent violence was not enough to keep them from celebrating the tremendous victories God had brought through the recent preaching of the Gospel.

"We were amazed as we found Foursqure churches, sometimes in small villages, with 600 to 800 people jammed inside, eager to hear the preaching of the Gospel," reports Greg. "We even heard of one congregation, less than three years old, with more than 5,000 in attendance."

Greg and David traveled throughout the country and took turns addressing crowded churches, preaching and praying with people to receive Christ. "One Sunday morning," recalls Greg, "I preached from 1 Kings 18:21, where Elijah went before the people and said, 'How long will you waver between two opinions? If the Lord is God, follow Him; but if Baal is god, follow him.' We addressed the same issue of witchcraft and the power of God to break its bondage. People began to weep and call out to God in repentance. Several came to the front of the crowded village church and repented and found salvation."

The words of Jesus indeed ring true—there are wars and rumors of wars. But the Gospel of the kingdom—the good news that God reigns and is victorious over the power of Satan—is being proclaimed even when things seem to be the darkest.

Foursquare World ADVANCE, 1999

> *Lord, I pray for those missionaries who find themselves ministering in war zones. Let nothing hinder their work...*

"The apostles left the Sanhedrin, rejoicing because they had been counted worthy of suffering disgrace for the Name."

ACTS 5:41

A young man who was dramatically saved in 1974 as Australian missionaries Graham and Irene Baker were beginning their work in Papua New Guinea showed up on their doorstep. Maringo had come from the island of Bougainville with a testimony of persecution and God's faithfulness.

For the past 15 months, Maringo, his wife, and their four children had been held in prison camps where they were tortured and beaten because of their love for Jesus. Maringo was forced to stand upright and open his mouth wide while rebel soldiers walked by and spit into the opening. Such was his punishment for not ceasing to witness about Jesus Christ.

One night Maringo's wife quietly told him, "We need to go to bed early, as tonight at 10:30, we will be escaping." The parents awoke and aroused their children from sleep, and without a noise departed from the camp. They passed the guards who all lay fast asleep.

This courageous family weaved its way through the brush, crossing a large river and arriving at a government forces camp where they hoped to find safety. Maringo walked ahead of his family with his shirt tied to a pole as a flag of peace.

Unknown to him, just the day before the Lord had given the camp sergeant a vision, showing a Bougainville family coming out of the jungle to their camp. When the sergeant met them, he rejoiced. "This must be the family the Lord told us about."

Undaunted by the persecution, Maringo and his family prepared themselves to take the Foursquare Gospel back to the distressed, wounded and battered people on the island of Bougainville.

Foursquare World ADVANCE, 1993

> *Lord, many are suffering persecution right now for your sake. I pray that you would give them courage, strength, and hope in the midst of their trial...*

"Sow your seed in the morning, and at evening let not your hands be idle... the seed that fell on good soil is the man who hears the word and understands it. He produces a crop, yielding a hundred, sixty or thirty times what was sown."

ECCLESIASTES 11:6...MATTHEW 13:23

*I*t was always interesting to watch the people as they responded to the Gospel. Often during a church service people would descend from the bus and pause to listen to the Word. The next time, they might venture through the door to sit in the back of the church. For some it took time for them to answer the call to come to the altar to accept Jesus as Savior. There were few services when no one came to the Lord.

While ministering at the Bible Institute in San Cristobal, Venezuela, a young Bible college student and I drove thirty miles through winding mountain roads to Cucutá, Colombia, to conduct a radio program every Sunday in the early morning. We then returned to San Cristobal for Sunday school, morning service, and the afternoon outreaches to parts of our city. A children's meeting and the evening service usually closed the day's activities.

Serafin Contreras, the young Bible student who so capably conducted the radio program, completed his Bible school training and became a pastor. Today he and his wife serve as missionaries in Central America and his radio ministry is heard on more than 80 stations throughout that area.

Praise the Lord! The seed that was sown years ago has produced a bountiful harvest!

Dorothy Buck
Former Missionary to Latin America

Lord, I ask that my life would be fruitful for you. Let me influence young men and women to serve you and dedicate their lives to you...

"He will give beauty for ashes..."
ISAIAH 61:3 (NLT)

*I*n the fall of 1994, the Sri Lankan Army marched north to the Jaffna Peninsula to do battle with a militant rebel group. As the armed forces attacked, everyone was forced to flee into the jungle. Among these more than 250,000 refuges were many Christian believers, including Foursquare Pastor Lazarus, his wife, and their four children. At nighttime, they settled in under the trees. In the morning, he would make a temporary house for them and then try to find the other members of the congregation.

The next months were hard. They scavenged for things to add to the small food supply they had been able to bring with them. In spite of the difficulties, believers grouped together to worship and pray. Small congregations of believers formed in the jungle. Many who were displaced were now finding their peace in the beauty of a new relationship with Jesus, their Savior.

Some weeks later, as the bombing moved south and east, Pastor Lazarus and a fellow pastor returned to the city to see if they could salvage any of their household goods. There was little left, but Pastor Lazarus did find his guitar and some clothing for his family. He and his pastor friend joined a group of other refugees to walk back to their jungle lean-to. As they came to an open field, the bombing began again and they were thrown to the ground. Suddenly it was silent. They sat up and realized no one else was moving. In horror they looked to see that everyone in their group of walkers had been killed. Their clothes were splattered with debris and blood, yet they could not find a wound.

In the midst of the ashes of war, their lives had been spared.

Eloise Clarno
Former Missionary to Sri Lanka

Lord, I pray for those who live where war is causing havoc. I ask you to help those who must flee from their homes, especially those who are my brothers and sisters in Christ...

"The words I have spoken to you are spirit and they are life."
JOHN 6:63

"*B*ellas Palabras de Vida" (Wonderful Words of Life) are words you could have heard every morning over Radio Tegucigalpa in the late 1950s. For one half hour we preached the full message of Jesus.

This program had aired for about two years when one month we did not have the $75 fee. It seemed we would need to discontinue the program for a while.

My husband always said, "When we have a real need or problem, I always ask the women of the church to pray." And when he did that, one of the women said, "We will stay here in this church and pray until the money comes in."

Oscar, our young assistant pastor, stayed and prayed with us until 2:00 a.m., when he went to stand in the open front door of the church. Soon a man walking by heard us praying and asked, "What are these people doing?"

Oscar gave him the simple answer, "They are asking God to send the money to pay for our radio program this month."

"What radio program is that?" the man asked.

"Bellas Palabras de Vida," Oscar responded.

The man was immediately interested, "I am a Catholic and a lawyer here. I listen to that program every morning. It is very uplifting and a good way to start the day. How much money do you need?"

When Oscar told him, he immediately wrote a check for $75. Oscar came back inside, waving the check. God had supplied our need.

Vonitta Gurney Boylan
Former Missionary to Latin America

> Lord, you always supply everything that is needed to do your work. Your promises are wonderful...

> *"...unless you change and become like little*
> *children, you will not enter the kingdom of heaven."*
> MATTHEW 18:3

"*I*n the country of Santiago, Chile, five-year old Martita asked Jesus to give her a tea set. When asked how it was going, she would say, "I'm still praying!"

Missionaries Leland and Barbara Edwards wanted to "help God out." One morning Barbara told Martita's father what she planned. The father chuckled, "Just this morning she told me she wasn't going to pray anymore because God hadn't answered." Then Barbara told Martita that on Wednesday evening she should look on the platform by the pulpit. Martita was sick that evening, so her father took home the gift. She opened the gift, saw what it was, and got down on her knees. "Thank you, Jesus, for the tea set. Now, where's the little stove?"

In Panama City, pretty nine-year-old Emilia received Jesus as her Savior during Vacation Bible School. She was such a happy, bubbly little girl and faithful to attend the church. When Christmas came, she had her first part in the program. What a delight!

Just before the service, a somber little Emilia came to the missionary. Her arms had been scratched and pinched. With tears she said, 'My mother did this. She didn't want me to come tonight; she thought I would be ashamed to come with my arms so bruised. But I couldn't stay away. We are celebrating the birth of Jesus."

Then this little girl profoundly said, "But that wasn't really my mother that did that. She just doesn't know Jesus. And when she does, she will be sorry."

Barbara Edwards
Former Missionary to Panama

> *Lord, bless the children in my life. May each one know you*
> *and serve you. Lord, I bring before you each one by name...*

*"For you make me glad by your deeds, O Lord;
I sing for joy at the works of your hands."*
PSALM 92:4

I had the opportunity to minister with my husband many times—it was the joy of my life. On one of these ministry trips to Panama and Colombia, Dr. Courtney carried a $2,000 bank draft for the purchase of property in Bucaramanga, Colombia.

En route from Panama to Colombia, he realized he had lost the check. He prayed and, as soon as possible, he telegraphed the office to stop payment and issue a new check.

A few days later we received a letter from Arthur Edwards, who was a missionary in Panama. A man he had never seen before had found the check on the street. Since it had the word "Foursquare" on it, he thought of that missionary who was so well known and took the check to him.

Of course, we rejoiced over finding the check. But, we also were delighted that the life and ministry of our dear missionary was so well known in Panama City.

Vaneda Courtney
Wife of Dr. Howard Courtney, Missions Director, 1944-1950

Lord, I thank you that you give favor to your servants. Let my name be identified with your name here on earth as I serve you and tell others of your goodness...

"And we know that in all things God works for the good..."
ROMANS 8:28

I had been ministering in Hong Kong for only three years when the American Consul requested that all Americans leave the nation due to the expected Chinese communist take-over. I went to Japan, settled in the city of Oizumi, and began language study.

At that time there was no Foursquare Church in Japan. I played badminton with the neighborhood children, served them tea and cookies, and learned some Japanese from them. Before long we had a Sunday school in my home with 100 children attending weekly. The landlord requested that either the children stop coming or that I move. We rented a nearby school and the number of children grew to 145.

I then began an adult Bible study in my home. Many young people and adults began attending these meetings. As a result a church was necessary. The college students made a church bank and took it to the merchants in the town, asking for donations for the first Foursquare church.

God showed me the land where we were to build the church. When we went to talk to the owners, a father and his adult son, the father agreed to sell but the son said no. The third time I went back, I told him that God said this land was for the church. He gave his consent. We signed the papers.

Over the months, God provided the money for us to build. God did it! Today a Foursquare church continues to minister in Oizumi.

Billie Charles Francey
Former Missionary to Asia

Lord, I thank you for the work you continue to do among the Japanese people. I pray that you would deliver even more of them from the power of darkness into your glorious light...

"The people walking in darkness have seen a great light; on those living in the land of the shadow of death a light has dawned."

ISAIAH 9:2

I was out strolling in the neighborhood, hoping to make new friends when I came to a gathering of women. I greeted them and asked if I could join them. Because they wore an unusual amount of beaded jewelry and skirts of the locally woven traditional red cloth, I knew I was at a special function.

"We are visiting and praying together," one said.

"Oh, I like to pray," I responded.

"Then come and pray with our jaaja (grandmother) inside." They took my hand and guided me into a courtyard with several small dwellings. The entrance was narrow, flanked by spears and attended by spear-wielding guards. I was whisked through before I could ask questions.

We bent low to enter a small hut. The small dark room was crowded with people. Candles lit one corner and a smoldering fire glowed in another. Seated on the ground, completely caged-in by a conical structure of spears was an old, old woman. Surrounding her was a group of people, all seeking her blessing. The old woman was a medium. Peering through the spear shafts with half-blinded eyes, the jaaja greeted me warmly. To the room full of people she announced I was the muzungu (white person) she'd predicted would come. Then she asked that I pray a blessing.

I replied that I only prayed in the name of Jesus. She hesitated, but then agreed. I prayed loudly so all would hear it was Jesus I to whom I spoke. I prayed that the true light would come and expose the works of darkness. I believe He will answer that prayer.

Sarah Adams
Missionary to Uganda

> *Lord, I pray for these people who seek spiritual truth, but are looking in the wrong place! I bind the forces of darkness that keep them from seeing the true Light...*

"For you were once darkness, but now you are light in the Lord.
Live as children of light..."

EPHESIANS 5:8

*A*fter I met with the jaaja and her followers (see yesterday's devotion-al story), I discovered that this group of people gathers every week near our home. Their leader claims to be the last king of the Luganda dynasty, resurrected. The jaajas are the ones by whom prayers are delivered and witchcraft practiced. Many of their number are people who claim to also be Christians or Muslims. People are being led into all sorts of evil traps and deceit.

The day I was invited into their gathering, after the jaaja invited me to pray, I was escorted out of the crowded, dark room and into the courtyard where people sat huddled in groups. I was led to three more fires in differ-ent booths about the courtyard. At each I was requested to pray in the same manner as before. Each time I prayed earnestly, calling on the name of Jesus and praying for the true light to come and expose the works of darkness. I prayed in the name of Jesus against the powers of deceit and evil. I prayed out loud, gaining more and more courage each time.

My spirit was troubled that night as I tried to rest. In the wee hours I rose and opened my Bible, asking God to speak to me through His Word. Without knowing where to read, my eyes fell on Ephesians 5:8-14, which speaks of walking in the light so that we expose the works of darkness. Peace flooded my soul; I knew God had been with me throughout this experience, with the purpose that His light would shine in their darkness.

Sarah Adams
Missionary to Uganda

Lord, may your true light shine into the darkness of these
people in Uganda. I pray that you would be victorious in
this struggle for their hearts and allegiance...

> *"There is no wisdom, no insight, no plan that can succeed against the Lord."*
>
> PROVERBS 21:30

During the 1950s, the Protestant Church in Colombia suffered under the religious system that dominated the government. The Foursquare Church in the city of Barrancabermeja was no exception. Joe and Virginia Knapp were missionaries in this city.

The authorities in this city ordered the church to be closed and a seal was put across the front door. While the believers could not meet as a full congregation, they began meeting in small groups in homes. Then the authorities passed a law that it was illegal to have more than 10 people gather in homes. That limited the number who could meet together, but reinforced the determination of all believers. When the doors of the church were finally reopened, the congregation was twice as large as before the doors were shut.

One evening Joe Knapp and Fred Beard, a pastor from the U.S., decided to take a walk down by the Magdalena River. The authorities had been seeking a time when they could kill Missionary Knapp, and they realized this was that opportunity. As the two men walked along the river, they heard a mob of men coming their way. Knowing there was nowhere they could hide, they stepped aside, off the trail, where they prayed and waited.

The mob came towards them, and then stopped in confusion. They knew they had seen the two, but could not find them, even though the two stood beside the trail only a few feet from them. Finally, with much frustration, the gang went on ahead and dispersed. God had hidden the missionary and his friend from the view of these men.

Dr. Leland Edwards
Missions Director, 1965-1988

> *Thank you, Lord, that the schemes of men cannot thwart your plans and purposes for my life. Hide me from those who would harm me or distract me from your purposes...*

"I know through your prayers and the help by the Spirit of Jesus Christ, what has happened to me will turn out for my deliverance."

PHILIPPIANS 1:19

A.J. Gordon said, "You can do more than pray after you have prayed, but you cannot do more than pray until you have prayed." Our national leader in Papua New Guinea, Timothy Tipitap, testifies to this.

Timothy was a man who persecuted the Foursquare Church. In fact, he even tried to put pressure on the government to have it closed. Then Timothy discovered the Lord Jesus, whom the Foursquare Church preached, and his life was changed. After training in the Bible Institute, Timothy became a pastor.

The people from a neighboring warring tribe were looking for Timothy in order to settle a family dispute. They set up a road block, knowing Timothy would pass this way and they could kill him. They had seen him often, and knew what he looked like.

When Timothy came that way, he was stopped. The men searched his vehicle, even looked straight at Timothy, but did not recognize him. They moved the roadblock and the vehicle started to drive away when Timothy began hearing them shout, "That was Timothy!"

Later Timothy learned that God had blinded the eyes of this mob, causing them to see a young Filipina lady named Jessica, not Timothy.

It was the prayers of the saints and the pursuasion of the Holy Spirit that delivered Timothy Tipitap from the powers of darkness and brought him into the light of Jesus Christ. It was the prayers of the saints and the power of the Holy Spirit that blinded those who would do him harm at the road block. And it is the prayers of the saints and the work of the Holy Spirit that will bring continued salvation, deliverance, and healing to the many tribes of Papua New Guinea.

Wayne DeCosta
FMI Personnel and Training Coordinator

> *Father, help me to remember the power of prayer and the authority you have given me in Jesus Christ. Come Holy Spirit, and lead me and guide me as I pray for the nations...*

"You were shown these things so that you might know that the Lord is God; besides him there is no other."

DEUTERONOMY 4:35

A young Foursquare church planter was sent to a remote area that had been liberated from Khmer Rouge control in early 1999. He had been born in that area and his desire was to take the Gospel to his people. When he arrived, he testified about his faith and several young men were converted, but he noticed that none of the girls would respond. When he asked why, he was told that the Buddhist monks had convinced the girls that if they became Christians they would become pregnant. This was partly a result of the monks' misunderstanding of the virgin birth and partly a scare tactic to keep them from Christ.

He began to pray for a miracle to show the power of Jesus. In that village there was a seventeen-year-old boy who stood about three feet tall, had a distended chest, and was partially paralyzed on his right side. The Christians gathered around the young man and prayed. Immediately his head straightened and he could walk and talk normally. Many people responded to the Gospel because of this miracle, but still the girls were unresponsive.

News of the miracle reached the headquarters church and the national leader went to investigate. At the same time, I sent Gkim San, a young woman involved in the orphan ministry. When the girls in the village saw this young woman worshiping God and observed that she was not pregnant, there was a mass conversion of more than a dozen girls!

Ted Olbrich
Missionary to Cambodia

Lord, you work miracles because of your great love for your children. Thank you for your love and for your miraculous works in my life...

"I urge you, brothers, by our Lord Jesus Christ and by the love of the Spirit, to join me in my struggle by praying to God for me."

ROMANS 15:30

The most precious of all the gifts a missionary may receive is the gift of prayer. We know people were praying on our last day in Colombia, where we served as missionaries.

That day I went out to take some pictures. I was able to get some shots of people as they walked down the sidewalk. After a few minutes, a Jeep pulled up and out jumped three men with machine guns.

One soldier asked me for my ID, which I didn't have with me due to the confusion caused by our packing. One of them told me to get into the Jeep. I had no choice. As we drove out of town on an isolated dirt road, I thought, "This is it. I'm glad I'm saved."

Finally we pulled up to a run-down old building and they told me to get out. We went inside and I was told to sit on a wooden bench. It seemed like I waited forever. I had plenty of time to think, and to pray! Finally one of the men came back and told me the "Capitan" wanted to see me.

The "Capitan" identified himself as a member of the Colombia's secret police and said I had been seen taking pictures of their headquarters. I assured him I wasn't a spy. They finally agreed to let me go.

The Word reminds us to "pray one for another." I am so glad that someone was faithful to pray for me that day.

Dennis Pendergast
Missionary to Mexico

Lord, today someone needs my prayers. As I wait upon you, impress upon my heart those people for whom you want me to pray...

> *"...give thanks in all circumstances,*
> *for this is God's will for you in Christ Jesus. "*
>
> 1 THESSALONIANS 5:18

The day for the children's outreach was here. Seven of us, dressed like clowns, packed into two cars to leave the church parking lot. We had no idea what the fruit of that day would be. We had no sooner moved into traffic than a motorcyclist came out of nowhere and slammed into the side of the car I was riding in. We were stunned!

The only one not dressed like a clown was Charlie, and he was in the other car. Whatever would this man think to be confronted by a carload of clowns? But Charlie had seen the accident and returned to help.

Thankfully, no one was seriously hurt so we continued on to the outreach. The cyclist was taken to the hospital to be sure there were no serious injuries. Our Christian insurance agent discovered he had been in four accidents in the past four months. The man had been a Christian but was not living for the Lord.

His encounter with us "clowns" brought him in touch with our Christian insurance agent, who boldly asked him, "Are you waiting for the devil to kill you and take you to hell, or are you ready to give your life to Jesus?" This man rededicated his life to the Lord and the very next Sunday took his wife and family to the church.

Charlie and Darla Finocchiaro
Missionaries to the Dominican Republic

> *Help me to praise you Lord, in every circumstance in which*
> *I find myself. Let me bring your grace into difficult situa-*
> *tions and see your power to transform bad things into good!*

"...always giving thanks to God the Father for everything..."
EPHESIANS 5:20

Give thanks for everything? When traveling around the Philippines we often had accommodations that could be termed "primitive." However, while many had little to offer materially, we found an abundance of love and graciousness that made it easy to be thankful.

The first mattress-less bed we slept in was an unforgettable experience. The bamboo floor might have been softer, but our Filipino friends knew that Americans do not sleep on the floor. As the bed was narrow, we synchronized our turning, and because it was short, our feet hung over the end.

Taking a bath was another challenge. Usually the bath consisted of a bucket of water with a dipper. It is amazing how well you can bathe with such little water! At one place, the community bathed outside at the water well pump. The men wore shorts; the women discreetly bathed while wearing loose fitting dresses; the children didn't bother with clothes. However, they had thoughtfully taken care of this American lady by making a special place for me to bathe.

At the side of the house, burlap bags were draped around poles and crushed shells were scattered on the ground. I felt secure enough to bathe freely since the "walls" of my bathroom covered me from shoulders to knees. I enjoyed my bath!

As I was finishing and redressing, I glanced up. To my surprise, several men stood on a second floor balcony of a house across the street. I was the entertainment of the day!

Don and Sharon Nicholson
Former Missionaries to the Philippines

> *Lord, your word says that in everything I am to give thanks. Today I offer thanksgiving and gratitude to you in every circumstance and situation of my life, no matter how difficult or trying they may be...*

> *"Know therefore that the Lord your God is God; He is the faithful God, keeping His covenant of love to a thousand generations of thosewho love Him and keep His commands."*
>
> DEUTERONOMY 7:9

When Alva and I arrived in Nicaragua in 1990, we found a poor and wounded church, but one faithful to God because of the faithful work of its pastors. Three of these heroes were Foursquare pastors Juan Ruiz, Juan Campos, and Jose Centeno. They had many stories to tell of how they worked to care for their flocks during the war with the Sandinistas and how God cared for them.

During this war, Pastor Ruiz often walked hidden among the trees. Sometimes the bullets whistled near him. He protected about 300 people by hiding them in the church. It was illegal to do this but the people were homeless because the bombing had destroyed their homes. Pastor Ruiz hid, fed, prayed and preached to them. In all the weeks they were at the church not once did the police look there, for him or the people.

In their own towns, Pastors Juan Campos and Jose Centeno also faced these same difficulties with great faith. Each can testify of God's care during the difficult years of the war. For 13 years the Foursquare Church in Nicaragua went through difficult times, but these shepherds remained faithful.

These three pastors have served God and ministered in the Foursquare Church in Nicaragua for nearly 40 years. They represent many throughout Latin America and around the world who serve in dangerous and difficult situations and with great faith and grace. What makes these men heroes of the faith is that they are obedient to God's call on their life and they trust God to remain faithful.

Serafin and Alva Contreras
Missionaries to Nicaragua

> *Lord, I thank you that when I go through difficulties, you remain faithful. As you bring me through tough times, help me to reach out to others and think of their needs...*

*"Utterly amazed, they asked: '...how is it that each of us
hears them in his own native language?
...we hear them declaring the wonders
of God in our own tongues!'"*

ACTS 2:7,8,11

I was invited to go to an Assemblies of God church in Puerto Rico to preach the Gospel. The minister of the church knew both Spanish and English and would interpret for me. Although I had taken Spanish in high school, I was not fluent in the language.

After the pastor had introduced me to the congregation, he walked away leaving me without an interpreter. I didn't know what I was going to do. There was a three or four minute rehearsed testimony that I could tell without an interpreter, but then what?

As I started to tell my testimony, all of a sudden, the anointing came upon me and I began to speak perfect Spanish. I preached for thirty minutes without an interpreter that day!

Dr. Nathaniel Van Cleave
Former Missionary to Puerto Rico

*Lord, I pray that you would put the words in my mouth to
tell others about you...*

*"...my preaching was not with enticing words of man's wisdom, but
in demonstration of the Spirit and of power..."*

1 CORINTHIANS 2:4 (KJV)

During the ministers' conference in the various districts of the
Philippines, a gracious moving of the Spirit was evident. Rev. Evelyn
Thompson was invited by Field Director Mason Hughes to be guest speaker
in each conference. God wonderfully honored her ministry and that of the
district pastors and missionaries. Literally hundreds were slain by God at one
time. Broken homes were restored, and sinners cried out to God for forgiveness. Church people and members went to one another, confessing their
own faults. The gifts of the Spirit became active in many with tongues, interpretations, prophecies, miracles, and other manifestations being evident. "It
has been just like living in the book of Acts," was the report.

The fire did not die out with the conferences but is still going, and without doubt there will be a great increase in the number of souls saved in the
Philippines as a result. Missionaries and pastors are convinced that when
the price is paid and men are committed to the harvest, they will see one of
the greatest revivals ever to come to East Asia. They are anticipating persecution and trial in the wake of such a moving, but there is confidence that
the people will be ready when it comes.

Update: Revival did come—at the beginning of the year 2000 there
were 4,349 Foursquare churches and meeting places in the Philippines, and
Foursquare Asia now includes 6,822 churches and meeting places in 24
nations!

**Dr. Herman D. Mitzner
Missions Director, 1950-1965**

*Lord, bring revival, and begin with my own heart. I ask you
to forgive my sins that I now confess to you...*

> *"Then they were glad because they had quiet,*
> *and he brought them to their desired haven."*
>
> PSALM 107:30 (RSV)

A twenty-one foot open "banana boat" with a forty horsepower outboard engine is an adventurous way to travel the open seas. On a trip to the island of New Ireland from the neighboring island of New Britain, we loaded our gear and set out on the 20-mile trip across the Bismarck Sea. After several days of teaching with a newly formed group of churches, we set out on the return trip. To quote from Gilligan's Island, "The weather started getting rough, the tiny ship was tossed. . ."

The waves, wind and rain were nonstop and when it came time to cross the strait that separated New Ireland from New Britain, the skipper announced that the visibility was too poor and since there was no point of reference to steer by, we would have to wait on the beach until the storm cleared. At this point we were wet, cold and weary, and when missionary Keith Bickley pulled out his GPS (Global Positioning System) device and got a lock on New Britain, we were ready to try anything to get back!

Guided by satellite we bounced and splashed our way back across the sea and were relieved to see a point of land after more than an hour. I found myself wondering what would happen if the batteries died or if there might be another New Britain somewhere in South America, but we made it back just as night was setting in. Just as the GPS device got us through the open sea.

Jesus is the fixed point in the universe, the One who points us in the right direction and guides us through the storm! He knows how to get us to the right destination!

George Butron
Missionary to Papua New Guinea

Lord, may you be my only point of reference as I navigate through this life. Help me keep my focus on you...

> *"In the sheet were all sorts of animals, reptiles, and birds. Then a voice said to him, "Get up, Peter, kill and eat them."*
>
> ACTS 10:12-13 (NLT)

*I*n the light of the kerosene lamp I saw Pastor John sitting in the far corner of the hut eating something from a small paper bag. We had just finished a great meal of eggs, kasava, greens, and bread. I wondered if this was a hidden sweet my host was enjoying.

Seeing my interest, he offered some to me. I took a small handful and tried to identify just what kind of dessert this was. The lamp wasn't bright enough to illuminate this delicacy so I just popped it into my mouth. I was surprised at the sweet and crunchy taste—what a treat! I tried to get another handful but he told me I should take it easy on this high protein food. I am curious by nature and so I pressed him to tell me what this delicacy was.

He began a lengthy discourse about the rainy season, how rain came down so hard that the 'dudus' [the Kiswahili word for bug] would fall to the ground because the rain knocked off their wings.

I realized the bug he was talking about was the termite, as I remembered how we had to put a rug in front of the door to keep them from coming into our house. He went on to say that after the rains children go out and pick up the 'dudus' from the ground by the hundreds. Momma fries them over the fire and they are a great source of protein.

Glen Mickel
Former Missionary to West Africa

> *Lord, I thank you for the variety of foods in this world, and your servants who have willing hearts and stomachs!*

*"I will give you the treasures of darkness, riches stored in secret
places, so that you may know that I am the Lord,
the God of Israel, who summons you by name."*

ISAIAH 45:3

The recent ministers conference in Davao, Philippines, opened with
over 200 registrations. Every message seemed to be kindled with fire
from above. The last night of the conference, Rev. Evelyn Thompson was
led of the Lord to have a heart-breaking service with Communion. The
Spirit of God moved in such a way that people sought forgiveness and
release from grudges they have carried. Nearly the entire congregation was
slain under the power of God, including our missionaries who later
declared, "This was the greatest visitation from God ever seen in all our
years of ministry."

God had promised by messages and interpretations that there would be
special treasures and also there would be dark days that would cover the
land. The special treasure came through the great visitation of the Holy
Spirit, preparing the workers for whatever lies ahead.

Dr. Herman D. Mitzner
Missions Director, 1950-1965

*Father, I praise you that when there will be trials ahead for
me, you have a way of preparing me so that I will be able to
go through them. Your Holy Spirit is with me and is in me...*

"You are not your own; you were bought with a price."
I CORINTHIANS 6:19,20 (RSV)

*M*any of the local high school students attended a youth meeting in the Eastern Highland town of Goroka, Papua New Guinea. This is when one young man, 14-year old Paul Ihanimo, heard the Scripture, "You are not your own; you were bought at a price." He committed his life to Jesus.

Paul began going to his home village, where he led many to the Lord and built a Foursquare Church. Then he trained people to lead that church so he could go on to other villages. Many people were saved and other churches started. Miracles of healing resulted at the teaching of the Word.

At age 16, Paul graduated from high school. He went to the English Bible School at Hageri to prepare for the ministry. After only a few years, as we traveled through the Highlands, it was not hard to find someone who had been saved through the ministry of Paul Ihanimo.

Paul and his family later were sent as missionaries to serve in northern Australia, ministering to Aboriginal people.

What if all Christians took that Scripture as literally as Paul? We are not our own!

Larry and JoAnn Six
Former Missionaries to Papua New Guinea

> *Lord, help me to live for you, recognizing that my life is not my own and looking for ways to serve you in everything I do and in every decision I make...*

> *"So make every effort to apply the benefits of these promises to your life. Then your faith will produce a life of moral excellence. A life of moral excellence leads to knowing God better."*
>
> 2 PETER 1:5 (NLT)

A friend gave us a subscription to National Geographic just before we left to live in Africa. I looked forward to many enjoyable evenings of browsing through it. The first one came to our post office box two months past the date on the cover. That was the last one we received while in Africa.

While waiting for the light to change on one of the main roads in Nairobi, young men would walk among the waiting cars selling everything from cassettes to magazines. I saw the distinctive cover and waved to the young man who ran over. It was the current issue of National Geographic and only about a month old. I was happy to get it for twice the cover price. The back part of the brown mailing cover was still attached. As I drove off, I glanced at it and noticed that it had been mailed to someone here in Nairobi. I almost ran into the car ahead of me as I recognized my own name. It was too late to go back and ask the young man where he got my issue.

Later I discovered that this type of activity goes on in major cities around the world. While I was protesting to the Lord about how wrong this was, the Holy Spirit gently whispered to me that this is the way of man on the earth. He also assured me that He would never rip me off and that all He had for me was mine for the taking.

Glen Mickel
Former Missionary to West Africa

> *Teach us, Lord, to give up all injustices to you, whether they be great or small. Help me to forgive anyone that comes to mind right now...*

"You are my hiding place; You will protect me from trouble..."
PSALM 32:7

The little settlement of Pajonal is in the interior of the Republic of Panama, about 100 miles from Panama City. In the days when we were missionaries in this nation, we left our car in the town of Penonome and walked five hours up the mountain, crossing rivers five times in order to reach Pajonal. Because of the heat, we traveled at night. When we arrived the church was packed with people. We began the service at midnight. The people had walked up to nine hours to get there and they were hungry for God's Word.

One Saturday night as the pastor and two helpers met in this same one-room church to pray, they heard a commotion outside. Three drunken men with machetes yelled, "We know you evangelicals are in there; we heard you praying. We are going to kill you." With no windows or a back door, there was no way the men could escape the building. They separated, one in one corner, another in another and the pastor in the middle. The drunken men broke down the door and staggered in, cursing their threats. They looked around and wondered among themselves where the Christians were. They knew they had been in there, but now wondered how they had gotten out. Finally, they staggered out. God had blinded the eyes of those men so they did not see the believers.

Dr. Leland and Barbara Edwards
Former Missionaries to Panama
Missions Director, 1965-1988

Lord, you have such creative ways of keeping me safe! I
thank you, Lord, that you take such good care of me...

"Jesus said to the people, 'I am the light of the world. If you follow me, you won't be stumbling through the darkness, because you will have the light that leads to life.'"

JOHN 8:12 (NLT)

Our Friendship Center in the Muslim community of one Middle Eastern country drew young university students. They would stop by after classes to take advantage of the weight room, a ping-pong table, television and the like. As we built friendships, we were able to share the love of Jesus.

Christmas presented a special opportunity to share the Gospel. One of the young men who came announced one day, "I know why you Christians put lights on the Christmas tree." We were curious to know his thinking, since for us it was tradition more than anything else that motivated us to put lights on the tree. So we asked him, "Ahmed, why do we put lights on the Christmas tree?" His answer was, "Because Jesus is the Light of the World!"

How quickly we forget why we decorate, why we celebrate during the Christmas season. This Christmas—may we be reminded that Christmas is about celebrating the "Light of the World" and his name is ... JESUS!

Scott Winter
Missionary

Thank you, Jesus, that you are the light of the world and the light of my life. Help me to never forget it and to walk in your light and to be a light to others...

"All this is from God, who reconciled us to himself through Christ and gave us the ministry of reconciliation."

2 CORINTHIANS 5:18

As we drove up to the small village in our mini-van, we looked out on a sea of human faces, evidencing a dimension of spiritual hunger rarely seen. I remember it was this fact that brought me to Africa 11 years ago. The area where we were traveling in Burundi was just outside of the town of Kirondo, very near the Rwandan border. It was an area where local inhabitants have experienced unspeakable atrocities by both Hutu rebel militias and the Tutsi-led Burundi Army forces.

Every time I have driven this steep, winding mountain road from Bujumbura to Kirondo, I've witnessed heavily armed Army units along the roadside. It was sobering to hear later that these same Hutu rebels killed others using the same road. However, the Burundi pastors that rode with me never seemed worried. They reasoned that if they suffered death having done an important ministry, it would be God's will—so why worry?

The national leader of the Foursquare Church in Burundi, however, has been a messenger who preaches reconciliation between the Hutu and Tutsi tribes. When tribal people hear this message of reconciliation and forgiveness, they become convicted and repent quickly, asking the Lord Jesus Christ into their lives. Since it started in 1993, the Burundi Foursquare Church has become the third largest Evangelical church in this tiny mountain country in the heart of Africa.

Greg Fisher
Missionary to Uganda

> *Thank you, Lord, that you have given me the ministry of reconciliation. Help me to follow the example of my brothers in Burundi, and to boldly go wherever you lead me to proclaim the reconciliation that is available in Jesus Christ...*

> *"Now is the time for judgment on this world; now the prince*
> *of this world will be driven out. But I, when I am lifted*
> *up from the earth, will draw all men to myself."*

JOHN 12:31-32

There are millions of people in the world who have not had the chance to hear the Gospel even once. The prince of this world has blinded their spiritual eyes through false religions such as Islam, Buddhism, Hinduism, and other polytheistic traditional religions. Many of these people live in a belt that stretches across North Africa, the Middle East, India, and Asia that is known as the 10/40 Window.

In a village in a 10/40 Window country radically resistant to the Gospel, the only Christian living in the village died, and he was buried in a cemetery on top of a hill outside the village. After the graveside service, the man's neighbors saw a stranger walk away from the cemetery, come into the village and look into many of the houses. Later on, a team came to the area to show the Jesus Film. Politely watching the film, the villagers were amazed by the scene of Christ's baptism. Seeing the face of Jesus, they exclaimed, "That's the man we saw going from house to house!" They all received Jesus that day! In this country 15,000 new believers are baptized each day.

FMI Communiqué, 1997

> *Jesus, you are amazing. I am thankful to you for your*
> *incredible love that reaches into the darkest corners of the*
> *earth. Lord, continue to use your people to drive out the*
> *enemy...*

"...your Father knows what you need before you ask him."
MATTHEW 6:8

R ose was a Bible student in the city of Willowvale, South Africa. She had debts that her parents insisted she pay. They ordered her to quit her studies and search for a job. While she was concerned about the debt and wanted to please her parents, she knew of no work available. And, she wanted to continue her studies.

She approached Foursquare missionary Howard Manthe. He was able to direct Rose and several other Bible school students towards employment as "peace monitors" during the national elections. Monitors were paid very well, and Rose was chosen for one of these positions. In her willingness to please God and her parents, God blessed her and provided for her needs.

Immediately following the election, Rose went home to give money to her parents and to pay off her debt. She returned to Willowvale. At the close of the Sunday morning service, Rose remained in the pew, sobbing. Terry Manthe, Howard's wife, went to investigate and discovered a joyful Rose. Rose exclaimed, "I've seen the hand of God. My father has received two unexpected checks and I see that He is blessing my family."

Our Father knows what we need—even before we ask. He is our faithful provider!

Foursquare World ADVANCE, 1994

Lord, you know exactly what my needs are today. In fact, you know better than I myself know! I trust you to meet all my needs...

"Then the disciples went out and preached everywhere,
and the Lord worked with them and confirmed his word
by the signs that accompanied it."
MARK 16:20

God is waiting for people to believe His Word so that He can confirm it with signs following. Had we not known the Scriptures as well as we did when we went to the field, we could never have seen accomplished what we have, for the Lord was waiting to confirm His Word, and since we believed His Word, God could not help Himself.

With the authority of the Word of God that gave us the right to do exploits, we stood in the rain one day in Davao City. We did not know anyone. Through a misunderstanding, our money had not been transferred into the bank of Davao, so we didn't have any finances. To top it off, we were in a place where we didn't understand the language. Yet we felt something inside of us that was joy unspeakable and full of glory.

I remarked to my husband, "Aren't we a little 'touched in the head'? Here we are in a place we don't know anything about. We can't understand anybody. It's raining and we don't have any place to go. We haven't a building to hold a meeting in. The banks have our money tied up. Now how can we do anything?" Still we laughed—it wasn't a foolish laughter—it was in the knowledge that God was with us.

Dr. Evelyn Thompson
Former Missionary to the Philippines

> *Lord, I do believe your word! I want to be joyful in every cir-*
> *cumstance, trusting that you will keep every promise you*
> *have made...*

"Then the disciples went out and preached everywhere,
and the Lord worked with them and confirmed
his word by the signs that accompanied it."

MARK 16:20

We were standing there in the rain, not knowing the language or the city, and without access to our money and with no place to go, but we were confident in the Word of God and laughing with the joy of the Lord.

Suddenly I noticed an empty building nearby. A man was there who spoke English well. He acknowledged that the building was for rent. The cost seemed prohibitive, but we knew that if God had prepared the way, and if He was going to confirm His Word, we had no worries. All we had to do was to walk in the light and the knowledge that He had given us and He would fulfill His promise and have a place for us.

Rev. Thompson went to see the man that owned the place and he quoted him his own price, one that he knew we could afford, and the man said, "Yes." He couldn't help himself because he was in the hands of God! We were God's servants and He had to confirm His Word.

Rev. Thompson said, "We will take the building, but we don't have any money yet." However, he quickly explained how the money would come. If you knew the place, as we know it, you would realize it was a miracle that the man replied, "Never mind, you take the place and I'll trust you."

It is almost unheard of for people there to trust one another. But he said he would trust us. Why? Because God had prepared this place before we arrived!

Dr. Evelyn Thompson
Former Missionary to the Philippines

Lord, I want to have greater faith in you. Use every circum-
stance in my life to increase my ability to trust in you...

"Each man should give what he has decided in his heart to give...
This service that you perform is not only supplying the
needs of God's people but is also overflowing in
many expressions of thanks to God."

2 CORINTHIANS 9:7,12

We have all wondered if our missions gifts really matter. The Foursquare Church in Roanoke, Virginia, had a heart for missions and gave systematically. As the pastor I wondered if our gifts were all that significant.

We knew the Roanoke church had made one quite significant gift— Mattie Sensabaugh, the first member of that church and the first one to be filled with the Spirit—had left for Bible College soon after the church was started. A few years later, though hindered by a stiff leg, Mattie served as a missionary in San Pedro Sula, Honduras, where she labored faithfully for more than 20 years.

Knowing Mattie's leg hindered her work—although she never com-plained—the church sent $15 each month to help support Miguel, a man who assisted her. Not knowing his full name, we often prayed for Miguel, aware that his help made Mattie's ministry more fruitful.

Some years later, Misael Argenal and I were speaking at a pastors' con-ference in Guayaquil, Ecuador. Misael, from San Pedro Sula, pastors the largest Foursquare church in the world. My curiosity was aroused. Did he know Miguel? Was he still alive?

No, Miguel was not alive. But, yes, Misael did indeed know him. He was Misael's father-in-law, a great influence and encourager in his life.

How rewarding to know that in those lean years when we were strug-gling to be faithful with what now seems such an insignificant monthly gift, we were making an investment in the life of a nation-changer by giv-ing to a man few would ever know.

Dr. Harold Helms
ICFG President 1997-1998, pastor of Angelus Temple 1981-1999

I praise you, Father, that you take our gifts and use them...

"Jesus answered, "I am the way and the truth and the life..."
JOHN 14:6

AIDS is robbing Africa of its future. In our work in the hospital the number of infants and children with AIDS seems to increase every day.

A young mother and her six-month-old baby Christopher came to be treated. John tenderly held him, whispering prayers and speaking words of love into his tiny soul as he breathed his last. The mother was too traumatized to hold her little one. We thank God we could be there to comfort and care for both of them.

Pelakazi is also six months old. She too is dying of AIDS, but unlike Christopher, her mother has abandoned her in the hospital, choosing instead to take the healthier twin home. We are praying Jesus will enable us to do more, perhaps open a home for children suffering from AIDS.

Door-to-door outreach is a vital way to reach people who are hungry for prayer and often, when they hear who Jesus really is, they gladly receive Him into their hearts. During one outreach, three of our co-workers were approached by a woman who begged them to pray for her. As they prayed, the woman fell to the floor crying, "There's something inside my stomach."

The group went to war in the spiritual realm until the woman was calm. When her boyfriend came to take her, she rebuffed him saying, "This is the truth. Go away. This is the truth…"

The truth of Jesus is so powerful. The truth sets the captive free, brings healing to the hurting, and love to the unlovable. Jesus is truth!

John and Dianne Shober
FMI Associates to South Africa

I praise you, Jesus, for you are the truth and the way and
the life. Lead me into greater and greater understanding of
your truth; lead me in paths of righteousness...

"I will go before you and will level the mountains; I will break down gates of bronze and cut through bars of iron."

ISAIAH 45:2

*W*e were about to leave Nigeria to be reassigned as missionaries to Papua New Guinea. Joe and Betty Babcock were replacing us, and we were working with the government to secure their visas. This was during the Biafra war and the government had been very firm that they would not issue new visas to American missionaries.

Every day one of our pastors or businessmen went to the immigration department to check on the status of the Babcock's application for visa and to encourage its approval. The same answer always came back, "We are not giving any visa approvals for missionaries. Stop bothering us!"

After many days of this, our Bible school students were praying one evening when a word of knowledge came forth: "The governments of this world are still in My hands."

The next day, one of our pastors once again made the trek to the immigration office. He received the same message, only more emphatically, "No visa! Don't come back! It won't do you any good!" Then, as though unaware of what he was doing, the officer picked up the visa application and stamped the "Approval" on it.

We are convinced that God will make a way—He will level any mountain and break down any gate—with Him nothing is impossible!

Larry and JoAnn Six
Former Missionaries to Nigeria

> *I praise you, Lord, for nothing is impossible for you. You know the mountains in my life that I need you to make level, and you know the gates that need to be opened. Go before me, I pray...*

"Jesus Christ is the same yesterday and today and forever."
HEBREWS 13:8

God is doing some awesome things in Chile! We praise the Lord for miracle healings and the gifts of healing that have been in operation.

A woman named Rosa was prayed for because she had a tumor. When she returned to the doctor it was confirmed that the tumor was completely gone!

Ana Maria, a lady who tried to kill her son with a knife and was sick because of witchcraft, was completely delivered. She has been incredibly transformed by God's power.

These are only a few reasons we can't help but praise our Lord! He healed in the Bible and He heals today. Jesus Christ is the same yesterday, today and forever!

Sheila Ransford
Missionary to Chile

Thank you, Lord Jesus, that you are the same today as you were when you did great miracles through the early church in the book of Acts. Help me to follow the examples in Acts and to believe you to do great things in my life and in the lives of others through my prayers...

"I thank Christ Jesus ... that he considered me faithful, appointing me to his service. Even though I was once a blasphemer and a persecutor and a violent man, I was shown mercy because I acted in ignorance and unbelief."

1 TIMOTHY 1:12-13

*I*n 1977, I began preaching in one of the worst areas of San Pedro Sula—a section of the city known for its cantinas, bars and brothels. At first, the going was tough; I preached to only three to five people in the church. When I took my message to the streets, things became even more difficult. There was great persecution. The owner of the bars and brothels paid people to attack our church and stop me from preaching the Gospel.

Forty young men bonded together to kill me. However, each attempt backfired. A turning point came when Ramon, the ringleader of the group, discovered that he had the HIV virus. He became extremely ill, and towards the end of his life, he called me to pray for him. Ramon accepted Jesus and so did his entire family. He asked for forgiveness and then passed into heaven.

Several of the other young men died from accidents or illnesses as well. This brought fear upon the others, and they all came to Jesus as did their families. Today, many members of that group are leaders in the church. A large number of prostitutes, as well as owners of brothels, came to Christ during those early years and are now elders and leaders in the church today.

Misael Argenal
Pastor in Honduras

I praise you, Father, that you radically change lives and even the worst of sinners can find grace and mercy in the cross of Jesus Christ. I pray today for those who seem far from you, and need you to grab ahold of them and change their lives...

Then the Lord asked him, "What do you have there in your hand?"
EXODUS 4:2 (NLT)

he church building had about 300 people in it. All were trying to wor-ship in singing and dancing. As an individual, you could have danced if there were only 150 people in the building. But with 300, we all danced together in one accord, so to speak. Even though there were a lot of natu-ral odors coming from 300 people dancing on a hot African afternoon, there was a smell that rose above the rest and challenged identification.

From my childhood, I remembered the cow barn, and recognition came. The walls of the church were made from small poles and plastered with cow manure. It was dry on the wall, but had turned green on my arm as I leaned against it. But that is the material they had to use to make a place of worship.

What was going on inside the building and in me had nothing to do with the building materials used. It was the same as when God confirmed to Moses that all he needed to go to Pharaoh was what he already had. A walking stick.

Ordinary things—whether they are church buildings made out of cow manure or a walking stick used in herding sheep—are brought into use in order to bring God's people into use. Swaying in dance and worship with those 300 people took an ordinary place to do an extraordinary work in my life.

Looking at a picture of that building now reminds me that all my efforts to make things "just right" for God to do His work in my church is at best a misguided effort. Why not allow the common things of our lives to be supernatural in our Creator's hands?

Glen Mickel
Former Missionary to West Africa

Father, help me to take the simple things you have given me
and use them to bring glory to you...

"Teach me your way, O Lord, and I will walk in your truth..."
PSALM 86:11

As the congregation on the island of Boca Chica, Colombia, began to grow, the Lord spoke to us about teaching missions giving—and about giving ourselves.

When God first talked to me about this, my response was, "We are missionaries, we surely don't have to give to missions. After all, we don't have very much." God ignored my arguments. He said, "Give." And He told me to give 25 pesos, a lot of money at that time.

As I came through the house, Claire came rushing toward me, "I have something to tell you. The Lord wants us to give to missions." If there had been any doubt, we knew then that this was God's will—we were learning to do things God's way and we would be obedient by giving to missions personally and by teaching that to our congregation.

That same day a man knocked on our front door. He had heard about our church and while on a fishing trip he had stopped by to meet us. He hadn't gone to church that morning, so he wanted to leave his Sunday offering with us. The amount was twice what God had told us to give! Once again we felt that God had confirmed HIS WAY.

When we learn God's way, we learn the best way!

Virginia Martin
Former Missionary to Colombia and Bolivia

Lord, I ask you to speak to me today about giving to you sacrificially. Lead me in how much I am to give and to whom...

"He even makes the deaf hear..."
MARK 7:37

*T*he weekly women's group at the Foursquare Willowvale Mission is called a "Manyano." At the Manyano, women are discipled by missionaries and taught to disciple others.

Recently, the Manyano women heard that a Foursquare woman from a remote area had lost her husband in a mining accident. They went to the woman's home to console and encourage their mourning sister, since she was the only Christian in the family.

When the Manyano group arrived at the woman's home, they met the dead man's mother, an unsaved woman who had been totally deaf for many years. The women were concerned about the deaf mother, knowing that although they had been sent to this place with God's message, the message was falling on truly deaf ears. So they prayed for the deaf mother. They prayed for comfort for the loss of her son, but also for her spiritual and physical ears to be opened so she could hear the Gospel.

Nothing obvious happened immediately, but not long after the prayer, the women noticed new interest in the mother's face. She was tilting her head towards sounds, rather than just towards light and movement. Then the mother began to smile. In the midst of losing her son, she had gained her hearing! The Manyano women happily shared the Good News of Jesus the Savior, the Baptizer, the Healer, and the Soon Coming King to a woman whose ears and heart had been closed to the truth, but now were open. The following week, the mother received Jesus as her Savior.

Sharman Stockton
Mission Team Specialist to South Africa

*I praise you, Father, for your miracle power that makes the
deaf to hear and brings to pass good things in my life...*

"You will be blessed more than any other people..."
DEUTERONOMY 7:14

Foursquare missionaries are blessed people. We were blessed over and over again by the women's groups and the churches here at home. They especially remembered our birthdays and Christmas. We owe so much to those who loved and encouraged and prayed for us.

When we first went to the mission field our girls were very young, and we did not have a television. On the way home for our first furlough we stopped in Costa Rica to see the missionaries there. They had a TV. Our children were fascinated. Of course, when they got home they had opportunity to see more of it.

After our second furlough, our children were older and as we left for Panama, they had become accustomed to television and really wanted a set. We told them to just pray about it; the Lord would need to provide the money.

Our first Christmas after furlough, a sizeable check came to us from one of our churches. We decided to buy a television. When we priced them, the price was the exact amount we had received in that check.

What a surprise it was for the girls on Christmas morning! God had answered their prayers.

Darlene Coombs
Former Missionary to Venezuela

> *Lord, you love to meet my needs and even some of my wants*
> *as I follow you. Thank you for blessing my life and my family's*
> *lives...*

"Give, and it will be given to you."
LUKE 6:38

One of the great joys for Foursquare missionaries is the generous out-pouring of love and gifts they receive from Foursquare churches at home, especially during the Christmas season:

Our first year as Foursquare missionaries we were in Papua New Guinea. Suddenly we began receiving gifts from churches at home. They wanted us to know that we were remembered and they wanted us to have a good Christmas away from home.

At the same time, we began noticing that our Papua New Guinean pastors had little at this season. Our family decided to pass on the blessings that God was giving to us. By mid-December we were overwhelmed by the generous gifts we were receiving, and we began giving gifts to our pastors so they could have added joy at the celebration of our Savior's birth.

Our blessings didn't stop, though. Through the weeks ahead God continued to bless us, until we had received more than ten times the gifts that we had given away.

The sorrow over missing the pinecones and fir trees paled in the light of the joy we received from sharing with others.

Phil and Diane Franklin
Former Missionaries to Papua New Guinea

Thank you, Lord, that I can never outgive you! Teach me to have a generous spirit and guide me in my giving...

"...and she gave birth to her firstborn, a son. She wrapped him in cloths and placed him in a manger, because there was no room for them in the inn."

LUKE 2:7

As we approached our first Christmas as missionaries, we were lonely. We hoped another missionary family or someone from the church would invite us to celebrate with them, but no one did.

We had made one friend, however. The *elote* man passed our house everyday selling corn on the cob. Our children loved this corn. When he came by, our children would run out to meet him, even if they weren't buying anything. We usually greeted him as well, when we could.

We learned this man was a new Christian, but his wife was not yet saved. One day as he passed by, he invited us to his house in the poor section of town for Christmas Eve. We accepted and went with great anticipation.

This family's home had but one room. We sat on beds with a table placed in the middle. The kitchen was a cubbyhole with a portable gas stove. The bathroom was a community outhouse, and their only running water was a community faucet. It was a humble way to celebrate Christmas, but a blessed time. This experience bonded us to the people of Mexico in a special way.

This turned out to be one of our best Christmas memories. We were reminded of that first Christmas and the humble beginning of our Lord Jesus, born in a manger!

David and Nancy Stone
Former Missionaries to Latin America

Lord, you choose to dwell with those who are humble in heart. I pray that I would be one of those in your eyes...

"I bring you good news of great joy that will be for all the people. Today in the town of David a Savior has been born to you; he is Christ the Lord."

LUKE 2:10-11

One of our cherished memories of the pioneer days of Calvary Foursquare Church in Manila, Philippines, is the celebration of Christmas. We can well remember our wonderment of our first Christmas, December 1949.

Just a year before, on Christmas Eve 1948, we left the United States on the maiden voyage of the President Wilson, a luxury liner. We were on a luxury liner because of a serious longshoremen's shipping strike up and down the west coast. To shorten the delay in our departure for the Philippines, the Missionary Board booked us on the President Wilson, which was not involved in the shipping strike. Christmas Day on the President Wilson was a day to remember, as the passengers were given a beautiful Christmas celebration.

One year later in Manila, though, there was a different atmosphere. There were no street decorations and no Christmas trees with lights nor gifts wrapped in beautiful paper placed underneath them. However, the simple decorations we did see were beautiful and the spirit of the people was joyful. The Filipinos made large stars and hung them in their windows, reminding us of the Star of Bethlehem announcing the birth of Jesus. The frame of the star was made of bamboo and covered with colored paper with paper tassels hanging down from three corners of the star. There was Christmas caroling and witnessing, and then all the family members gathered in their homes at midnight to partake of a delicious meal and enjoy family fellowship.

Everett and Ruth Denison
Former Missionaries to the Philippines

> *Father, thank you that Christmas isn't just about decorations and gifts—it's all about Jesus and relationship with God...*

"For unto us a Child is born, unto us a Son is given...
and His name will be called Wonderful..."
ISAIAH 9:6 (KJV)

Christmas season in the Sahel region of West Africa was usually rough on our family. Being away from our family and our own traditions was hard, and dragging out the miserable little plastic Christmas tree didn't help much. The needles, what was left of them, looked sort of real, but they just smelled like closet mold—no fresh evergreen scent here.

Living in a Muslim area, we discovered Christmas was almost a clandestine ritual practiced by only a handful of pilgrims. Almost, that is, except for the fact that traders knew the season was good for making money—prices doubled, even tripled during Christmas. Food and fuel "shortages" developed as the time for the holiday meal drew near. One holiday dinner the five of us gathered around a skinny chicken, some overripe tomatoes, and lukewarm orange soda. But Jesus came and joined us anyway.

In this fairly depressing environment, one year we ran across a carved nativity scene for sale in a market stall. In it there appeared the holy family, the magi, and a few animals. What was precious to our hearts was that they were all African, wearing native dress: Mary with a lovely Yoruba headress and skirtwrap; Joseph wearing an agbada with its glorious embroidery; the magi as tribal elders decked-out in their finery, carrying their goat tail fly whisks; all of them admiring the newborn baby, surrounded by a couple of curious goats and a few chickens. This little scene said it all— unto us a child is born, Emmanuel, God with us! Even in Africa!

Bill Kieselhorst
Regional Coordinator to Africa

Father, I pray for missionaries who are away from home
during this Christmas season...

"Trust in Him at all times, O people; pour out your hearts to Him, for God is our refuge"

PSALM 62:8

*I*n 1973, while serving as a missionary in Guatemala, I decided to spend Christmas in Nicaragua with a friend. Another missionary planned to go with me. We intended to leave on Dec. 22, but circumstances made it impossible, so we decided to leave a day later. On the 22nd we traveled to Guatemala City and stayed at a house for missionaries. In the morning, the hostess told us, "There was an earthquake in Managua last night."

My reaction was, "So what? There are always earthquakes there." It wasn't until we arrived in Honduras that we realized that it was a bigger quake then we had thought. People were weeping as they boarded the plane, and we were told it was possible that we would not land in Nicaragua since the airport was damaged.

We did not know what to expect. When we landed we were greeted with chaos. We didn't know where to go so we went to our central Foursquare church. Everything was destroyed including the church building. We found Brother Pritchett and he helped us find a place to stay with some others—under some trees, since all the buildings were unsafe. We spent Christmas Day doing all we could to assist others; the city was completely destroyed.

God protected us. If we had gone on the 22nd as planned, we would have been in the very center of disaster. When we arrived in Nicaragua we had to trust him every moment we were there. I learned to trust in God's timing and to wait upon Him.

Jackie Coppens
Former Missionary to Guatemala

Lord, I do trust in you. Your timing is so perfect, and you do all things well in your perfect timing. I pray that today you would order my steps

"The grace of our Lord was poured out on me abundantly,
along with the faith and love that are in Christ Jesus."
1 TIMOTHY 1:14

Vladimir was thirteen years old when he started experimenting with marijuana and LSD. By the age of twenty he wanted something stronger so he started taking heroin and cocaine. By the time he was twenty-five years old, Vladimir was using heroin every day.

In the midst of his addiction he married Barbara, a wonderful drug-free woman. They had a beautiful baby girl, but Vladimir still felt the strong urge to escape reality and he continued to use heroin. Six years later Barbara started using heroin every day with her husband and every morning for the past five years they would shoot up together.

Vladimir never thought about God, as he lived in a communist country until 1995. But early in 2001, Vladimir's best friend overdosed and died. At the funeral, his friend's father began screaming at Vladimir in front of everyone that it was Vladimir's fault.

Later that day, Vladimir returned to the cemetery to see his friend's grave, and as he was weeping and feeling so close to death himself, he prayed to God for the first time. Immediately a peace came over him like nothing ever before. A supernatural escape came, not from reality, but from the present pain and suffering he was experiencing.

Temptation and trials continued, but God gave him peace and rest when he asked Jesus to come into his life. "Grace is everything." Vladimir says. "I know that Jesus has given me grace and a new chance at life!"

Vladimir now faithfully attends the Foursquare Church in Pula, Croatia, with his wife and daughter. He and Barbara are now six months into the church rehab ministry and they are completely free from drugs!

Steve Mickel
Missionary to Croatia

Thank you, Lord, for your abundant grace and your ability
to change lives...

"...the God who gives life to the dead..."
ROMANS 4:17

lonzo and Cristobal were on their way to our home group meeting one Thursday evening. When they were almost there, they found the street completely blocked with a large crowd of people. They found a man and a woman fighting over a little five-year-old boy lying on the ground. He was their son who had been dead for about two hours and each was blaming the other for his death.

Alonzo stepped in and calmed the situation and offered to take them and the boy to a funeral home. They readily accepted. In the car the father was holding the boy in his arms. The Holy Spirit spoke to Alonzo and told him to stop the car, as He wanted to do something. They stopped the car and Alonzo turned around in the front seat and said to the parents. "God wants to do something in your boy's body." The father answered, "There is nothing He can do, my boy is dead and has been dead for over two hours."

Alonzo simply laid his hand on the boy's head and said, "Life, in the name of Jesus Christ, return to this body." Instantly the boy opened his eyes and began to talk to his parents. The parents were almost frightened out of their minds and asked, "Who are you people and how did you do that?"

That night Alonzo and Cristobal told two very overwhelmed parents about Jesus Christ, the giver of life. What joy filled that room!

Dean Truett
Former Missionary to Honduras

> *Lord, I pray that I would be a person who sees your resur-*
> *rection power at work in the lives of those around me. Make*
> *me a channel of life...*

*"He will yet fill your mouth with laughter
and your lips with shouts of joy."*
JOB 8:21

Sometimes you just have to laugh…
We went to the travel agency in Hong Kong to secure a visa for travel in China. The travel agent asked us if we had brought additional pictures for our visa, but then she said, "Oh, never mind, if you forgot to bring a picture for your visa, it's okay. I have a box of pictures of you round-eyed, white-skinned, long noses and we can just use one of those." I guess we all looked alike to the travel agent!

And laugh some more…
The bus drivers in Hong Kong drive furiously. One Sunday as I boarded a bus, I went up to the top floor of the double-decker bus. As I was proceeding down the aisle carrying my umbrella, a 40 pound (or so it seemed!) Holy Spirit Bible, and my purse, the bus driver hit the gas pedal and the bus began to lurch forward at about 90 miles an hour. I lost my footing and began a backward race.

I grabbed for the bar that goes across the back of each seat and makes a handle. Out of the corner of my eye, about three feet behind me, I saw, what looked like, an empty seat. Leading with my back, I threw myself into that seat to keep from falling. Unfortunately, the seat was occupied by a Chinese man. I ended up squarely on his lap. I said, "I'm sorry!" and quickly jumped up and stumbled into an empty seat. The man sat stoically, never said a word, and looked like the whole thing had never happened.

Carol Dawson
Former Missionary to Hong Kong

*Thank you, Father, for laughter. Help me to laugh today
and to rejoice with you in every situation. Give me victory
today and fill my lips with shouts of joy as I live triumphantly
for you…*

> *"Because he loves me," says the Lord, "I will rescue him; I will pro-*
> *tect him, for he acknowledges my name."*
>
> PSALM 91:14

*T*he military convoy of three civilian vehicles and 100 trucks slowed to an eerie stop. Pop, pop, pop, pop, pop... The repeating rifles shot out into the Mozambique bush from the armored truck in front of us, which was leading the convoy through Mozambique to Zimbabwe. We were returning to South Africa from a ministry trip to Malawi and were traveling the Tet Beira Corridor, a dangerous road where travelers are often ambushed. Most travelers, however, have few options, as it is the only direct road between the two countries. The road is riddled with potholes and lined with buildings bearing the marks of war, and we knew that we were in hostile territory.

"We are being ambushed!" we exclaimed to each other. As we crouched down in the front seat of the car, we began to pray. We had heard many stories of people being ambushed and forced to walk by night with little or no food, and then being compelled to hide with their captors during the day.

Feeling unsure at what would happen next, we memorized our passport numbers and Terry changed into her tennis shoes in case she was captured and forced to walk. After further military help arrived, the road ahead was cleared of trees and landmines. After many hours of waiting throughout the heat of the day, the convoy cautiously began to move forward again.

We knew that God had protected us from capture or even death. We had considered the option of not traveling with the military convoy, and had we not joined the convoy, our lives might not have been spared.

Howard and Terry Manthe
Missionaries to South Africa

> *Lord, I acknowledge your mighty and powerful name, and*
> *ask you again today for protection for all those who serve*
> *you, especially our missionaries...*

"...you meant evil against me; but God meant it for good..."
GENESIS 50:20 (NKJV)

On New Year's Eve in 1998, May Gabong was driving a missionary utility truck in a poor area of Morata when he was held up by thieves. During the robbery, a knife was held to May's throat and he was badly beaten. Young people from the church were able to locate the truck the next day, and with some minor repairs, the truck was back on the road again. Later, they received news that one of the young men who had beaten May had been shot through the stomach by the police and was in the hospital.

May, who has adult children of his own, went to visit the prisoner. Walking up to him, he gently said, "I have come to tell you that God loves you and that I forgive you for what you did." Tears filled the young man's eyes.

After they had talked for a while, May prayed for him and left, promising to come back again. During May's next visit with the young man in the hospital, the young man repented of his lawless lifestyle and asked Jesus into his heart.

May continues to visit this new believer, teaching him how to appropriate the promises of God and to walk in the freedom he has in Christ. The enemy's plan was to bring evil but God had a different plan. May and this young man experienced the goodness, love, salvation and healing of God!

Bill Page
Missionary Pastor in Papua New Guinea

Teach me, O Lord, to pray for those who hurt me. Help me to forgive and see your purposes accomplished in those who sin against me...